MW01626424

How to Understand Everything

Consilience: A New Way to See the World

TOM BEAKBANE

How to Understand Everything: Consilience, *A New Way to See the World*

First Book edition: January 12, 2021

Beakbane Publishing, Toronto, Canada
https://howtounderstandeverything.beakbane.com/contact/

ISBN: 978-0-9735288-4-8 Electronic book
ISBN: 978-0-9735288-5-5 Paperback

Cover design: Dale Moser
Editor: Carolyn Jongeward
Proofreader: Readable Ink

In the beginner's mind there are many possibilities; in the expert's mind there are few.

Shunryū Suzuki, 1904–1971

Even the gods took fright at the Deluge,
they left and went up to the heaven of Anu,
lying like dogs curled up in the open.
The goddess cried out like a woman in childbirth.

The Epic of Gilgamesh

Ceaselessly the river flows, and yet the water is never the same,
The foam that floats on stagnant pools, now vanishing,
now forming, never staying for long.
So, too, it is with the people and dwellings of the world.

Hōjōki

Try and penetrate with our limited means the secrets of nature and you will find that, behind all the discernible concatenations, there remains something subtle, intangible and inexplicable. Veneration for this force beyond anything that we can comprehend is my religion. To that extent I am, in point of fact, religious.

Albert Einstein

We are now Gods but for the wisdom.

Eric Weinstein on The Joe Rogan Experience

Those who know do not speak. Those who speak do not know.

Lao Tsu, Tao Teh Ching

Table of Contents

Preface

ANXIETIES ARE RUNNING HIGH. There are demonstrations in cities across the Western world protesting about climate change, racism, inequality, political correctness, lockdowns, new deals for society, contested elections, and counter-demonstrations protesting against high fuel prices, law and order, freedom and nationalism. Where is all this leading? While it is unwise for anyone to predict the future, we can be certain that new issues will arise, and they will not be solved through current modes of political discourse.

This book, *How to Understand Everything*, explains a new approach to making sense of what is going on.

The quest to understand everything might sound overblown, and the first questions likely to pop into your head are, "Who is this author Tom Beakbane?" and "Why should I spend time reading this book?"

I have a particular perspective because of my interests and my job, which is branding and marketing communications. Think about it like this. Imagine you are at a World Cup soccer final between your national team and the worthy adversary, Brazil. The entire crowd is transfixed on where the ball is and the movements of each of the players. The noise is thunderous, and the mood of the crowd ebbs and flows following the game's momentum. I happen to be at the same match, but my mind is wandering. I'm thinking about the logos on the jerseys and musing about the amount paid by the various companies to reach a deal. I am visualizing the business meetings and the backslapping that was undoubtedly involved. I'm also looking at the products the players and coaches are using, and trying to figure out where they were manufactured and the technologies that make them possible.

Personally, I prefer playing sports rather than watching them, and my mind is occupied with everything other than the outcome of the game.

This is because I likely suffer from mild ADD and ADHD – which was, thankfully, never diagnosed when I was at school and my teachers viewed me as just an inattentive and, on occasion, mischievous pupil. From an early age, rather than studying schoolwork, I liked observing people making things. For example, when bricklayers came to our house, I would shyly watch them for hours. I'd watch my father build yachts and steam engines. As I grew up, I found making things myself deeply satisfying, so I made ties, suits, parachutes, rockets, model airplanes, an amplifier, clay pots, an aluminum chess set, a bee house, a kayak, soy sauce and malted barley. When a university student, I was a competent-enough cook that one summer I made good money working as a sous-chef in a restaurant in Juan-les-Pins on the Côte d'Azur. I also tried, and failed, to make money as a street artist in Paris. Another summer I worked as a machinist in an engineering facility in Philadelphia. As I enjoy making things and appreciate different technologies, I often learn the details about how my business clients run their enterprises. That means I like spending time with business owners, touring their facilities and asking questions about their operations. The result is that when I see a can of Labatt beer or Schweppes tonic water, a Toyota car or a Duracell battery, a Gillette razor or a Lindor chocolate, a carabiner or an intravenous drip, or hundreds of other products, I not only see the product but I can also picture how the components were sourced, how they were manufactured and how they were shipped.

Because I studied biochemistry and neurophysiology at university, I often think about what is going on in the minds of the soccer fans, half of whom will end up happy at the final whistle and the other half unhappy. I ask myself, "Why is that? How are everyone's eyes tracking the ball so perfectly? Why does everyone's mood change in the half-second it takes for the kick to go this side or that of the crossbar? What exactly is happening in the brain?"

So if we met in a bar after the match and you commented on the winning goal, I wouldn't know much about it. I might be daydreaming about the mechanisms at work in my own brain, and how this developed from the chance collision between a sperm and an egg. You would probably sidle off and find someone more engaging to talk to.

During the COVID-19 lockdown, I observed what was happening in the public arena and became irritated that the media focused on the position of the ball with little insight about what was happening at deeper levels of psychology and human interactions. The implications are worrying. To my mind, if people are only paying attention to who is winning the game, inevitably half the supporters will end up disappointed because of circumstances such as shortsighted politicians, the power of online communication and academic theories that are disconnected from reality, and there will be consequences that are a complete surprise — possibly catastrophic.

This book describes a way of looking at the world known as "consilience," enabling us to fuse together different domains of human experience. We are at a unique moment in history because scientists now have tools that enable them to see the workings of the cells that make up the human body, including the brain. We no longer need to speculate about the nature of human reason and consciousness — we can see how the neural systems work. The many discoveries enable us to become ruthlessly scientific about human behavior and acknowledge its unending complexities. But at the same time, we are forced to acknowledge that science can never be completely objective as it cannot be disentangled from human interactions.

Consilience requires that you see beyond the labels we attach to things. It doesn't matter whether some people are called "Americans" and others "British," or that we label anxiety about society as "climate change" or that we brand some things as "scientific" and other things as "religious." I am inviting you to join me on a multidisciplinary adventure that, if you stick with me will, I hope, change how you think about everything.

Where did the idea for consilience come from? It came from the same fellow who invented the word "scientist": William Whewell. He was an intellectual giant, a polymath, a poet and a mathematician of the first order. He coined the word "consilience" in 1840, but the word has since been largely forgotten because his ideas were not as appealing and easy to grasp as ideas of other thinkers.

On account of my job, I have spent tens of thousands of hours coming up with various ideas with the purpose of changing people's behavior. These ideas have related to foods, beverages, toys, educational products, pharmaceuticals, sexual health, educational products, software, professional services and many others. My objective has always been to make things work to everyone's mutual satisfaction, and I have not cared one iota about the source of good ideas. I have therefore cultivated curiosities that do not discriminate between the arts, sciences and every other realm that explains and enriches human life.

I am not a scientist, a researcher or an intellectual; I enjoy, however, the challenge of understanding how complex things work. My situation is somewhat different to that of people who have been working on the frontlines of research in that I feel no loyalty to a particular discipline, and I can pick and choose ideas as necessary without conforming to the normal codes of academic decorum.

Also I have been running my own business since age 29 and don't have a boss, which means I am not stifled by the need to be politically correct. I speak the truth as I see it. In this book I will be stating some uncomfortable insights about human behavior, so please be prepared for perspectives that are not self-affirming.

Join me on a mind-altering journey. Afterward, you'll better understand the things we probably both care about: our well-being, our countries, our families and future generations. You'll be able to discuss current issues with greater confidence and, if you wish, join those who are working toward changing the game.

Acknowledgments

This book is largely a compendium of other people's ideas. I have chosen not to include a bibliography because the 1,400 entries would reflect only a tiny proportion of the books, articles, papers, podcasts, videos, movies, public talks, meetings, teachers and inspiring people who have contributed to forming my mental landscape from which the ideas presented in the following chapters have flowed.

Also, my aim has not been to represent other people's ideas as they might wish, but instead to use them to support the argument that humanity is at an extraordinary, singular moment in history because for the first time we can see how our brains work — matter-of-factly, which lays bare our vulnerabilities and enables us to thread together various realms of existence that would otherwise remain disconnected.

I glanced through thousands of references, like a magpie looking for gems, while writing the book, that have enriched the narrative. Many of the concepts I mention are complex, yet I deal with them in a quick sentence or two. There should be enough keywords mentioned if you wish to track them down.

As an avid reader of scientific journals since my teenage years, it is impossible for me to recall the many issues of *The New Scientist, Scientific American* and *Nature* that I have read, sometimes cover-to-cover. I still treasure the last issues of the award-winning journal, *The Sciences* published by the New York Academy of Sciences whose marriage of science, art and poetry sent me into a trance every two months until it ceased publication in 2001.

A rich source of knowledge were my grandparents' books on veterinary science, botany, evolution, ethology and primatology. I shared their curiosity about the philosophy of science and as a student I devoured most of the books by Kuhn, Popper, Lakatos, Koestler, de Chardin and Fleck.

I also owe a debt to the many highly accessible books I have read that deal with subjects relating to philosophy, psychology, history, travel, medicine, economics by writers such as Pirsig, Zukav, Ridley, Winchester, Bryson and Gladwell.

In the text I do not mention books about business, marketing, communications and the biographies of leaders, yet I have studied many of them carefully, and they inform my perspectives.

A list of all the people I have worked with through my career whom I have learned from would take over 40 pages — suffice to say — *thank you*! I hope this book gives us another reason to reconnect.

I also acknowledge the organizations I have belonged to: The Executive Committee, Strategic Leadership Forum, the American Marketing Association, TechConnex, IN and the United Way, where I encountered many highly intelligent and hardworking members.

There is a soft spot in my heart for the Mindcamp family led by Tim Hurson. Under the guise of promoting creativity, the divisions between art, imagination, drumming and productivity dissolve.

Thanks to those who waded through early drafts — Rob McKenzie who instructed me to add the World Cup, my journey and Tipsy; Nadya Markin who, along with two other professors of mathematics, checked over my take on number theory; Tyler Cohen who noted that postmodernism isn't an easy villain; John Puffer who read the manuscript three times and rewrote key paragraphs. Stephen Shrewsbury, Alan Middleton and David Hickman provided many helpful and supportive comments to this headstrong author.

Credit for the book's readability should go to editor Carolyn Jongeward, who brought understanding and sensibility to weave a narrative from my disparate ideas and jumbled words.

And thanks to Victoria Reed for her typographer's eagle-eye — not dimmed since we worked together in the days of desktop publishing 30 years ago.

I will be giving credit to the many I have not acknowledged above who have helped me, and wish to promote consilience, on the website https://howtounderstandeverything.beakbane.com/.

Introduction

Consilience is a paradigm that opens up liberating new ways to think about everything relating to science and the natural world, including human behavior. It is more challenging to undergo than other paradigm shifts because it concerns the human brain, which we use to understand — everything.

LET US SAY THERE ARE THREE SPECKS. We can understand them in different ways.

A writer might describe them poetically as being like pollen grains glinting in the rising sun. A painter may represent them in a picture with bright splashes of color.

A chemist could describe them as a specific collection of atoms, and a physicist would define them by measuring various properties, such as their mass and temperature. The relationship of the three specks to each other and to their container can be described mathematically by using equations such as the inverse-square law and Boyle's law.

Another way to understand these three specks would be to recount their history from moments after the big bang, documenting every step until each was emitted from a volcano and swept up by the wind, and eventually coming to our attention.

The three specks could also be apprehended as having religious and spiritual significance. Can our mortal souls ever understand the symbolism of this trinity and its origins in deep time?

We might also consider the etymology of the word *speck,* which originated in the Old English word *spic,* meaning "bacon fat." We need not restrict ourselves to English; we can look at the differences in how other cultures might term the tiny objects, including grain, motas, fleck, пятнышки, קעפס, 斑点, флек.

We could ask who owns them, or what is their legal status and economic value. As a business person I might consider how to brand the specks: creating a trademark such as "Trion," figuring out a consumer benefit such as everlasting health, packaging them with others, selling them profitably and living happily ever after.

Consilience is an all-embracing perspective that acknowledges the value in each of the many ways of understanding things. However, consilience takes us both higher — so we understand the power of ideas — and deeper — so we see how things work at the level of neurons in our brain and body, and how our ways of thinking come into existence and change our behavior.

Many years ago when I started on the path of writing this book, I thought consilience could be understood from a purely scientific standpoint. My reasoning went like this: frontline researchers have discovered many of the details about how animal nervous systems work. They have also deciphered many of the facts about the genetics and biochemistry of cells. Researchers in diverse fields continue to discover details about human evolution. When these facts are arranged logically, it becomes evident how the human mind works and how distinctions between different aspects of human existence overlap. It is then a manageable step to see that apparently unrelated subjects, such as science, religion, sports and the arts, share the same neuronal mechanisms and are deeply intertwined.

This straightforward matter-of-fact way of understanding the human mind has been enabled by a stream of intellectual progress that has gathered momentum over the past two decades. Mathematicians and computer scientists have pioneered techniques that show how complex things can emerge from simple repeated steps. These insights show that functional and beautiful things can self-organize, creating themselves. This has opened a door to new ways of understanding everything in the universe.

Previously, the presumption was that complex things, such as the human mind, required correspondingly complex theories to describe how they operate. It is now evident that complex things can come into existence simply, and it is possible to figure out the steps that have led to their current form. This new way of thinking about everything is bottom-up, flipping our understanding of the physical world and, in the process, revealing that scientific modes of thinking – founded on categorizations and theories – are not optimal for understanding the peculiarities of human behavior.

Over the past few decades, without being conscious of it, my mode of thinking has flipped. Previously, whenever I tried to explain the scientific facts about the human mind, I encountered difficulties getting my point across. Now, I realize that it is *my* perspective that has changed and I think about many things, including science, differently than everyone else.

As we go through life, we build up patterns of understanding and, naturally enough, we become attached to our own way of thinking. Consilience offers a completely different way of comprehending nature and human behavior, an approach that demands we think differently.

Here is an anecdote to convey what I mean. As a young boy I was an introvert and, along with my playful cat, Tipsy, I would disappear for hours into my bedroom, where books lined the walls. I read voraciously, trying to understand basic scientific ideas, and I would marvel at the wonders of nature as I leafed through pages of *National Geographic*. I would explore drops of pond water with a microscope, intrigued by how the almost invisible hairs on little creatures propelled them through the water. And I was the proud owner of a dissection kit given to me by my grandfather, who was a veterinary surgeon and parasitologist in Africa.

That part is actually true, now the anecdote becomes imaginary. My parents, who were also scientifically inclined, set me the task of figuring out how the world worked, then shut my bedroom door, instructing me to come out only when the job was done.

Using ideas in all the books and the technologies in the room, I came up with insights that, at least to my satisfaction, explained how people think. Excitedly, I called out to my parents to come and look at my discoveries. When they opened the door, what did they see?

They might expect to see the pre-existing items in the room, including the books, arranged in a way that explained my new ideas. Perhaps the ideas would be expressed as mathematical formulas or diagrams on a poster or be presented in an intelligent essay.

But when they opened the door, they saw I had taken all the items in the room, including every word from all the books, plus the sheets, curtains, furniture, even the cat, and cut everything into the tiniest pieces. They would be greeted with a room full to the ceiling with nothing they recognized. It would be neither granular nor fluffy nor paste-like. It would be an amorphous gray-brown mass.

They cried out, "What have you done? Where are all the books? Where are the ideas and what in god's name have you done with Tipsy?"

I replied, "I found that the words we all use have meanings that get in the way of us being able to see clearly, so I hacked everything apart to their primal elements. Even the cat was confusing, so I deconstructed it."

Loving parents as they were, they tried to make sense of this destruction: "Why have you been so irresponsible? What on earth is the purpose?"

We cannot communicate with each other without using words, but I have found that words sometimes group complex ideas together in ways that bias our thinking. For instance, we readily understand a word such as "science," but it encapsulates many different subdisciplines and ideas. Furthermore, the word represents the work of many practitioners who are deeply engaged in their research and proud of what they do.

In this book, when I explore the limits of science — specifically, the point where scientific perspectives get in the way of understanding human beings — you may interpret this exploration as an attack on scientific methodologies and ethics, but this is far from my intention. Similarly, I question the usual interpretation of words such as "brain" and "thinking," and point out how their meanings impede our understanding of how they work.

The words we use are woven into a cloth of understanding. To understand the human mind, we have to look at the matter from new vantage points, ones that cut the threads we have grown accustomed to. Experts in particular are loath to reweave what they have come to know.

To try to understand the human brain and society with a bottom-up perspective, we need to arrange our thoughts in a new way. To sum it up, consilience is a new paradigm. "Paradigm" is a word that became popular in the 1960s after the physicist and science historian Thomas Kuhn published *The Structure of Scientific Revolutions*. He described how science was not just a stepwise process of making discoveries, like completing a jigsaw puzzle according to the picture on the front of the box, but periodically, when scientists have difficulty fitting the pieces together, it becomes necessary to find a larger box featuring a different picture.

Kuhn described the classic example of a paradigm shift that happened in 1543 when Copernicus showed that the earth was moving around the sun, thus overturning 1,400 years of certainty that the earth was the center of the universe. It is almost impossible to transport ourselves back to that time to grasp the magnitude of the mental shift. After all, it was common sense to believe that the earth doesn't move. People could look down and feel the ground beneath their feet to establish that as a fact. At the time of Copernicus, everyone in the Western world knew that God created Earth as the center of all things — there was no other credible explanation for how things had come into being. To be told that the earth was in fact whizzing around the sun did not make any sense at all. The Copernican Revolution completely changed the way people felt about themselves and their place in the universe. It turned their reality upside down.

Kuhn's book itself caused a paradigm shift in how science was viewed. He showed that science is not progressing to a point where all the pieces of the cosmic puzzle are filled in, but instead is moving away from points of ignorance, sometimes through the painful destruction of well-established theories. He quoted the physicist Max Planck, who remarked in his *Scientific Autobiography* that "a new scientific truth does not triumph by convincing its opponents and making them see the light, but rather because its opponents eventually die, and a new generation grows up that is familiar with it." To sum up, scientists don't easily change their minds.

Kuhn's finely argued book used the word "paradigm" in 21 different ways, so it was easy to misinterpret the point he was making. In the hippie spirit of the 1960s, the idea ignited revolutions of all sorts: cultural, political and musical. Paradigm shifts go far beyond the invention of new cultural movements. New paradigms change the structure of how we think and have not occurred often throughout history. When they do, they bulldoze old ways of thinking and lead to the creation of new explanatory landscapes.

Paradigm changes related to the motion of the earth and the nature of science are challenging to comprehend. To grasp the paradigm shift of consilience is even more challenging because the brain is implicated – and, as such, relates to everything we perceive, think, communicate and do. Consilience is about *everything* we care about.

This change in paradigm is illustrated by the definition of "consilience" itself. It would be psychologically satisfying to be able to define it as follows: *Consilience is the fusion of different disciplines that enables us to understand the human brain and explain both the achievements of human society and its iniquities, allowing us to move forward more productively, both individually and collectively.* An understanding of consilience, however, requires a corresponding understanding that the meanings of the words result from our social interactions and are constantly in flux. Therefore, consilience is best comprehended as a *process* toward improved understanding that can never be boxed in with a tight definition.

Consilience fosters a new mental landscape and creates new ways of seeing things. It cannot be fully comprehended by academic patterns of thinking alone; instead, it needs to build off one's own personal experiences. To help you understand consilience, we need to embark on a journey toward discovering its meaning and implications together. I'll use anecdotes about my personal struggle to reconcile different domains of my life, and I'll be forthright about how my perspectives have evolved and the uncomfortable mental unraveling I underwent.

Consilience is a perspective that is personal, social and intellectual. In my case, it has resulted in me thinking differently about everything — particularly the behavior of people. Initially, my changing viewpoint was disquieting. Subsequently, it has allowed me to organize my thoughts so I can express myself more clearly. It has become easier for me to recognize the limits of my own, and other people's, understanding. While I have a new confidence in what I understand, I have become certain that undue confidence in expert knowledge is rarely, if ever, justified.

My career has been in branding and marketing communication: typically viewed as divorced from the frontlines of scientific research. However, another way to look at the situation is that companies are petri dishes of human interactions and their markets are living laboratories of human behavior. Businesses are groups of people that intersect with other social groups that practice science and engineering — as well as the many other groups that play a part in our lives.

The genesis of consilience, for me, originated in musings about how to close gaps in evolutionary theory. When we observe an animal trait, such as a giraffe's long neck, it is easy to envision why it evolved. A longer neck enables adult giraffes to feed on leaves in trees that are out of reach of other herbivores. The developmental mechanisms that give rise to the giraffe's long neck are relatively straightforward. The genes that control the cells in the growing baby giraffe's neck cause the cells to replicate a few more times than those of its shorter-necked forebears — in a manner similar to the mechanisms commonly observed in all plants and animals where structures grow large and tall.

Likewise, it is easy to envision why traits such as human intelligence evolved: clever humans survive better than those less intelligent. But the developmental mechanisms at the level of cells in a baby's developing nervous system are not so easy to puzzle out. There is a vacuum in scientific knowledge, often unacknowledged, about the causal steps between the genetic code and how the cells in the growing body give rise to traits such as intelligence and social behavior.

The genetic mechanisms that give rise to human traits that evolved over the past few million years — an eyeblink during the timescale of evolution — such as our abilities to communicate and adhere to moral behavior, are unfathomable. By adopting a bottom-up vantage point and, instead of explaining traits that are significant to us, simply looking at the biological mechanisms at work in each of the cells, another picture comes into focus. Free of preconceptions it becomes possible to make sense of the ways that babies grow, learn language, and become adults, and then how groups of individuals work and cooperate with one another. With a bottom-up perspective, the dizzyingly idiosyncratic behavior of humans becomes less perplexing.

This book describes this new bottom-up way of looking at the world and explains how it enables us to see the similarities and connections between different domains of our lives that previously appeared to be disconnected. You will see that I don't stay within the confines of specific disciplines, but rather weave interconnections among topics ranging from human biology to sociology, politics, art, history, religion, and current pressing issues in the Western world.

The text is dense with ideas, and perhaps you'll want to ponder the points that resonate and explore them more deeply by using Google. Following is a summary of the overall content of the book and how the ideas are organized in three interlinked trajectories: first, my personal journey; second, an account of the scientific discoveries that reveal new ways of seeing; and third, a sweeping narrative of the human search for understanding and social well-being.

My business experiences are where we start. In the first three chapters I describe how the day-to-day practice of sales and marketing does not mesh with what's described in textbooks that relate to human behavior. I explain a key feature of our neural systems: that they are goal-directed.

Recognizing there is always a "point" allows us to make sense of how humans communicate, understand and behave.

In chapters 4–5, I describe how frontline science researchers have revealed how neural systems work, but at the same time unrecognized ideologies of science have held back our understanding. I introduce a challenging concept: consilience, which enables new ways of thinking about everything in the universe and the human body. Top-down methods of understanding using categories and theories are contrasted with bottom-up methods that are developmental and historical.

In chapters 6–11, I explain many topics of scientific research related to the human body: how every cell in the body knows its role; what consciousness is and how it evolved; how the brain works, including how we move, orient, see and hear. These chapters provide the scientific underpinning for controversial subjects explored later in the book.

In chapter 12, I describe how the brain makes sense of the complexity of human experience. I focus on the nature of words and highlight how they impede deep understanding.

In chapters 13–14, I illustrate how we learn to communicate and that speech evolved in lockstep with our ability to work in groups.

In chapters 15–18, I explain the neural mechanisms related to our social capacities; how the brain is inherently tribal, and how that leads to violence characteristic of human history; how our tribal nature along with our need to have a point lead us to oversimplify complex matters and "pointify" them into ideologies. I outline three tribal journeys of Western society that account for the deep rifts in political views witnessed today.

In chapters 19–21, I describe how stressors, particularly in early adulthood, can lead to epiphanies or tragedies, and how landscapes of ideas take form.

In chapters 22–25, I explain how the idea of consilience originated and how a chasm formed between the sciences and the humanities. I spell out six artifacts of thinking that impede our ability to understand. Then I venture into the dynamics of academia to illustrate how tribal divisions and anger have been amplified.

In chapters 25–27, I use the ideas of consilience to critique ideas of the natural sciences, which opens the door to the value of spiritual and religious practices. The Judeo-Christian genesis is recounted from a historical and political perspective.

In chapters 28–30, I deconstruct the current concern about climate change; offer some thoughts about education, particularly the importance of cultivating skills; and then suggest that each of us follow our own path to wisdom.

This book is particularly attentive to issues facing the Western world. In chapter 31, however, I introduce the significance of Eastern perspectives, and how certain aspects can help us regain strength and optimism.

The last chapter advances a novel way to conceptualize human beings, one that contrasts with the accounts in textbooks. An honest understanding of human nature will help us — individually and collectively — live together productively.

1

The Unraveling of My World

How I started on the journey to close the gap between textbook theories and my experience in business. The process of changing my way of thinking took time and was unsettling.

IN 1998 I WANTED TO WRITE A MANUAL for my marketing communications company; it would be called *Total Quality Communications*. At the time I thought it would take about three months and its purpose was practical. I saw how manufacturing companies were using a number of management approaches, including *Kaizen, Lean* and *Six Sigma,* to improve product quality, reduce waste and operate more efficiently. As the owner of a marketing agency I figured that we should implement something similar. The field of marketing communications was changing rapidly, with TV advertising no longer working like magic and digital technologies advancing on multiple fronts. We needed to get ahead of the online revolution and make sure the communications we produced for our clients achieved their objectives as reliably as possible.

In every case the approach to quality management begins with defining and quantifying precisely what is meant by "quality." If you are a steel bolt manufacturer, you need to specify the dimensions and the tensile strength. Once the machine operators know how quality is defined, they can monitor their own performance without the need for management or the quality control department to check their work. As I had a degree in neurophysiology and biochemistry I hoped to spell out some general science-like principles about human perception that my staff could use to evaluate their work. By that time I had also had the privilege of working with some of the world's leading packaged-goods companies and their advertising practitioners in London, New York and Toronto. I thought that if I bundled what I had learned together with scientific principles, my agency would be more successful.

I decided to start by taking a quick look in the most up-to-date marketing textbooks to harvest their best ideas. But nothing, literally nothing I found had any relevance to what my team was doing day to day. Every entrepreneur knows there's no substitute for practical experience; nonetheless, I found a puzzling, large gap between textbook theory and the kind of information that is useful for business people. The books written by advertising and marketing practitioners, of which there are many, do not overlap with traditional marketing theory. It is the same with leadership. Academic accounts of leadership theory are nothing like the skills needed to lead a group of people, nor are they like the approaches described in the biographies of great leaders.

The gap between business theory and practice has been particularly apparent to me because, by North American standards, my route into a marketing communications career was unusual. I was never taught business in an academic institution. When I joined the marketing department of United Biscuits in London, I was no different from the other three recruits who were graduates from Oxford and Cambridge universities with degrees in the equally un-business disciplines of geography, chemistry and politics. My lack of formal marketing credentials never bothered me, because even before I graduated I had a string of marketing wins, which included promoting a photo-customization business; successfully launching the Durham University Industrial Society; and being awarded honorary life membership of the students' union for running a student health food store, increasing its sales by 35% and working with staff so that it made a profit for the first time in its history.

Although I had never been taught business and marketing theory, if I ever came across anything I didn't understand I'd read books and journals until, at the very least, I'd get a measure of my ignorance. Plus, I enjoyed reading about science and technology.

While preparing to write the marketing manual, I found marketing textbooks unhelpful, and the latest marketing research papers in the University of Toronto and York University libraries equally unhelpful. Nothing I read was relevant to my goal of making marketing communications more scientific. I needed to come at the task from another angle.

When I studied neurophysiology at university, scientists had been making progress in deciphering how brains work. Twenty years on, I presumed there would be new discoveries, so I looked at all recently published books about the human brain. I enjoyed reading Steven Pinker's *How the Mind Works* (1997) and other similar books, but these left me perplexed. In trying to explain how the mind works, he wrote: "Thinking is computation, I claim, but that does not mean that the computer is a good metaphor for the mind. The mind is a set of modules, but the modules are not encapsulated boxes or circumscribed swatches on the surface of the brain." This is a literary conundrum rather than a scientific explanation. If thinking is computation, which is what a computer does, but the mind is not like a computer, then what is the mind really like?

Pinker muses about another conundrum: "Once we have isolated the computational and neurological correlates of access-consciousness, there is nothing left to explain. It's just irrational to insist that sentience remains unexplained after all the manifestations of sentience have been accounted for, just because the computations don't have anything sentient in them." From this viewpoint, there is nothing left to explain, except that it is impossible to nail down what *sentience* means or how consciousness evolved.

After reading several books that describe the brain as a modular computation device, I retreated to university libraries to read papers on brain neurochemistry in the hope of figuring out the conundrums. The papers by frontline researchers described remarkable advances that in their own right made sense, but the brain-chemistry discoveries were strangely disconnected from what Pinker and other authors had to say about widely accepted explanations of human behavior.

However, I discovered tantalizing insights in books by John McCrone and Michael Gazzaniga, who describe how our conscious mind could not be relied upon to report our motivations accurately. It was clear that *the way we think we think is not how we think*. The implication is that a manager's intuition about human motivations cannot be relied upon. Books by Joseph LeDoux and Antonio Damasio led me to the conclusion that emotions and reasoning – at the level of neurochemicals – are indistinguishable.

Rather than being able to understand what all this research was saying, I became progressively more confused. What had begun as a three-month project became an obsession. I spent days, evenings and weekends looking into what frontline researchers were reporting. I learned fascinating details about how the visceral nervous system was more complicated than the spinal cord, but also that this aspect of the nervous system had not been studied much. The gap between what was in the textbooks, what I was reading in the scientific journals and what would be helpful in running my business widened.

The literature on psychology was particularly puzzling. Dozens of jargon-filled journals with statistical gurgitations reported results of hundreds of student surveys, but the research approaches didn't fit with the techniques used by the marketing research professionals I had worked with; they also ran counter to the observations of ethologists, who study the behavior of animals in their natural habitat.

That prompted me to study the history of psychology. I read several books by Kurt Danziger, including *Naming the Mind: How Psychology Found Its Language* (1997). This book describes how the categorizations used in psychology are not objective, a realization that first came to him when he moved to Indonesia as a professor of psychology. There, exposed to academics whose psychology was grounded in concepts of the mind from Eastern cultures, he realized that alternative explanations of the mind were just as valid and, in their own way, as scientific as the psychological explanations he had been taught in the West. Categories such as *behavior, stimulus* and *response* are cultural. Danziger wrote, "Contrary to common belief, these categories do not occupy some rarified place *above* culture but are embedded in a particularly professional sub-culture." It is hard for us to see, but the language we use to categorize mental events is not the same as the mental event itself. "The entire investigative enterprise is so immersed in language that it is simply taken for granted and its role becomes invisible."

Marketing professionals are particularly attuned to the peculiarities of different cultures. It goes without saying that the tone and terminology needed to address an audience of cardiologists versus an audience of lip gloss purchasers is completely different. The brief booklet on *Total Quality Communications* that I had planned to write for my agency was turning into something much longer. I was uncovering ideas that would be useful for every business manager. Three months stretched into two years.

The more I read, the more bewildered I became. It was like noticing a piece of lint on an old woolen sweater. When I tried to pick the lint off, I found it was securely attached to the sweater; so when I pulled, out came a length of wool and another question. Why are marketing textbooks so unhelpful? That led to another length of wool and another question. Why are there so many graduates publishing psychology papers that have zero utility to managers of organizations?

I pulled at more lint and found this led to ideas in brain science that led to mysteries of sentience and consciousness. This led to me yanking on the wool leading to culture and linguistics.

Different scientific disciplines have distinctive cultures. Surgeons, physicists, biologists and every other discipline use contrasting vocabularies that are the result of their practitioners' interactions. I had always believed that science was essentially objective — a belief shared by many scientists — but its actual practice is social, and cannot be divorced from the ongoing influence of peers, research assistants and funders.

Catching Ourselves in the Act, a book written by a computer engineer who decided at age 50 to get a doctorate in cognitive science, was particularly mind-bending. Horst Hendriks-Jansen explains that people make sense of each other's actions by attributing intentions to them. For example, when mom hands her baby a block and the baby takes it, we assume we know what is happening. The mom initiates the behavior and the baby wants the block, so the baby reaches out. But the book explains that when you investigate the interaction as it unfolds with high-speed video, their hands move in concert. In other words the actions are emergent rather than intentional. The implication is that we make sense of human interactions using causal logic; however, the discoveries from frontline researchers show that the underlying mechanisms don't work like that.

Hendriks-Jansen's ideas hint at deeper questions about scientists' patterns of thinking that presume causality. Typical mechanistic thinking, where we assume one thing causes another, might describe how we make sense of the world, but not provide insight into the nature of reality itself. I started writing the first version of this book with a scientific mindset, but soon realized that science itself is built upon neuronal tricks that I could not fathom.

The sweater I started out with was now a big pile of wool. Everything I had previously been certain of was lying in a mess on the floor. It was a pile of confusing ideas. After three years, I finished the book. It was called *Consilience: Marketing and the Science of Persuasion*. At 123,900 words, it was 300 pages long. And the 840 citations were impressive. I was exhausted.

An editor cleaned up the manuscript, but it was a muddle of arguments against established ways of thinking. There was no way it could be salvaged, so I buried it on a hard drive and forgot about it. I was embarrassed that I had wasted three years of my life with nothing to show for it — not even a diploma on the wall.

With hindsight, I can see that the task I had embarked on to shed light on marketing practices using science was impossible for several reasons. First, I was trying to make sense of human communications and human behavior using scientific reasoning. Science can be viewed a few different ways. One way is that it is like a brand similar to the type that marketing professionals like me create. In this sense, it is a brand representing objectivity and truth. However, if one tries to make sense of the human brain with the precondition that the brain has to be capable of purely rational thought one quickly encounters a dead end. Scientists come to conclusions through a process of deliberation that is largely conscious, and therefore it is reasonable to presume that the ultimate goal of brain science is to understand human rationality. However, conscious deliberation turns out to be only a small part of what the human brain does. Brains have evolved for reasons of immediate survival — not to solve scientific riddles.

A second reason the task was impossible is because most people, particularly scientists, don't understand what marketing practitioners actually do. It happens that marketing practitioners and scientists use similar techniques. Science journals often depict marketing as a collection of tricks designed to subvert otherwise rational minds. For instance, an article in *Scientific American* called "The Science of Persuasion," starts out, "Hello there. I hope you have enjoyed the magazine so far. Now I would like to let you in on something of great importance to you personally." And the article ends with, "Surely, someone with your splendid intellect can see the unique benefits of this article. And because you look like a helpful person who would want to share such useful information, let me make a request. Would you buy this magazine for 10 of your friends? Wait, don't answer yet. Because I genuinely like you, I'm going to throw in — at absolutely no extra cost — a set of references that you can consult to learn more about this little-known topic... And I love that shirt you are wearing." The inference is clear. Persuasion is a form of trickery, little different from the bleating of a fairground hawker complete with obsequious asides.

As my route into marketing communications was unorthodox, my view of the practice contrasts with those represented in textbooks. The clearest way to sum up the differences is to say that the textbooks are concerned with creating gaps, whereas the real-world practice works toward eliminating gaps. To make this clear I'll describe a project from my agency's early days.

The Canadian brewery, Labatt, wished to relaunch a brand of beer called Kokanee to reverse its market share, which had been declining steadily in British Columbia. The label featured a line drawing of a small glacier under a craggy peak in the Selkirk Mountains. We decided to replace the line drawing with a photograph. We hired Alec Pytlowany, a local photographer, who, on a clear, sunny day, right after three days of blizzards that covered the mountains with gleaming white snow, rented a helicopter and provided us with hundreds of images. Those were the early days of computer graphics — it took weeks of work to scan the photographs and assemble several options that we felt were appealing, along with different versions of the logo and other wording. Then we went through a process of refining the design and working with the technical staff, printers and production staff, until around four months later we saw millions of bottles and cans pouring off the production lines. Subsequently, the beer regained its share of the market, and was launched into stores and bars across Canada, the northern United States and in London.

If you were to study this relaunch from textbooks you would need to read books that at least cover the following: project management, marketing strategy, branding, copywriting, design, typography, photography, sales, market research, brewing, distribution, film separations, label printing and packaging manufacturing. Much of the content of the various textbooks originated as scientific ideas that, through history, have been turned into technologies for creating products such as bottles, cans and computers, as well as subject areas such as "consumer behavior." Those textbooks clearly distinguish the manufacturing aspects from the cerebral aspects of strategy and management, which, in turn, are different from the creative aspects of design. Textbooks on accounting and project management would lay out various distinct stages and define the economic entities, where clients are completely separate from their agencies, suppliers and consumers. That all seems to be perfectly logical, except that the actual process went down nothing like that.

The brand manager at Labatt, Rick Shaver, had the beginnings of a vision and, through his encouragement, the design we came up with hit the right emotional chord among beer drinkers. The whole process involved several teams of people with diverse skills cooperating as if we were building a house. The construction was collaborative from the start, and there was no demarcation between the thinking, the art, the technicalities, the production, the sales and the distribution. All of these meshed together. The end result was successful because there were no gaps.

The way that textbooks might have characterized this relaunch would be that its purpose was to sell more beer. The beer sale would occur when the salespeople persuade retail and foodservice outlets to order the product, which means the transaction would be consummated financially. Yet that perspective would miss the pervasive interpersonal interactions that involved some degree of persuasion. My agency persuaded the client that we were capable of handling the job. Shaver influenced us to develop the design approach of using photography on the labels and cans, which at the time was technologically innovative. Each design we submitted was accompanied by an explanatory rationale. Really, every time anyone communicated they did so with the purpose of selling an idea or persuading someone to do something. The words *sales* and *persuasion* are overstatements. Perhaps a better description would be to say that throughout the process there were many thousands of instances when there needed to be a "meeting of minds."

The situation and the people involved determined the precise details of each of the instances of the meeting of minds, but the details of the interactions mattered in every case. The whole process could have been derailed by just a few instances of people misunderstanding each other, or becoming impatient and rude.

The sensitivity of interaction to precise details throughout the process is illustrated by the beer label itself. Labatt organized multiple rounds of consumer research to help us pick and refine the packaging design. Small adjustments to the design made big differences in how beer drinkers felt about the product. For instance, the perspective of looking down at a mountain, with lines of peaks behind stretching to the horizon would engender feelings of freedom. If the perspective was from below, looking up to the peak, the respondents themselves would feel less significant. If the sky was crystal-blue, the beer looked refreshing, whereas if there was any tinge of gray, the beer would be unappealing. Emotions were affected not only by the image, but also by the juxtaposition of the elements and the exact words used to describe the product. We ended up saying: *B.C.'s cool, crisp, glacier-fresh taste.* The market research professionals did not treat the label as a scientific matter, but instead were sensitive to how beer drinkers reacted. Tiny details made the difference between respondents looking at the label with a snort of appreciation or glancing away.

At every point in business, and in life generally, the details of human-to-human interactions are critical. The meeting of minds is the glue that closes gaps. The glue of human relationships is profoundly significant, yet textbooks are strangely silent about this fundamental aspect of human behavior.

— ▪ ○ 2 ○ ▪ —

Gaps Between Theory and Reality are People

This chapter lays the foundation that business, art, science and everything we care about involve interpersonal communication. Textbook marketing has been based on psychological theories that are supposedly scientific, but are often counterproductive.

WHEN I GRADUATED FROM UNIVERSITY and joined United Biscuits as a marketing trainee, I had to undergo an eight-month stint in the salesforce. I wore a blue suit and went from store to store in West Birmingham and the Cotswolds. I quickly realized that the stereotype of sales wasn't the same as practice. The salespeople who were training me treated the store managers as friends, and the feeling was mutual. I was a typically anxious 22-year-old — although by that time I was emotionally hardened. That's because I had been sent to an all-boys boarding school when I was eight; had been with people in different countries, including spending time among several tribes in East Africa; and had worked in France and rough neighborhoods in Philadelphia, where I witnessed occasional adrenaline-pumping moments when the bars were closing. In Britain, your accent immediately defines your station in life, and mine was different from those of the store managers I visited. My way of speaking betrayed that I had been to boarding school. As a salesperson I was treated courteously, but I felt I was on foreign territory.

The sales dynamics were nothing like I had imagined. Even before I started speaking, I could sense that each store manager had sized me up. Exactly how they reacted after that depended on a myriad of factors. Did they like the company I worked for and our products? Were they busy or having a bad day? Were they bored and felt like giving the trainee a hard time because they preferred dealing with their regular sales representative? Occasionally, store managers gave me a large order, likely because they saw I was nervous and took pity on me.

Human-to-human interactions are the currency of life, so why haven't scientists and academics progressed in understanding how they happen? Certainly, sales managers and marketers would find it useful to understand basic principles of human interaction.

The birth of marketing as a business discipline coincided with a period when psychologists were becoming confident that human behavior could be figured out scientifically.

In the 1800s, the mild-mannered, deep-thinking physicist Hermann Ludwig Ferdinand von Helmholtz demonstrated that nerves work somewhat like electrical wires. He speculated that the brain might be like a telephone system, so it seemed reasonable to him that one could figure out how the brain works using the laws of physics.

In 1904, a pioneering young Russian researcher named Ivan Pavlov was awarded the Nobel Prize because of his discovery that dogs could be stimulated to start producing saliva when the ringing of a bell coincided with feeding time. In his acceptance speech, he referred to this as a *conditioned* reflex. Pavlov suggested that study of conditioned reflexes offered a way of understanding the mechanisms at work in the brain. In North America, an ambitious researcher named John Broadus Watson read reports of Pavlov's speech and was inspired. He reasoned that maybe "the conditioned reflex as an object methodology could be used to investigate sensory problems that were previously thought to be accessible only through introspection." Watson believed that it was possible to bypass the question of what was happening in the brain by measuring the effect that different *stimuli* would have on the output — or *response.*

At the start of his career, Watson tried to conduct research on babies, since he figured their behavior would be simpler to understand than adult behavior. After grappling with realities of babies kicking and crying in their cribs, however, he realized it was impossible to get consistent and quantifiable results, so he turned to rats instead. In his dissertation, he mused, "If you could understand rats without the convolution of introspection, could you not understand people the same way?" This approach to the study of behavior was termed *behaviorism.*

Some of Watson's theories have become famous because of their boastfulness, such as his claim that he could take any child and "train him to become any type of specialist I might select — doctor, lawyer, artist, merchant-chief and, yes, even beggar-man and thief, regardless of his talents, penchants, tendencies, abilities." At the time, even though this claim was outlandish, the methodology appeared to be sound. The brain could be understood using the laws of physics and by viewing it as a switching device much like a computer. The leading college-level textbook of the time, *Psychology: A Study of Mental Life,* written by Columbia University psychologist R.S. Woodworth, states: "Stimulus-response psychology is solid, and practical as well; for it can establish the laws of reaction, so as to predict what response will be made to a given stimulus, and what stimulus can be depended on to arouse a desired response." He adds that this predictive "'knowledge is power.'"

Academics at universities of the northeast United States became avid proponents of behaviorism. B.F. Skinner, a professor at Harvard University, picked up the mantle from Watson, continuing his quest to make the study of stimulus-response quantifiable and thus inarguably scientific. He studied animal learning by putting rats in mazes to see how quickly they could navigate their way out to find food or avoid electric shocks. In an effort to eliminate unpredictable behavior, he developed the Skinner box — a cube about a foot square, insulated against sound and light —

into which he would put a lone rat that learned to get rewards or avoid punishments by pushing a lever.

These supposedly scientific approaches to understanding behavior were destined to fail. Animal behavior is unpredictable; otherwise, a predator could easily anticipate an animal's movement and pick them off. The reality of Skinner's experiments is that the rats are starved before being put in the maze, and even then some cower in a corner while others navigate their way out seemingly intelligently. Some dogs will salivate at the sound of a bell, but others less amenable to having their stomach wall pierced by a tube to collect the saliva will quiver with terror, losing control of their bowels and suffering from so-called experiment neurosis.

Nonetheless, the theoretical approaches of behaviorism were adopted in the marketing community. In the 1950s, TV advertising worked so well it was commercial magic: spend a million dollars on advertising and you would get a return of many millions. Consumers absorbed TV stimuli in their suburban homes just like rats in their Skinner boxes and, instead of pressing a lever to get a food pellet, they would drive to the new emporium of consumer choice — the supermarket — and load up their shopping cart with the packaged goods they had seen advertised.

Throughout the 1970s, the search to bypass unpredictability in human behavior spawned the use of statistics in seemingly endless volumes of academic journals, including the *Journal of Marketing Research*, the *Journal of Advertising Research*, the *Journal of Behavioral Decision Making* and the *Journal of Business Economics & Statistics*. Once it was understood that the number of advertising stimuli to which consumers were exposed did not correlate well with their behavior, other angles were explored. For example, could human behavior be understood by categorizing people according to their values and attitudes?

Marketing by definition is all about *markets*, which allows practitioners, at least in theory, to sidestep the idiosyncrasies of individuals. I have observed, however, that when practitioners embrace marketing theory, it often leads to failure. For instance, suppose Fernando has invented a $2 widget that attaches to the toe of soccer shoes that makes every kick of the ball go in the intended direction. If he reasons that the market of soccer players worldwide is 300 million and nearly every player wants to kick the ball better, this means that if he can get 10% of the players to buy a pair of widgets his sales will be $120 million. Wow! Fernando will make lots of money.

I'd counsel Fernando to forget the market and start from the bottom up. How many soccer players does he know? If he hired a salesperson, how many clubs could they visit? If he used online advertising, how many ads could the company buy and what conversion rate might be possible? This bottom-up approach could provide sales forecasts that would be less impressive, but more likely achievable.

Rather than thinking in terms of markets, a more fruitful approach is to view business as a "chain of satisfaction." Fernando first needs to hire someone to join his team. Can he express his vision in a manner that will persuade the bright young executive, Sofia, to sign up? Can Sofia persuade the buyer at an online retailer to promote the item? And further along the chain to the soccer player, Carli, how will she feel about buying the widgets? But it doesn't stop there. How will Carli feel when she walks onto the pitch and her teammates start laughing at the geeky-looking lumps on her soccer shoes? When Carli ends up outscoring them, their ridicule will turn to envy. What then will they say about the widgets as they down a beer after the team celebrates their first win of the season?

Successful communications practitioners have been disdainful of treating people as aggregates. Claude Hopkins is arguably one of the most successful and influential marketers of all time. In his still top-selling book *My Life in Advertising*, penned in the 1920s, he wrote that selling to "markets" was a mistake: "We must treat people in advertising as we treat them in person. Center on their desires. Consider the person who stands before you with certain expressed desires. However big your business, get down to the units, for those units are all that make size."

David Ogilvy, an influential and high-profile industry practitioner, who was kicked out of Oxford University, cut his teeth selling AGA cookers in Scotland. To the end of his life, he said, "I'm a salesman." Another high-profile advertising leader, Rosser Reeves, insisted that "If a copywriter isn't a salesman, then he is a bad copywriter."

There is a marketing mythology that says brands such as Coca-Cola were created through mass-market advertising; however, in their early years they were built through face-to-face selling. Asa Candler hired farmworkers in their off-season, sending them to conquer new territories. He used advertising to lessen the skepticism of soda fountain owners and reported spending "considerable sums in territory which has not yet yielded any returns." The purpose of the advertising was not itself to persuade consumers to buy Coke, but instead was used by the salesman to persuade retailers they should start selling Coke, otherwise they would lose out to soda fountains up the street. Sales grew because of up-close human interaction set in motion by Asa Candler's leadership and missionary zeal, convinced as he was that the drink he had invented had magical curative properties.

Coke became a worldwide mega brand as a result of U.S. military activity during and after the Second World War. The corporation built bottling plants close to U.S. military bases around the world and supplied soldiers with bottles for just a nickel each, barely covering costs. Product sales grew through social interaction.

The huge gap between theory and practice related to human behavior can be bridged by an understanding of human relationships. So a study of differences between marketing theory and its realities is instructive, but the matter is far from straightforward, which I realized when I became an assistant product manager after my sales training.

In the United Biscuits marketing department there was a room with floor-to-ceiling shelves of binders filled with data about the cookies and biscuits that consumers were buying. The data was compiled weekly by a research company that would collect, from a representative number of households, their grocery bills and all the wrappers they had put in the trash. We referred to the data as a "dustbin audit." Keen young thing that

I was, I decided to mine this trove of data to define different types of consumers and understand their purchasing habits. It was obvious that rich people buy more expensive biscuits such as Carr's Table Water and people in lower socioeconomic groups bought McVitie's Rich Tea and Crawford's Pennywise brand. After spending weeks sorting through the data, the marketing director, Jim Laird, got wind of what I was doing and called me into his office. In his soft Scottish brogue, he said, "Tom, don't waste your time. Read this." He reached into a drawer, pulled out some papers and slid them across his desk toward me. It was an analysis of consumer behavior in the cookie, biscuit and cracker market authored by Andrew Ehrenberg.

The late Ehrenberg had cred. He held the rare distinction of having been awarded the Gold Medal of the British Market Research Society twice, first in 1969 and again in 1996. He also held the honorary fellowship of the Royal Statistical Society. In December 2005, he was awarded an honorary doctorate by the University of South Australia. In 2010, he received the Lifetime Achievement Award of the (American) Advertising Research Foundation.

Over a career that spanned 50 years, Ehrenberg had carefully analyzed the purchasing patterns in more than 300 markets across five continents. He found that key market attributes, including market share, purchase frequency, market penetration, levels of cross-purchase and measures of consumer attitudes, move in concert and can be modeled using a single mathematical equation, known as the Dirichlet formula. He said, "Repeat-buying of any item from any frequently bought branded product-field tends, within certain broad limits, to follow a common pattern and can be dealt with by one single theory, irrespective of what the brand or product is and irrespective of what other brands its buyers may or may not have bought as well." He found these patterns not only in packaged-goods markets but also in business-to-business markets, including aviation fuel contracts, ready-mix cement, cars, computers and medical prescription.

He stated that the finding "is noteworthy, given the large variety of different conditions under which buyers make their purchasing decisions."

Consumers buy from habit, not persuasion. Incidentally, he was scathing about the use of multivariate statistical techniques.

If you choose to accept his findings, then you have to toss out a lot of standard marketing dogma. For instance, when marketers see a consumer buying one brand repeatedly, they presume the customer is "loyal." But Ehrenberg's findings show that loyalty is more accurately labeled as habit, and habits initially develop principally as a result of social factors. His findings also show that advertising does not work by increasing levels of awareness and by changing attitudes, including those that are evaluative, such as "it tastes better than the other brand." Instead, awareness and changes in attitude follow changes in purchase behavior.

How did Ehrenberg explain his findings? He didn't. He was a painstaking statistician, who advocated simplicity but disliked sweeping theories, saying, "I have never had much time for über theories." He even found fault with well-established scientific laws, such as Boyle's law, which describes the relationship between pressure, volume and temperature; he called it a generalization that does not hold when there are "leaks, or condensation, or absorption, or a temperature change, etc."

One implication of Ehrenberg's findings is that consumers don't think much about each purchase decision. They have a habit of purchasing from a stable of brands, then the final purchase choice happens as a result of immediate circumstance and chance, not because of conscious deliberation and attitudes. When looked at in aggregate, purchase decisions end up looking the same as if they are random.

Ehrenberg was dismissive of mainstream marketing theory. "Marketers complain that their business colleagues and the public don't take their work as seriously as they would like," he observed. "But marketers have only themselves to blame. They tend to set goals that cannot be fulfilled: sustained growth; brand differentiation; persuasive advertising; added values; maximizing profits or shareholder value; and instant new knowledge based on just a single set of isolated data."

"Marketing people not knowing about this," he stated, "is like rocket scientists not knowing that the earth is round."

Marketing as an academic discipline is an attempt to make human behavior understandable so it can be taught to business students using science-like theories. It would certainly be useful in all realms of life if we could understand humans by applying categorizations and theories in the same way that physicists and engineers explain systems that are mechanical and electrical. However, it is a futile quest because the mind does not operate like a human-built device. Everything that human beings do, including communicate, is a product of the human mind; therefore, to understand everything, we need to use modes of thinking that stretch beyond those used in science laboratories and for teaching.

—▪○ 3 ○▪—

Always a Point

Whenever humans communicate there is always a reason, or point. Often the point is unconscious.

EDUCATORS, IN ORDER TO MAKE DIFFERENT SUBJECTS EASIER to teach, demarcate ideas in various ways. There are demarcations between disciplines, and ideas placed in the textbooks of different disciplines are further split between chapters and subject areas; for example, biology and the study of human communication are presented separately, with little crossover. Marketing research is not regarded as having similarities to scientific research — for example, selling beer has nothing to do with explanations of Boyle's law. While distinctions are needed so that we can communicate and understand one another, they do not accurately reflect the complexities and commonalities we experience in our daily lives.

Ideas have their own structure and dynamics. Just because an idea is true does not mean it will be easy to communicate or that it will stick in someone's mind. For an idea to stick, it must largely conform to what people already understand, and it needs to be useful in some way — that is, it must have a *point*. The fact that all communications need to have a point is itself not sticky. It does not stick for two reasons. First, this fact applies universally and therefore does not fit neatly into any subject categorization. Second, it infers that we humans are not fully in control of the data in our heads and therefore is not self-affirming.

However, the fact that all communications need to have a point is important because it helps explain how the brain handles complexity and how ideas evolve over time. It also explains how ideas graduate from being a personal insight to becoming something other people understand and, from there, passing into general acceptance and becoming so-called common sense.

After three years of attempting to write *Total Quality Communications*, I felt that I had uncovered a number of insights that business leaders would find useful, including how to manage company communications and make ideas stick. At the time I was a member of an organization called The Executive Committee, where each month groups of about 12 CEOs would gather for a full day to discuss their business and offer each other advice. As members of each group got to know each other, they would speak about matters that were stressing them. The list of issues was never-ending. Most of these were related to interpersonal matters such as friction from business partners or pressures in their private lives of every sort, from children behaving inappropriately to marital breakdown. Before discussing business issues, we would spend half the day learning about a new management technique presented by an expert in a particular field.

I began delivering workshops on how to evaluate marketing communications. The purpose of my seminar was to "understand the human brain and make better decisions about marketing communications." I started the sessions by showing the CEOs eight different concepts for a homepage for an organic fruit smoothie company, then I asked them to pick the ones they judged would be the most successful in the market. All the designs were well executed, but very different from each other. One was clean and elegant. Another made the fruit the hero. Another was steampunk and so on. When each executive rank-ordered the designs, there was no consensus on which design would be the most successful or the best criteria by which to judge them. So I established there was a need for the seminar.

To create a framework that would improve their ability to make decisions, I described a universal characteristic of effective communication:

the use of a narrative chain to make a well-defined point. I used books as a metaphor to explain the importance of choosing a *point* with a single sharp focus, as well as several techniques writers use to communicate, such as avoiding words that are nonspecific, including the words "quality" and "value," and using concrete visual metaphors, rather than adjectives. I also described that, when we see an image, our eyes jump around the interesting parts in steps called *saccades*. I explained how to pick images that attract attention. I spelled out the cardinal rule for good decision-making, which is to look at communications through the eyes of the target audience and recognize that they'll register meanings that are different from their own. I also explained the principle of coherence, and the need to maintain a consistent style and tonality.

I spent two hours going step by step through practical tools for making better decisions. If I had left it at that, the session would have been satisfying and worthwhile. But I could not resist expounding scientific findings about how the human brain works, and how it does not operate using reason independently of emotions. I presented certain facts about *feelings* and why these are so important. As soon as I said, "The way you think you think is not the way you think," the narrative chain was immediately broken. The point of the session switched from being about helpful tools for improved decision-making to "he says the way I think is unreliable."

These CEOs were under constant stress dealing with the pressures of running a business. They did not wish to hear that their ability to reason logically is not how the brain really works. Daily, they need to make decisions, and need approaches and management tools that strengthen their position and build their confidence. Being told that they should become more aware of feelings did not provide the self-assurance they craved.

The statement, "The way you think you think is not the way you think," is problematic for at least three reasons. First, our mind is linked with our self-identity, which is deeply personal and something each of us cares about. We don't need someone acting like they have figured us out. Second, most of us have an idea of what our mind does. Every waking moment we are, at least to some degree, thinking. So it is reasonable to believe that most of what we do is the result of conscious deliberation. And third, human reason and free will are concepts that underpin much of the academic enterprise and the merits of higher education.

By questioning the solidity of generally accepted presumptions about how the mind works, I had deviated from what is common sense, without explaining, step by step, why they should believe what I was saying. I should have anticipated the impasse, because for my entire career I have been coming up with new ideas, including new brands, as well as marketing messages, and guiding audiences through the steps that lead to a mutually beneficial mental destination.

The techniques for getting ideas to stick are worth recounting because they are applicable to all types of ideas, including those that are scientific and political. First of all, for an idea to be remembered it needs to be represented by a word. In the world of business, the word is generally the name of the company or product, in which case it is referred to as a "brand." The idea, or brand, needs to be associated with a *benefit*. In order to get the idea or brand to stick in people's minds, all the messaging has to have a single *focus*. The requirement that communications need to have a benefit that can be summed up succinctly is the same as saying there always needs to be a clear point. The point of something could be summed up by the answer to a question such as, "Why should that be of interest to me?"

The need for a clearly defined point applies not only to seminars... but also to companies. Not only that, it applies to *all* communications, including fiction, movies, documentaries, newspaper articles, business presentations, sales pitches, advertising, sermons and scientific papers.

Every famous book, play, movie, TV series and documentary can be summarized in a single sentence. This is remarkable given that some are monumental in length and have complex plots. For instance, the epic *War and Peace* by Leo Tolstoy featured 580 characters in 365 chapters and can be summed up as, "Story of five families set against the backdrop of Napoleon's invasion of Russia." Likewise, the TV series *Mad Men,* which ran for seven seasons with 92 episodes, can be summed up as, "Creative director at a New York ad agency tries to balance exceptional professional life and wavering personal life."

If an author wishes their communication to be remembered and to hold the attention of their audience, a single point will sum up the entire work, and be reflected in the title and subtitle. Writers and creative artists recognize that the benefit — that is, the *reason* for their creations — is to inform and entertain.

In the field of marketing communications, figuring out a single, clear point with an inherent benefit is not easy. This is why agencies go through a process of defining a creative strategy before they create any brand communications. This can be frustrating, because inevitably there are many facts that need to be communicated, and some business clients believe the purpose of communications is to convey information. The client has to settle on a single focused point. Just one. If the client decides to communicate several points at the same time, the effectiveness of the communications will be compromised.

It may sound far-fetched that there is *always* a point to human interactions, because sometimes we seem to chat for no good reason, but there is always an underlying motivation. For instance, when a mom pinches a baby's cheek and says, "Aren't you the cutest li'l thing," the point of the interaction is to express her love. When you ask someone to "please pass the salt," the point is clear.

You can prove that all communications have a point by trying this at your next dinner party: say something where only you know its point. Start looking at a fork on the table and, with an even tone, begin describing it. "A fork is a metal implement. This one is stainless steel. Forks have handles and the pointy parts are called tines. I call them prongs, but take your pick — tines or prongs." Your guests will pause their conversations and look at you with curiosity. Then, without smiling or laughing, continue, "Forks are used for lifting food to mouths. They are also used for cooking, and sometimes they are used in gardens." Your guests will likely be asking themselves what fork in the road are you at and whether you need to lie down. If you resume, perhaps poetically, "Dinner forks, fish forks, like a bird's foot, are beakless and blind...," nothing you have said is factually incorrect or crazy, but your friends will, at the very least, be puzzled about why you are talking about forks. If you stay in character and plow on, they'll look at each other, push their chairs back and contemplate calling an ambulance.

When a seasoned communicator or salesperson persuades someone to believe a new idea or buy something, they always make the point clear; if they start talking about the merits of forks, you know it's because they're trying to sell you one. Either deliberately or intuitively, they take their audience, who might be a potential customer, on a mental journey to a mutually desirable destination. They structure their messaging in a manner that can be conceptualized in the following way.

Initially, the communicator sets a scene that the customer can visualize. It represents a place where both agree about what is significant. The situation might acknowledge a problem or a potential issue that needs to be avoided. The first objective is to get the customer to start saying "Yes," if not out loud, then at least in their mind. Then, step by step, they take them to a place that is more pleasing. The steps need to be close enough together that they require no leaps in logic.

In practice, the most effective way to get someone to buy something is to be polite, helpful, truthful, enthusiastic, and extremely sensitive to their needs and perspectives; you have to understand your audience, not in a glib, manipulative way, but sincerely. In a sales situation, customers are sensitive to being taken advantage of, hence the caricature of the salesperson with the loud plaid jacket who cannot shut up is an object of scorn, not because we encounter salespeople like that frequently, but because when we do it is jarring.

Dale Carnegie's 1936 book on sales techniques, *How to Win Friends & Influence People,* has sold more than 30 million copies worldwide, making it one of the best-selling books of all time. Its title is misleading because it sounds as though it explains how to get the better of people, when it actually does the opposite. Carnegie starts by making it clear that "When dealing with people, let us remember we are not dealing with creatures of logic. We are dealing with creatures of emotion, creatures bristling with prejudices and motivated by pride and vanity." He states that attempting to coerce someone to do something against their will is futile. Here are a few of the 12 principles he lays out: Never argue. Show respect. Admit when you are wrong. Be friendly. Let the other person do the talking. Honestly try to see things from the other person's point of view. And be sympathetic to the other person's ideas and desires.

The single most important skill of a salesperson is the ability to listen and become synchronized with the prospect's feelings. The salesperson needs to be able to ask questions that show they understand and they wish to move together with the prospect to a place of shared advantage.

Being able to ask good questions requires uncommon skills. These days, if you know who you are going to meet, it is expected that you will have looked over their LinkedIn profile and Googled their organization, so it would be sloppy to say, "Please tell me a little about yourself and your company." Good salespeople ask questions that have a clear point, steer clear of being nosy, but do not have obvious answers. A good salesperson responds to what the customer means, not just the face value of the words they use.

The best training for salespeople, in my experience, is to send them to learn improv with a theatre company such as Second City. The main skill an improv performer needs to develop is the ability to respond to what other players say and do. This isn't easy, because people start practicing their response, inside their head, before others have finished speaking, which means they stop listening. When taking part in an improv scene, you have to listen to the very last moment and then continue the story. The cardinal rule of the craft is to build on what the other person just said with a "Yes, and..." response. If they have just indicated you are a "crippled grasshopper," you need to start hopping around in a lopsided manner. You'd be breaking the rule to respond, "No, I'm not; I'm a praying mantis."

At the seminar I gave to the CEOs, when I said, "The way you think you think is not the way you think," I was not being sensitive to the needs of the audience. They needed tools to equip them for leading a business; they did not share my curiosity about human cognition. There was no reason for the CEOs to embark on a conceptual journey with me — especially one that contradicted their intuition — toward a destination that was ill-defined.

The notion that all forms of persuasion have underlying similarities does not square with how people imagine their mind works, particularly those who work in science, engineering and medicine. We tend to believe that most of our behavior is the result of rational deliberation.

For instance, if you ask someone why they purchase a particular product, they'll be able to provide an explanation. But that is not the complete picture. To illustrate this point, I'll pick two products, Pepsi and Coke, that are relatively simple, well-known brands. If I ask a scientifically minded person which they prefer and why, they might respond, "I couldn't really care, but I have a slight preference for Coke because of the taste." Built into that reply are some hidden presuppositions. The first presupposition is that taste is a significant criterion. What about more significant criteria they have left out? More important than taste are the relative microbial counts, the purity of the water, the amounts of heavy metals, the exact ingredients in each, the relative amounts of high fructose corn syrup, the latest health research and the companies' ecological footprint... and on and on. Near the top of the list of unacknowledged criteria is trust. How do we establish who and what is trustworthy? That is mostly determined by social factors. It's evident that many people drink both brands and do not stagger around bent double and retching, so it's reasonable to surmise that both brands are trustworthy.

When someone wants to purchase a car and wishes to select between say a BMW 328i and a Ford Fusion (Mondeo), and they are trying to be completely objective and don't trust any of the reviews, they would need to spend a lot of time evaluating all the data on each model. What are the dimensions that are most significant? Is fuel efficiency more important than reliability? Are the number of standard features most important? What about the quality? If the quality of the engineering is the most significant criteria, they'd need to check the quality of each of the 30,000 components from which each model is made. And whose data should they trust? They'd need to check the credentials of everyone involved in the supply chain and the regulatory bodies. Then there is the crucially significant matter of aesthetics — impossible to quantify. In reality they don't have time to thoroughly check all these significant criteria, and so they would make a decision based on their idiosyncratic feelings, having been illuminated by reviews and social factors.

Several additional criteria are both important and unacknowledged. One is that at every stage buyers would unconsciously play the scenario forward and visualize how the people they care about might react to the purchase. The other factor is habit and what they have grown familiar with. By definition, we are largely unaware of all the things we do that are habitual.

That we humans do not behave based on rational deliberation is demonstrably correct, but it is not a fact that sticks. It doesn't stick because it is hard to understand, and it fundamentally contradicts how we think we behave. As well, it is not mutually affirming to infer that human behavior results from factors that are unconscious and social, and there is little reason for people to accept this, unless we are embarking on a challenging mental journey that enables us to understand human behavior at deeper levels.

Novelists, screenwriters and actors are aware of the gap between what people know is true and what actually comes out of their mouths, and they make use of it. Love stories would be brief and boring if the characters said exactly what they mean. Crime dramas could be dealt with in a few minutes. Entertainment products are engaging because the players' motivations are unclear, sometimes even to themselves, and what they say, or don't say, is different from what they really want.

Over the years I have learned that when a manager spells out business objectives, it is necessary to go deeper. If they say they want to make such-and-such earnings before interest, taxes, depreciation and amortization (EBITDA), that is a proxy for underlying motivations. Money is never the motivator; what money represents is the motivator. There are always social dimensions. Does the manager want to hit targets and gain the approbation of their immediate manager? If so, what is the most significant criterion? At some point, the person who is the main driver of the endeavor has a vision. What is their vision? Is it to gain status in their community? Is it to pass the company on to their progeny? Do they want to become famous because of their new invention? What do they dream about?

In the same way, when we see young people demonstrating about climate change and racism — these issues are proxies for underlying anxieties. They want to embark on a journey to a more secure and harmonious place.

—▪○ 4 ○▪—

The Many Meanings of Science

Describes how scientific advances have made consilience possible, but the point of science has impeded understanding how the brain actually works. Science comprises categorizations and top-down theories whose roots are religious.

FOR CENTURIES, NATURAL PHILOSOPHERS and, more recently, psychologists have attempted to figure out the human mind through various means, including analyzing the shape of the skull, a practice known as phrenology, and through introspection. But their conclusions haven't proved to be scientifically robust.

The situation is now completely different. Scientists in multiple disciplines are enabling us to see what's happening in the human body with extraordinary precision. Geneticists are showing the relationships between different organisms. Cell biologists are revealing how DNA unzips and replicates, and how it operates as the blueprint for protein structures from which cells are made, and how proteins are catalysts for chemical reactions that power organisms. The details of how a cell captures the energy from sugars has been elucidated. Embryologists have been figuring how cells replicate and differentiate into the various cell types that make up the human body. The speed at which these different disciplines are progressing is remarkable and accelerating.

But when it comes to understanding the ways the human mind works, scientists have encountered roadblocks. Scientific papers and books spell out the details of structures, but they draw a blank when it comes to describing how neurons in the brain enable us to feel and think, and accomplish everything that makes up modern life.

The reasons for the roadblock are themselves challenging to understand. The human brain is powerful, but the world is unendingly complex, so the brain has to take various shortcuts. We do not notice the shortcuts because the brain is not a device designed for the purpose of introspection. The brain is like our eyes, in that they are designed to see out, but cannot look inward and observe their workings.

One shortcut the brain uses relates to the meaning of words and their point. Already established is the fact that when we communicate there is always a point. This means that when scientists, who often work in academic institutions, talk to students about a particular scientific concept, they do it for good reasons that vary according to the situation. Often they do it to help the student differentiate between sound logic and ways of thinking that are mistaken.

The requirement to teach students the difference between right and wrong has a crucial role in society, because it is counterproductive if people believe in things that are not right. For instance, if air traffic controllers believed the earth is flat, it would result in airplanes crashing. And if engineers believed that the power of prayer is necessary for the sound construction of bridges, it is unlikely they would construct well-engineered bridges.

Another shortcut is that when we use a word such as "science," each of us is fairly sure of what it means. We don't need to keep stopping the conversation to ask, "What do you really mean when you say 'science'?"

To understand the human brain, however, we have to unpack words such as "science" because they are more problematic than they appear. On the one hand, scientists provide methods by which we can unravel the biology of the brain, but on the other hand the practice of science has within it various codes of practice and beliefs that can get in the way of us being able to understand the mind.

Consilience requires that we understand science from a social standpoint of mutually understood meanings. One crucial step is to be sure of what materially exists, as opposed to useful concepts that we think are equally real, but are actually creations of the human mind.

Here are a few examples. *Temperature* is a useful concept. We know that if something is hot it can burn our skin. We can measure temperature exceedingly accurately and define it using the laws of thermodynamics. So, from a scientific and practical standpoint, temperature is a fact and it exists. However, when you get down to the actual behavior of atoms and subatomic particles, we can be certain that they exist, but temperature is merely a description of their behavior. In other words temperature is a useful idea, but in reality it does not exist.

It is certainly not helpful for a teacher to begin explaining to young students what temperature is by saying, "We are going to learn about temperature today, but first you should know that temperature does not really exist." The situation is different for university students who are studying physics. They need to be clear that temperature is a description of the behavior of particles, not a material thing itself.

The same distinction applies to the word *energy*, which we use as a synonym for materials that can produce heat and light, such as oil. Oil definitely exists, but energy itself does not exist. It is an invaluable concept, but energy is a property of matter and does not exist as an object.

To understand the brain, we must be clear about the distinction between reality and the concepts we use to describe things: particularly because scientists, and everyone else, do not make a habit of making this distinction clear.

The word *information* is a key example. In most books about neuroscience it is presumed that the brain handles information much like a computer. Information is a useful concept, especially in computer science, where computers use the ones, zeros and Boolean functions to manipulate and store information. It is reasonable to presume the brain uses similar methods to pack away memories and to enable thinking. The brain can also do simple computations like a computer, so similarities between a brain and a computer are unmistakable. From the standpoint of consilience, however, information is an idea that in fact does not exist, in the sense that it is not a material thing. In the case of computers, information is produced by magnetic and electrical interactions that are real. However, in both computers and the human brain *information* is an idea that has no material existence.

In a strange but important way, the discussion is the same with the word "science." Science is an important and useful concept, but when considered carefully it slips through one's fingers. Scientists exist. The products of science exist. The ideas furnished by science are useful, but *science* itself is a categorization and an idea that has no material existence.

The meaning of the word "science" changes according to the knowledge of the people who use the term and their particular motivations. Rarely do we need to define *science* when it is used as part of everyday vernacular. However, a core precept of consilience is that when we use a word such as science, we do not presume that everyone understands it in the same way.

There is no point in telling high school students that science does not exist or that the word's meaning changes according to its context. For them it is good enough to define science as a body of knowledge with proven theories that have been developed by experts. It is useful for students to learn that everything can be proven to be true or false, and that scientific knowledge is cumulative and connected like a tree: with roots grounded in objectivity and each branch representing a different discipline growing toward greater understanding. This view of science can be conceptualized as *top-down,* in that it has been clearly defined by experts as a real entity. *Science* for high school students is quite simply a *fact.*

To understand the human mind more deeply than previously, we have to question what we really mean by "science." Much of the time when we use the word we are unknowingly describing an ideology. The ideology of science is a belief in the power of objective, rational thinking, where theories can be verified through observation and experiment. In science, opinions lose out to facts. Many educated people see the scientific enterprise as being central to the Enlightenment endeavour, where humanity is progressing away from realms of superstition to one of reason and truth.

From the standpoint of consilience, it is a simple fact that "science" is a word. It is a well-demonstrated fact that the meaning of words is constantly changing; for proof, just open the voluminous *Oxford English Dictionary* that tracks the ever-mutating usage of words from their origins to their present-day meanings. Science cannot exist independently of words, including the ones you are reading. When I write that science is defined by what scientists *believe*, I need to make clear that, in this instance, the word "believe" means a mutually shared understanding. I do not mean to imply that science is equivalent to a belief in superstitions such as voodoo.

The word *science* as well as being an ideology is a category — a superset — that takes in many disciplines, subdisciplines, institutions and practitioners. The question arises about what should be included in the superset. Should the disciplines of psychology, economics, sociology and politics be thought of as sciences? Scientific ideology and practices have been highly productive in the domains of physics and chemistry, where levels of predictive certainty are greatest, but the ideas that make up other domains haven't attained the same success. Nonetheless, psychologists, economists, sociologists and political scientists sometimes position their discipline as *scientific*. They conceive of science-like theories that allow their practitioners to project a sense of certainty that's rarely justified.

Consilience is a *bottom-up* perspective that allows us to investigate specific things, people and ideas, and make judgments about their correctness and utility. Rather than being a metaphorical tree of knowledge, science, with its many, often disconnected disciplines and ideas, can be likened to a living, breathing, ill-defined collection of organisms, made up of millions of practitioners, hundreds of thousands of institutions, countless numbers of competing ideas and zettabytes of data. And it is evolving in countless directions. Each area of inquiry is like a single growing or shrinking organism, and each is made up of cells — that is, the specific ideas and data that are explained in scientific papers, emails, lectures, podcasts, videos and other interpersonal communications.

From the perspective of the consilience paradigm, the use of the word "science" should be defined in each instance by describing which scientists and findings we are referring to. Saying "gravity is a proven science" is almost a meaningless statement, unless you also know what aspect of gravity is being talked about and at what level. In high school, you may have learned of Newton's inverse-square law as an established fact that can be used to model the movements of projectiles, celestial bodies and ocean tides. That fact may be correct-enough for that particular audience. Among physicists, the nature of gravity is defined differently. The inverse-square law does not operate at the scale of quantum physics nor at cosmic levels where Einstein's law of general relativity is more accurate.

The word "gravity" is an example of how the meaning of words changes over time. For experts, its meaning is different from what it was just a few years ago. Einstein conceptualized gravity as a warping of the field of space-time. He predicted the existence of gravitational waves and in 2015 these were detected by the LIGO detector, which picked up perturbations in the fabric of the universe 1,000 times smaller than the nucleus of an atom. Now physicists believe that gravity is quantum in nature, and it might be possible to detect gravity particles called *gravitons*. In fact, it is likely incorrect to term it as "a force." The confirmation of Einstein's theory by LIGO changed how particle physicists understand the word "gravity." This is an exciting time in cosmology, because it looks like researchers are on the verge of discoveries that may further transform their understanding of gravity.

Change in the meaning of words is also illustrated by the word "atom." The physics book published by Sampson Low in 1962 that I browsed as a child showed atoms that look like billiard balls with shells made of electrons. Nowadays, atoms are portrayed as clouds, with the electrons explained as probability distributions. Particle physicists don't consider atoms to be objects.

— ▪ ○ ● ○ ▪ —

In upcoming chapters, I'll describe how the human mind makes use of the similarities between different things or ideas to make sense of them. As an example, we might say that we understand what science is because it is *like* completing a puzzle or it is *like* a growing tree of knowledge. These metaphors are not merely a superficial literary device; rather, they provide a feeling of "got it" that colors what we think about two things that would otherwise be unrelated. Science is physically nothing like a puzzle or a growing tree. It is, however, almost impossible to shake off the biases implicit in the metaphors we inherit.

In school, children are taught that science is made up of interlinked facts. Their mastery of science is measured using multiple-choice exams, so they come to believe that science is composed of facts. This perspective has the unfortunate consequence that schoolchildren come to believe that scientists are moving to a point where experts are completely certain and they will someday understand everything.

The reality is much different. I would argue that the truth is closer to the opposite. The more scientists discover, the more we realize how little we truly understand. Marcelo Gleiser, cosmologist and Templeton Prize winner, explains this using a metaphor: "As the island of knowledge grows, so do the shores of our ignorance." He writes, "Learning more about the world doesn't lead to a point closer to a final destination but to more questions and mysteries."

I'll give one brief example here, and later I'll describe other instances relating to nutrition, anatomy, mental health and climate change. The answers to simple questions, such as, "What is in empty space?" become harder to answer the more scientists know. Newton believed that empty space was filled with a liquid-like matter called aether that caused objects to float toward each other. Around 1900, the scientific consensus was that empty space, by definition, contained *nothing*. That position changed with Einstein's theories that showed there was some sort of field at work. The picture changed yet again with the discovery of the quantum nature of matter. More recently, it has become clear that empty space is filled with high-energy particles, called *neutrinos,* that are passing through everything from all directions. Now there is abundant evidence that empty space is a bubbling froth of quantum field fluctuations. These days, if you ask particle physicists what is in empty space, they are likely to tell you that no one is completely sure, but the answer is categorically *not* nothing.

Using the metaphor of a puzzle, we can see the pieces of the scientific puzzle are coming together. Scientists are deciphering the chemical reactions within cells without regard for traditional divisions between the disciplines of physics, chemistry and biology. At the same time, at the outer fringes of science, the more we discover the more we realize we do not know and may never know. Perhaps it will prove impossible for humanity to understand the nature of space and the stuff we perceive as solid matter.

A particular tool and mode of thinking has inspired scientists with confidence to believe the human brain has the power to figure everything out. That tool is mathematics. Mathematical formulas can be created and manipulated with certainty, which means answers to questions are either correct or incorrect — almost completely irrespective of language. Terms in pure mathematics can be defined in ways that are entirely divorced from the ever-evolving meaning of words.

Mathematics is a human conception. Numbers and mathematical formulas are ideas that, like temperature, do not exist in the real world. Their correspondence to observable patterns and their predictive power, however, are so exact and remarkable that it becomes easy to imagine that mathematics is just as real as the physical world it models. Ancient Greek philosophers, Enlightenment thinkers and present-day cosmologists have mused about how the complexities of the world can be compressed into simple formulas, but they have not arrived at any clear answers. Arguably, this correspondence is one of the very deepest mysteries in the universe.

These days, while mathematicians and scientists focus on their own discipline, they rarely have time to look back at the history of how their shared ideas were hatched. Historians of science, on the other hand, relish seeing how the great minds of the past thought about their ideas, which lets us track how science ideas have evolved to give form to our current understanding. Without this vantage point, it is easy to miss the religious root implicit in the phrase "law of gravity."

Isaac Newton wrote *Mathematical Principles of Natural Philosophy* in 1687. It spelled out the mathematical formulas that describe the laws of motion, including the inverse-square law. Prior to that, people believed things moved because they were finding their natural level and were being acted on by God's hand by way of the invisible aether. When an apple fell from a tree, it was finding its natural place, which was lower than air, because it was more earth than air. Planets moved because of the swirling aether in the heavens. Newton, who referred to himself as a natural philosopher – not a scientist, because at that time the term had not been invented – replaced the hand of God with the concept of *laws*. Newton explained that everything in motion was already moving or it was subject to an invisible force called gravity, exerted by everything.

We can no longer comprehend the world in the same way as Newton when he conceived the laws of motion. From our modern-day perspective, belief in God was being replaced by belief in science. But to Newton that idea was unthinkable, as crazy as someone today saying they don't believe in gravity. In Newton's time there was no doubt that the law of gravity, and its mathematical representation, the inverse-square law, was the creation of God; the laws of motion were God's laws.

The inverse-square law is now considered to be a fact, but implicit in that idea is that something is enforcing the laws of the universe, otherwise the earth would break free from the sun and go spinning off into deep space. For the laws of motion to work, mass and distance need to be measurable. But who is doing the measuring? How do the earth and the sun "know" how to move? Of course they do not know, but over time people have become comfortable with the metaphor of a higher power enforcing laws.

Another metaphor that has deep roots in the history of science is the notion that knowledge and information exist independently of the human mind. The origins of this idea are spiritual. For thousands of years it has been believed that there is a realm above us, separate from the physical matter of the universe. When René Descartes stated, "I think, therefore I am" and articulated the idea that the human spirit is separate from the human body, he did so at a time when the spiritual world was just as real as *information* is to us today.

The idea of a nonphysical force in the brain lives on and has been promoted by many wonderfully articulate and influential academics. Among them are the late Stephen Jay Gould and Richard Lewontin from Boston, a city that has "long considered itself the Hub of the Universe" with Massachusetts Institute of Technology being "the Vatican of High Church Computationalism," according to Daniel Dennett, one of the foremost thinkers about theories of the mind.

That there is a higher realm that exerts an organizing force on every living thing is an idea that can be traced back to Aristotle's biological and anatomical treatise, written 2,300 years ago. At that time the thought was that a prime mover was at the top of the ladder in an eternal domain, followed by angels, then man, then woman, then warm-blooded quadrupeds, then birds and so on.

The theory of evolution is often conceptualized as humans climbing a ladder of sophistication and complexity away from primitive organisms. The idea goes that, through knowledge and reason, humanity has thrown off the shackles of biology. "...[Man] is unique among the animals," Jacob Bronowski, an erudite mathematician-physicist wrote, "...unlike them, he is not a figure in the landscape, he is [a] shaper of the landscape." Man has achieved this through "a different kind of evolution — not biological, but cultural evolution."

When Charles Darwin conceived the theory of evolution, he was familiar with how farmers selected animals and seeds with the best traits. In the opening chapters of *On the Origin of Species,* he described how pigeons could be bred either to have exotic plumage, and therefore be sought after by collectors, or to be unremarkable, in which case they would be culled from the flock. The subtitle of Darwin's book, *Preservation of Favoured Races in the Struggle for Life,* makes it clear that evolution is a process of *natural selection.* He thought "Nature" did the selecting, much like a person would, only natural selection would be truer and bear "the stamp of far higher workmanship."

But natural selection is not what is observed in nature. One of the longest and most complete studies of evolution was conducted on the Galápagos Islands, the islands that once inspired Darwin to write *On the Origin of Species.* The subject of research were various species of black finches that Darwin, when he was there, hardly noticed. Peter and Rosemary Grant, researchers based out of Princeton University, painstakingly tracked the fortunes of each individual, measuring their size and, in particular, the size of their beaks. They measured the effects of the environment from one season to the next and how individuals survived, reproduced and died. The forces of evolution were at work all the time. Every species is at the mercy of changing weather, food sources, disease, and competition with other species and other individuals. Their research, which spanned 40 years wrapped up in 2003, is recounted in *The Beak of the Finch,* a Pulitzer Prize-winning book by Jonathan Weiner. He wrote poetically,

> Most of us think of the pressure of life in the wild as being almost static. Robins sing in an oak tree year after year. We imagine that life puts more or less the same pressures year after year on the robin and the oak. But the lives of Darwin's finches suggest that this conception of nature is false. Selection pressures may oscillate violently within the lifetime of most animals and plants around us, so that the robin must cling to the oak, and the oak to the ground, in chafing and contrary winds. It

> is as if each living thing on earth is holding on at the very shore of an ocean, in rough and invisible seas, swaying in place as each wave shoves it toward the shore and then tottering as the broken surf drags it back again.

In other words the metaphor of a God-like, top-down force that selects the fittest of the species is not what occurs. Organisms that are operationally defective don't last long, but after that the processes of evolution are largely haphazard and directionless, which is a conception that is psychologically unsatisfying.

Gould, a paleontologist, evolutionary biologist and historian of science, was one of the most influential and widely read authors of popular science of his generation. In *Wonderful Life: The Burgess Shale and the Nature of History*, he writes with grace and panache about fossils trapped in a layer of sedimentary rocks in British Columbia's Rockies, dating back to the Cambrian explosion 508 million years ago. At the time, a vast new panoply of soft-bodied life forms arose that were nothing like those that had appeared over the preceding three billion years, and nothing like the animals alive today. Gould acknowledged how the animals were bizarre, almost random, saying, "Life is a copiously branching bush, continually pruned by the grim reaper of extinction, not a ladder of predictable progress."

And yet he chose to explain the evolution of the human brain using processes that were self-affirming and spiritual. He supposed that consciousness was a recent development unique to *Homo sapiens*. Consciousness, he said, was like a "spandrel," a piece of a cathedral ceiling created by building a dome on a couple of arches. The space between them, when covered and decorated, exists not because the architect needed this space for a specific purpose, but because it is a byproduct of how cathedrals are built. He proposed that consciousness is like this, suggesting that when the brain evolved, there was a gap — a freak of nature that, magically, came to be human consciousness. Consciousness then allowed humans to create society, technology and art.

As Mark Twain joked about mankind's exceptionalism, this is like imagining that the Eiffel Tower was built for the purpose of the paint at the top. "If the Eiffel Tower were now representing the world's age," he wrote, "the skin of paint on the pinnacle knob at its summit would represent man's share of that age; and anybody would perceive that the skin was what the tower was built for."

It is hard to come to terms with the fact that much of science has been built using religious metaphors that make presumptions that the world is organized according to top-down categorizations and laws. Those presumptions are being overthrown by new ways of thinking.

5

Science Turned Bottom Up

New developments in mathematics and computing are enabling us to reconceptualize how everything in the universe is organized. Natural systems are inherently unpredictable.

IN RECENT YEARS, A REVOLUTION IN APPLIED MATHEMATICS, spurred by advances in computing, has been upending how scientists conceptualize everything in the universe — including humanity.

The mathematics was popularized by James Gleick's debut book *Chaos: Making a New Science* in 1987. He explained the work of Edward Lorenz, a professor in the department of meteorology at MIT in the 1960s, who found that, contrary to typical mechanistic logic, minuscule differences in the initial parameters of climate forecasts resulted in wildly different outcomes. "A small numerical error was like a small puff of wind — surely the small puffs faded or canceled each other out before they could change important, large-scale features of the weather," Gleick wrote in describing the mechanistic view. And yet Lorenz found that small changes could have huge effects, "cascading upward through a chain of turbulent features, from dust devils and squalls up to continent-size eddies that only satellites can see." This was the *butterfly effect,* where the flutter of a butterfly's wings in China can cause a rainstorm in Central Park.

Previously, mathematics had been applied in two different worlds. One was random, like the motion of particles in a gas or the flipping of a coin. The other was deterministic and mechanistic, such as the movement of the earth around the sun or the behavior of a piston in an engine. Chaos theory was the start of a deeper understanding of a world of patterns that exist between the two. It is a world described by exceedingly simple equations that generate unending patterns that in some cases are reminiscent of both living and nonliving things.

Gleick also described the discoveries of Benoît Mandelbrot, a mathematician working at IBM, who in 1962 looked at the patterns of ups and downs in the price of cotton on the Chicago Mercantile Exchange and noticed that the movements of markets had a characteristic form. He realized that these patterns were the same irrespective of scale. That means that large movements in the market always happen in the same proportion to small movements: a characteristic known as *self-similarity*. He also noticed that this was not just the case with cotton prices; it could be found in the price movements of all markets. Mandelbrot coined the term *fractal* for these never-ending, self-similar patterns.

Mandelbrot used computer graphics to produce the mesmerizing patterns known as the Mandelbrot set. You can become familiar with the Mandelbrot set by spending some time online observing its beauty, everchanging and infinite. When you do this, bear in mind that the patterns result from a mathematical equation that is shorter than the word *equation*.

For some time, it wasn't clear how the mathematics of chaos and fractals relate to natural forms. That changed when Stephen Wolfram, a British-American physicist and computational entrepreneur, spelled out what he terms *A New Kind of Science*. He found that he could take a single square that was either black or white, then duplicate it, changing its color according to the color of the squares around it. In his words, "I did what is in a sense one of the most elementary imaginable computer experiments: I took a sequence of simple programs and then systematically ran them to see how they behaved. And what I found — to my great surprise — was that despite the simplicity of their rules, the behavior of the programs was often far from simple. Indeed, even some of the very simplest programs that I looked at had behavior that was as complex as anything I had ever seen." Some of these *cellular automata,* as he called these black-and-white patterns, had an eerie resemblance to the natural world.

At the beginning of 2020, Wolfram upped the ante by launching a "project to find the fundamental theory of physics." It is a ridiculously audacious project to use computer programs to find a theory that reveals how the fabric of the universe came into existence, uniting the general theory of relativity with quantum mechanics. A few years earlier he would have been considered crazy. He wrote, "Let's try to make this the time in human history when we finally figure out how this universe of ours works!" The project has been progressing more quickly and easily than he ever imagined. Recently, he exclaimed he is getting close to explaining "quantum mechanics at the kind of level of middle school."

Only three requirements are needed to produce the patterns that exist in between random and deterministic. The first one is the most intriguing. Systems need to be made up of tiny parts such as grains of sand or cells of living bodies. This seems basic, but it points to one of the deepest mysteries of the universe and the reason why physicists, including Wolfram, are able to model reality with such uncanny precision using mathematics.

Our intuition is that if we were infinitesimally small and walked along the edge of a ruler from zero to one, it would be a smooth journey and every point we passed over would correspond to a number. Mathematicians are familiar with manipulating numbers that describe this smooth journey. They refer to them as *real* numbers, which is a confusing term as most of these numbers cannot be written down using a finite sequence of digits. These unwriteable numbers are called *irrational* and they are needed to describe many concepts encountered in the natural world including the relationship between the diameter of a circle and its circumference, known as π or *pi;* the golden ratio φ or *phi;* and the square root of 2.

And, that means that as we travel along the edge of the ruler our progress using digits can only be recorded as discrete points not as a continuum. And it is the same with reality. Physicists have established that the fabric of the universe is effectively granular. What appears to be empty space is in fact gridlike. When particles move through space, they don't move smoothly; they move in a series of jumps from node to node. It is the same with time. While the hands of a clock appear to sweep through each second in a smooth arc – at the unimaginably tiny dimension of the Planck constant – the elementary particles on the clock's hands are jumping through time.

The mathematics describing discrete distances does not need the smoothness of irrational numbers. Numbers happen to be granular, and so is everything in the universe.

The second requirement needed to produce the patterns that exist in between random and deterministic is recursion – meaning that each step is repeated in such a way that the results of each calculation are used in the next and next and next step. This is no different than saying that one thing causes another thing to happen in the future. It is similar to feedback, with the difference that it feeds forward in time.

The third requirement is nonlinearity. In linear systems, changes happen to propagate in a linear fashion, and the complexity of the system doesn't change: order remains order and randomness remains random. Chaos deals with systems where the complexity of the system changes as the system evolves. This means the changes are not linear.

These three requirements are found everywhere in the natural world: in nonliving systems as diverse as the formation of snowflakes, the process of chemical reactions, the erosion of shorelines, the frequency of earthquakes and the behavior of elementary particles. The same patterns are observed in financial markets and other human systems, such as in the pattern of the heartbeat, the distribution of rich and poor people, the dissemination of ideas, and the frequency and severity of wars. Similar patterns are ubiquitous in ecosystem dynamics where abrupt, impossible-to-forecast changes occur in populations.

This new branch of applied mathematics provides fresh ways to understand the world that are more realistic and instructive than the metaphors handed down from Aristotle, Newton and Darwin. The perspectives of their time are top-down; that is, they describe how things are organized, but with the implicit assumption that something is doing the organizing. The new mathematics associated with complexity is bottom-up, and it provides a way to understand how complex patterns emerge from simple things.

This fast-growing branch of knowledge is made up of overlapping concepts, variously labeled as *complexity, deterministic chaos, fractals, universality, complex correlated systems, criticality, catastrophes, dynamical, adaptive, cellular automata* and *emergent systems*. I'll refer to this new realm of knowledge simply as *complex-criticality*.

Complex-critical systems are emergent. That is, they are not organized by anything other than their component parts. The complex behavior of flocks of birds, colonies of ants, swarms of bees and schools of fish emerges from the interactions of the constituent parts of the respective systems. The behavior of bees in a hive does not happen because the queen bee organizes the worker bees and drones. Their collective behavior emerges from the reaction of individual bees to the environment, larvae, other bees, intruders, sources of food and waste.

As I'll describe later, the mechanisms at work in the cells of the human body, including brain cells, can be described by the mathematics of complex-criticality.

The plasma-physicist-turned-science-journalist Mark Buchanan writes in the book *Ubiquity*, "It is not chaos that historians should be turning to for instruction, but universality — the near miraculous discovery that under very broad conditions, systems made of interacting objects of all different kinds show universal features in their behavior."

In theory, the classical laws of science enable systems to be understood by reducing them to their simplest elements, allowing outcomes to be reliably predicted. It was thought that if outcomes could not be predicted in particular instances, then by looking at many instances and using probability theory and statistical analysis, it would be possible to obtain information in the form of averages and other measurements that are predictive for similar scenarios. The mathematics of complex-criticality reveals that the presumption of predictability in natural systems is rarely justified.

Statistics is a useful tool in many instances, but its functionality is not founded on underlying never-to-be-broken *laws* of predictability. Sometimes statistical analysis is used to obscure inherent unpredictability in natural systems leading to overconfidence in forecasts.

The ubiquity of complex-criticality helps explain Ehrenberg's observations about people's purchasing behavior. Everyone's behavior cannot be understood with reliability at the level of categorizations such as *attitudes* and *values*. Nor does people's behavior become easier to explain by attributing it to the mental processes of *rationality, consciousness, thinking* and *free will,* which are customarily used to account for our actions.

Everything can be understood, at least in specific instances, from the bottom up.

— ▪ ○ 6 ○ ▪ —

Complex-Critical Systems in Us

Understanding the world from the bottom up opens new doors to understanding how the cells of the human body organize themselves and how consciousness evolved to enable organisms to remotely sense what is happening in their vicinity and act accordingly.

THE MATHEMATICS OF COMPLEX-CRITICALITY PROVIDES NEW TOOLS for exploring and understanding the world and human beings. An example from art history illustrates the difference between top-down and bottom-up approaches to understanding, and opens a door to appreciating the deepest mysteries of life and the universe.

When Raphael finished the fresco on the walls of the Apostolic Palace in the Vatican in 1511, his painting, *The School of Athens*, featured the greatest thinkers the world had known: Aristotle, Pythagoras, Archimedes, Socrates and Zeno. He also included Leonardo da Vinci as Plato and Michelangelo in place of Heraclitus. Raphael composed the painting by incorporating various geometric proportions, including the golden ratio. The painting was a celebration of the rebirth of the Age of Reason and a growing reverence for the power of mathematics.

Viewing this work of art in a traditional way, we can see it represents a triumph of rationality and marks humanity's emergence from the Dark Ages. We can also see that it accurately displays newly discovered ways of representing three-dimensional perspective and the mathematical discoveries of Luca Pacioli, particularly a proportion represented by the Greek letter φ or phi and known as the golden ratio: 1.61803398... Pacioli's book The Divine Proportion, published in 1509, concluded that phi was a message from God and a source of secret knowledge about the inner beauty of things.

The *phi* proportion was considered divine at that time, and now we have the scientific tools to reveal how its powers are expressed at every scale of existence. *Phi* is an irrational number. Like *pi*, and all irrational numbers, its decimal expansion is an infinite, nonperiodic sequence. *Phi* can be found in nature and is approximated by the numbers of the Fibonacci sequence: 0, 1, 1, 2, 3, 5, 8, 13, 21..., where each subsequent number is calculated by adding the previous two numbers together. As the sequence progresses toward infinity, the ratio of ever-larger, consecutive Fibonacci numbers approaches *phi*. So 8/5 = 1.6 and 13/8 = 1.625, 21/13 = 1.615, and so on. The patterns made by these numbers are fascinatingly prevalent in nature, including the number of petals on flowers: lilies and irises have three, other flowers have five, eight, 13 or 21, and other numbers are less common. The patterns are also seen in the arrangement of leaves on stems, seeds on a sunflower, fruitlets on a pineapple, the shape of snail shells and even the shape of spiral galaxies. How and why *phi* is so ubiquitous in nature has always been a puzzle, that is, until scientists began to look at how nature is an emergent system that builds itself from the bottom up.

So we can view Raphael's creation from a top-down perspective and marvel at the flourishing of human thinking in the Renaissance, and we can also adopt a radically new perspective and tease apart what was going on in Raphael's brain, with perspectives that are biological and historical — from the bottom upward.

All macroscopic living things result from cells that repeatedly divide and organize themselves into an organism. This subject is known as embryology and, to get an immediate sense of how remarkable the processes are, you can watch short movies of cells growing into animals and plants. I recommend *Becoming*, a six-minute film by Jan van IJken that shows the miraculous genesis of a transparent egg into a complete, complex living organism, an alpine newt, with a pumping heart and bloodstream.

At the start you'll see how a single cell divides into two, then four, then eight, then 16, with a rhythmic coordinated beat, and each cell continues dividing until it forms a ball of cells. Then you see it form a small dimple as it becomes a cup, and a little later you see the cells fold into what will become its backbone and nervous system. While watching the movie, ask yourself how each cell knows what to do, where to go and how to differentiate into the 100 or so specialized cell types, including the skin, muscles, tendons, blood vessels, organs and nerves that are found in the adult body.

The mechanisms at play have always been a mystery, and to a degree they still are. When Raphael was painting *The School of Athens*, the accepted view was that each cell contained an invisible, completely preformed being. Long after Raphael's time, scientists have used powerful tools to see what goes on inside each cell. We now know that each cell has a complete complement of DNA, referred to as the genome. Geneticists can now decipher gene sequences of many living organisms, and they have uncovered many surprises.

Significantly, discoveries in genomics now show that human DNA is remarkably similar to organisms that are distantly related and apparently very simple. The genomes of several animals have been investigated in painstaking detail. One is the fruit fly; another is a tiny roundworm called *C. elegans*. Scientists choose to study *C. elegans* because it is transparent, and therefore it is easy to see inside its cells. They have mapped every cell of an adult worm's 959-cell body. And they know how every one of them develops from a fertilized egg.

This roundworm lives in soil and rotting vegetation, is thin as a strand of hair, and 10 million times smaller than a human, so one would expect that our genetic code would be correspondingly different. That is not the case. Humans have around 25,000 genes. The roundworm has 20,000. About 40% of its genes have been found in humans and, similar to humans, it has a brain and central nerve cord, but its entire nervous system consists of just 302 neurons. Its nervous system is so small and simple that every one of its connections has been mapped. It is the only animal so far to be so honored. Nonetheless, the patterns of behavior exhibited by this tiny worm are sophisticated. And in the words of the late Dr. John Sulston, former director of the Sanger Centre in Cambridge, England, where much of the gene mapping was done, "in a wonderful way, they are like miniature human beings."

According to the traditional top-down conception, life has been evolving toward greater complexity, and human consciousness is the ultimate creation. From this point of view, cells divide in ways that are essentially digital-chemical; that is, information encoded in the DNA within each cell's nucleus is transcoded into proteins that make up the structures of the human body. A cell was therefore conceptualized as a container of chemicals, where genes in the DNA are switched on and off according to a cell's function.

This way of viewing the workings of cells cannot be the whole story because it does not account for how each cell knows what function it needs to perform. Each gene needs to be told to switch on and off; however, if DNA is commanding the switches, this would be a circular process. It would be like learning how to read from a book that you cannot yet read. Another problem is that if cells worked like digital-mechanical devices, they would not be able to function reliably. In human-made systems, just one misplaced wire or incorrect line of code causes the system to break down.

Inside cells, there are microtubule structures that are almost invisible, even with high-powered microscopes. These structures are similar to the cilia, small hairlike structures that beat to clear material from the inside of our nose and lungs. They are also similar to the whiplike tail of sperm, only shorter. There are a multiplicity of these microtubule structures, and they play a central role in how cells split their DNA, either to form eggs and sperm, or to split a single cell into two cells. Because they are so small and nearly invisible, however, their significance has been largely overlooked. The sophistication of what they achieve is shown by how long it took for them to evolve — about 2.3 billion years. But once they did, all life on earth, including humans, took only 1.2 billion years to appear.

Now that scientists have an understanding of complex-criticality, as well as a battery of more powerful investigative tools, a new picture of how the magic of life appears is starting to come into focus. Structures within cells are tangled, and the terminology used in scientific papers is highly technical, so I'll explain how each cell figures out its role using the metaphor of a drum circle.

The cell can be viewed as a three-dimensional, dynamic, emergent system, like a room full of oscillating physical, chemical and electrical processes. The various oscillating reactions can be likened to a drum circle where people get together with a range of drums, triangles and castanets. Mickey Hart, the drummer from the Grateful Dead, explains how patterns emerge like this: "The drum circle offers equality because there is no head or tail. It includes people of all ages. The main objective is to share rhythm and get in tune with each other and themselves. To form a group consciousness. To entrain and resonate. By entrainment, I mean that a new voice, a collective voice, emerges from the group as they drum together."

From an evolutionary standpoint, microtubules have been beating rhythmically for billions of years. Scientists are in the process of figuring out the exact ways they work in living organisms. And since oscillating chemical reactions also occur in nonliving systems, the mechanisms of these will likely be unraveled as well. Nevertheless, because the interacting chemical reactions are extraordinarily complicated in living cells, the mechanisms may remain a mystery for a long time.

Each cell has millions of chemical oscillators, which you can picture as drummers beating with different rhythms. They don't beat completely independently; the vibrations from each interact, causing them to synchronize into a particular pattern. This pattern corresponds to a cell functioning in a specific way — say, becoming a skin or muscle cell. The cell is also sensitive to the beats of neighboring cells and can change their rhythm accordingly. Each drummer is sometimes inconsistent, but their cumulative rhythm is stable.

This new metaphor for how cells operate does not have an accepted name at this point. I'll call it the *cymatic* model. Cymatics is the study of the vibrational patterns that can be seen when particles are dropped onto a vibrating plate. At most frequencies the particles jump around randomly, but at certain frequencies self-similar patterns appear. The term was coined by Hans Jenny in the 1960s, to express the mystical aspects of the patterns that had been described by the German musician and physicist Ernst Chladni.

Cymatic patterns operate at the boundary between order and chaos. Their harmonics can be described by mathematics, and they are intriguing because each particle doesn't know what it should be doing, but at specific frequencies they behave in an orderly fashion. The behavior of individual particles is unstable and impossible to predict, but the overall pattern is emergent and stable.

This is where we see echoes of the deep, perhaps unsolvable, mysteries of the universe. The behavior of individual particles can be described using the mathematics of rational numbers, as particles can be seen as grains, a discrete set closely resembling the *natural* numbers 1, 2, 3... but to describe the harmonies emerging from particle systems, we require the mathematical smoothness and completeness of *real* numbers.

As each cell grows and splits, the microtubules in a developing multicellular organism have to constantly replicate, which is a process that needs to be tightly synchronized. Each microtubule is like a drummer that beats until the moment it replicates, at which point it quietens for a moment. The resulting rhythms would be like this: Beat-Split-Beat-Split-Beat... Each time it splits, the child microtubule would immediately join in, going Beat-Split-Beat... The timing is such that their beats are offset, so while the parent is on a Beat, the child would be on a Split. When you map the pattern, it starts with one player that splits into two, making a total of three, then five, then eight, then 13 and so on. Recall that these are the numbers that Fibonacci described in the sequence 1, 2, 3, 5, 8, 13, 21... They are numbers that move toward the divine proportion, and the mysteries of numbers and geometry that have transfixed mathematicians for millennia. Living cells remain on the edge between order and chaos, searching for perfect harmony, but never finding it.

When the system breaks down and is unable to self-correct, the cell starts replicating out of control, which results in cancer.

The above is a brief, metaphoric description of the dynamics of cellular biology that you can find in scientific papers with titles such as "On chaotic dynamics in transcription factors and the associated effects in differential gene regulation." My point is that scientists are now looking at the world from the bottom up. "It is unquestionable that we are at the threshold of a completely new era in the understanding of cell differentiation," writes Stuart Alan Newman, a professor of cell biology and anatomy at New York Medical College. It is now evident there is no unbridgeable gap between the physics and chemistry of the world and the development of a human being.

The cymatic model of cell development does not explain how human consciousness evolved. To understand consciousness, we have to let go of a pre-consilience meaning that implies it is something mystical. Looking at the evolution of consciousness from the bottom up, it becomes clear that it came about to satisfy some basic needs.

It isn't easy to comprehend how consciousness evolved, but I'll describe why and how it happened because consciousness is foundational to understanding *consilience* and how the mind works. Try to visualize the process by teleporting yourself back to the era when nervous systems such as the one found in C. *elegans* started evolving, and imagine you are a tiny worm that has simple taste sensors, but no eyes. To survive, you need to swim toward food. Each time you taste food in the water, you wouldn't know the direction from which the taste is coming; however, using a process of trial and error, you could swim toward its source. If you swim and the taste diminishes, you would change direction. Do this repeatedly, and you would swim up the concentration gradient, getting closer and closer until you bump into the source.

The technical term for moving toward something in this way is known as *taxis* – pronounced as though it has a double "s" at the end. The nervous system mechanism the worm needs to achieve taxis is quite simple. Plants exhibit taxis; they grow toward light. Even microscopic bacteria can swim toward food, and the chemical pathways are simple enough that biochemists have figured out how they do it.

But there is a problem with this method of finding food. You never know exactly which direction to go. When you swim using taxis, you might bump into the food, in which case you can eat it, but if you swim close by, you can only tell that you had been close when the taste starts diminishing. Then, when you change direction, you might still go in the wrong direction. It would be like trying to play the children's game of hide-and-go-seek with your eyes closed, your ears blocked and your hands bound to your sides. Imagine trying to find a fragrant orange using only your sense of smell and the sense of touch on your face and lips. Using trial and error, you would eventually find it, but it would take time.

Now imagine how much more successful you would be if instead of moving only toward or away from objects, you had a sense of where the objects were around you. You could develop this capability by sensing the light absorbed by or reflected from things. With several light sensors located behind a transparent lens, even without the need to move, you could sense where objects are situated.

Bear in mind, however, that your sensory apparatus does not know anything. It has to program itself. When you turn to the left, the object would appear to sweep from left to right. The beginnings of a brain would learn to direct the muscles to swim to the right. Through a process of trial and error, the components of the system could teach themselves how to swim toward particles of food.

There is a shortcoming with this system. It would be impossible for the sensory apparatus to distinguish between changes in the light source due to your own movement and those resulting from something moving "out there." This distinction is critical because something moving out there might be a predator that should be avoided, whereas sensations related to your own movement would be less of a threat. Very early in the evolution of mobile animals, the nervous system would have begun to distinguish between nerve impulses caused by "me" and those caused by "out there." Sensations that are caused by "me" can generally be ignored, but those caused by things moving out there could indicate danger or opportunity. If the object triggering the stimuli is large, it might be a predator ready to eat you or, if it is small, it might be food.

When considering this, think about it from the perspective of the cells themselves. "Me" is not an imaginary knower directing the process, but rather a cymatic cell responding to immediate feedback about the effects of internal versus external stimuli.

If you can get your head around this concept you can understand how consciousness got its start. It evolved for a basic reason. Consciousness allows animals to sense the world around them remotely and differentiate between "me" stimuli and "out there" stimuli.

In the minute-to-minute struggle to eat and avoid being eaten, the capability to sense what is around one and move accordingly would have conferred an immediate survival advantage. The ability to move through a dimensional world and act appropriately is what consciousness is for. The consciousness of a primitive animal is nothing close to human experience, but the differences lie along a continuum.

The development of greater visual acuity would allow more precise behavior. What started out as an array of light sensors eventually evolved into eyes with focusing lenses. Over long periods of time and with steady evolutionary pressure, this sensory device evolved into human eyes.

So far I have referred to sight and smell. You can go through similar thought experiments to consider sound and touch. Through trial and error your sensory apparatus would pick up tactile sensations and vibrations in the air that would contribute to a full-featured experience of what is around you. Seen this way, consciousness is a consequence of remote sensing. It is how an animal builds up a picture of the world so it can move around purposefully.

Consciousness is not a recent evolutionary invention: it evolved a long time ago. As well, each sensory realm would have gone through evolutionary steps that linked the different sensory domains together. Comparative neuroanatomists estimate that the integration of the senses happened at least 300 million years ago, when amphibians evolved from fish and ventured onto land. At that time, a region of the brain called the *dorsal pallium* started to develop. This part of the brain, located near the middle, is where all sensory inputs converge and become interlinked with the nerves involved with movement.

In recent evolutionary history the *dorsal pallium* mushroomed in size. In humans it became the two lobes of the cerebral cortex: the wrinkly parts of the brain (pictured on the cover of this book) that handle the senses and thinking. The *dorsal pallium* also includes the part of the brain that handles smell and the amygdala, which is often described as the part that handles emotions.

There are many ways of going about understanding Raphael's painting on the walls in the Vatican. We can approach it from within the confines of different academic disciplines. The artistic aspects are transfixing. The history of the period is endlessly fascinating, particularly when it is understood at the level of individuals and their interactions. The buildings themselves are worthy of study from architectural and engineering standpoints. We can also study the theological and scientific beliefs of that era, and how they are expressed in the details of the painting. The history, geography and economy of the Renaissance are also worthy of expert attention.

We can also discover useful insights by looking at the painting from the point of view of psychological and sociological theories. But these insights would not be scientifically robust because theories and categorizations are human-generated, top-down concepts. Instead, I'm describing how humans grow from a single cell into the complexities of the body, and that society and everything we do results from bottom-up, emergent processes.

In one sense, as scientists probe the inner workings of cells, we get a measure of how much we do not yet understand and may never understand. In another sense, we can see that, from the bottom up, everything can be understood in completely matter-of-fact terms, without the need for categorizations and theories. We can get the jigsaw puzzle to fit together, but each piece we assemble leads us to new puzzles that we didn't know existed.

If we really want to understand Raphael, his painting and everything else in the world, we have to let go of familiar labels. Every human endeavour, including art, mathematics, science and religion, is a product of the human mind. And to understand the human mind, we have to step through a door into the paradigm of consilience, knowing the labels we affix to things are necessary for us to communicate, but acknowledging they do not accord with how things work in the world — and in us.

— ▪ ○ 7 ○ ▪ —

We Move Before We Think

The nervous system of human beings is essentially similar to that of other animals and enables us to react in the moment. Our behavior happens in small increments far faster than conscious thought processes, as evidenced by sports.

GENE SEQUENCING HAS TRANSFORMED how we can understand our genetic relationship with one another and with other organisms. Not only can evolutionary geneticists draw family trees that show relationships between members of the same species, they can also see similarities between different species and even between far-flung branches on the tree of life. Gene sequencing provides unambiguous evidence of these relationships.

As a result, the evolutionary family tree has been reshaped. Animals once thought to be distantly related to humans because they look completely different from us — such as worms, octopi, snails, insects and fish — are now considered first cousins. Our truly distant relatives are the *archaeplastida*, which include algae and plants as well as a number of large groups of ancient, mostly tiny, organisms that many people won't have heard of, such as *alveolates, heterokonts, rhizaria, amoebozoa* and *excavata*. Bacteria are far distantly related, as are a huge group of organisms known as *archaea*, which straddle the border between life and nonliving systems. Archaea might have arisen as life forms independently and may be completely unrelated to animals and plants. Viruses, including the novel coronavirus, are yet another group.

Genetically, chimpanzees and other apes are like family siblings. Their DNA is about 99% the same as ours, and in key respects the human brain is identical, except for the size of the cerebral cortex – and the areas connected to the fingers and vocal apparatus, which I'll describe later.

The brain of our forebears served practical functions, such as enabling purposeful movement through a three-dimensional world, foraging for food, procreating and avoiding predators. Speed of response would have been most important. A difference of a few tenths of a second between the time it takes to decipher what is happening and acting appropriately would make the difference between eating and being eaten.

We might imagine that we think before we act, but here is an example from sports to show this is not true.

Any fast-moving sport could illustrate the point, but I'll use tennis as an example. When an elite tennis player – Roger Federer for example – returns a serve, a lot of things happen very quickly. Let's say he chooses to step forward, take the ball on the rise and hit it down the line. His eyes have to follow the ball off the server's racquet and figure out its trajectory. He has to change the alignment of his feet, pick which side to swing, take his racket back, all while adjusting his balance. Finally, he will accelerate the racquet toward the incoming ball and, in Roger's case, hit it right in the middle of the strings. All this will be achieved in the time it takes the ball to travel the length of the court moving 130 miles an hour: about one-fifth of a second.

Through the use of powerful fMRI, MEG and EEG technologies that can register what is happening in a functioning brain, neurobiologists have established that conscious awareness and thinking lags behind reality by approximately half a second. Conscious thinking is *slow*. If Roger had to go through the process of thinking about how to hit the ball, before he started to move, it would already be somewhere up in the stands. Through many thousands of hours of training, Roger's neuronal apparatus anticipates the ball's trajectory and his muscles work as a team, far faster than anyone can think.

While reviewing studies on how the body's motor systems work, I recalled spending hours at university looking down a microscope at slices of muscle tissue and drawing *muscle spindles*. The head of our zoology department, Professor David Barker, was an expert on spindles and one of very few scientists interested in these structures. To this day, there are not many scientific papers about muscle spindles. Now, four decades later, I realize that muscle spindles are emblematic of discontinuities between what frontline researchers discover, what makes it into textbooks and what people see in the media, and from there become part of everyday understanding.

Based on a presumption that human behavior results from the brain thinking and then telling the muscles what to do, you would expect to find lots of nerves running from the brain to the muscles. But that is not the case. Human anatomy has many more nerve fibers running in the other direction: from the muscles toward the brain. These are called *afferent fibers*.

Afferent fibers account for proprioception, which allows us to know the position of our limbs. If you didn't have proprioceptors, you would feel numb — the same feeling that happens when blood circulation to a limb is restricted and it "goes to sleep." If you close your eyes and imagine your whole body has gone to sleep, you would have no idea about its position. You would not be able to touch the end of your nose, unless you ran your fingers over your face as though it were someone else's.

Proprioceptors also have other functions, such as to ward off injury and to force us to take the weight off damaged muscles, tendons and bones, allowing them to heal. We experience this when we twist an ankle and immediately start to limp.

What is rarely appreciated is the remarkable complexity of the afferent system. Some nerves are thick, some are thin. And nerve endings vary strangely: some are splayed out like bunches of flowers, some are bulbous and others are straggly. Muscle spindles are particularly complicated. As a specialized muscle fiber, they have a motor nerve coupled with a sensory nerve that runs back toward the brain. Different types of spindles have inelegant names that reflect their appearance down a microscope. "Dynamic bag" spindles look like a bag filled with a few grapes; "static chain" spindles look like a chain of beads.

Another important function of afferent nerves relates to how the entire nervous system develops from a fertilized egg. In the early stages of cell development in a developing embryo, all cells are stem cells, which means they can grow into any one of the hundred or so types of cells that make up the human body. Stem cells that become nerve cells undergo a transformation. They eject one of the little hairlike cilia that are characteristic of other cells, and this enables them to break free and behave differently. They are like a teenager who throws away the front door key to their parents' home and puts down roots at a college and a friend's home. In terms of the cymatic model of cellular activity, ejecting a cilium changes the chemical harmonics of the cell. Once this happens, the nerve cell grows, with the head holding on to other nerves and the tail holding on to cells of skin or muscle tissue that form fingers and toes. As the fetus develops, the neurons elongate, which means the nerve head and tail grow to become far distant from each other.

As neuronal development is a self-organizing system, without a blueprint, neurons — with one end in the brain and the other elsewhere in the body — don't know what they are connected to or what their effect will be when they fire. And so they start a dialogue. The brain neuron sends a signal outward. If it is received by a muscle spindle, the muscle responds and sends a message back. The conversation might go something like this, figuratively speaking:

Brain neuron: Are you there?

Spindle: Yes.

Brain neuron: OK. Do what you do.

Spindle: Doing it.

Brain neuron: Good. I'm marrying that up with other sensory inputs.

Eventually, after weeks or months of experimentation, the brain neuron concludes: "You must be working with other nerves associated with closing the right thumb." Or more specifically, "You must be operating in *opponens pollicis*" – which is one of the four muscles that close the thumb.

After a baby is born, if the thumb encounters a sharp object and squeezes it, the brain neuron would receive signals from pain proprioceptors at the same moment it hears from the spindles in the four muscles that close the thumb, at which point the brain neuron would send a message to its colleagues in the brain who are active at that moment, saying, "Don't do that again!"

In this way, the nerves that control the muscles in the body become coordinated with the sensory nerves from the eyes, ears, mouth and skin, as well as pain sensors that are strategically located throughout the body. The chatter between all the nerves starts from the moment they form in the fetus. Then the nerves refine their functioning as the baby develops and learns. The process continues into adult life and is fully operative whenever there is physical activity. If at any point a neuron ceases to hear from one of its connections, it will listen out for others, then redeploy itself.

There is another intriguing purpose of the afferent nervous system. The muscles are continually feeding the brain a report on their state and position. Think of it like this: at the same time that Roger's eyes are tracking the trajectory of the ball, his brain is getting a report on the state of the muscles and tendons. From second to second, the brain is receiving a prioritized list of the choices of movements that are going to be the most efficient and use the least amount of energy, minimizing stress.

The muscles are, in effect, telling the brain what they want to do. Significantly, this sequence doesn't fit the classical view that the brain rules human behavior. And indeed, if you flip open a typical undergraduate kinesiology textbook, the complexity of the afferent nervous system is nowhere to be found. A leading textbook states, "Because of the complexity of the human body, we have developed a simplified model of the components of the motor system that are essential for movement. This simplified model is called the single joint system." This is typically accompanied by a diagram showing how a single nerve works with a single muscle.

The human body has more than 600 separate muscles with nobody-knows-how-many millions of afferent nerves that work together to twist and shape our core, limbs and hands into any number of positions and accomplish extraordinary feats of dexterity at speeds faster than our eyes can register.

Let's revisit Roger returning a serve. The complexity starts with the sensory system, and the lightning-fast and flawless coordination of the 12 muscles that control the eyes. As well, there is synchronized coordination of the muscles: more than 48 muscles in the shoulder and arm, another 68 in the trunk, and another 26 or so controlling the orientation of the head and neck. In every case the muscles are not evenly matched; they are different strengths and lengths, and they work at different angles to each other. Each is required to make continual adjustments, either moving or holding steady. When Roger makes a slight movement, virtually every muscle in the body feels the reverberations and makes minute, compensating adjustments.

All the muscles work in perfect coordination, always pulling against each other so that when some contract, others loosen. The muscles are maintained in a state of tone, so they are always ready for action. They do not waste energy tugging against each other needlessly, yet they are always taut, ready to make hair-trigger adjustments. Even when we feel relaxed all our muscles and neurons remain on constant standby, gently chatting with each other.

How important is conscious thinking in this whole process? In the case of Roger playing a point in a tennis match, very little. He has practiced for thousands of hours, so his senses and muscles react with lightning speed by themselves. The speed and precision of the system is refined through hours of physical practice, where the athlete repeats each step and swing, again, again and again. In the book *The Inner Game of Tennis,* Timothy Gallwey explains that as a coach his job is to stop the athlete thinking. He would say to his students, "I want you to focus your mind on the seams of the ball. Don't think about making contact. In fact, don't try to hit the ball at all. Just *let* your racket contact the ball where *it* wants to and we'll see what happens."

The act of concentration is best understood as allowing all the neurons in the motor and sensory system to become excited so they are chattering with each other and on the threshold of activation. When a player focuses their eyes on the seams of the ball, the neurons in the cerebral cortex that are attending to other matters quieten down.

Now let's go back to Roger Federer and ask him to describe how he returned the ball. He might say something like "I could tell the serve was going wide with a high bounce, so I stepped in and crushed it down the line."

Given that the events happened in less than half a second and his conscious mind takes about half a second to think, it is impossible that his actions were the result of his conscious thought processes.

We are not aware of it, but the brain has a remarkable ability to provide explanations for our actions after the fact. This was demonstrated through an intriguing experiment conducted by Michael Gazzaniga, a veteran of neurobiological research, dating back to his days at the California Institute of Technology in the 1960s. He conducted research on patients who had had the two halves of their brain separated to treat epilepsy; this research was the origin of the popular conception that the left brain is logical and the right brain is creative. He could show each side of the brain different pictures and elicit the patient's explanation from the side that controls verbal communication. The two halves of the brain couldn't communicate with each other and, so to speak, get their stories straight. In the book, *The Mind's Past*, he recounts a specific experiment. "A picture of a chicken claw was flashed to the left hemisphere and a picture of a snow scene to the right hemisphere." He recounted how the patient would pick an image by pointing at it, and how the other hemisphere would fabricate an explanation. "Of the array of pictures placed in front of the subject, the obviously correct association was a chicken for the chicken claw and a shovel for the snow scene. One of the patients responded by choosing the shovel with his left hand and the chicken with his right. When asked why he chose these items, his left hemisphere replied, 'Oh, that's simple. The chicken claw goes with the chicken and you need a shovel to clean out the chicken shed.'"

"What is amazing here," Gazzaniga stated, "is that the left hemisphere is perfectly capable of saying something like, 'Look, I have no idea why I picked the shovel. I had my brain split, don't you remember? You probably presented something to the half of my brain that can't talk; this happens to me all the time. You know I can't tell you why I picked the shovel. Quit asking me stupid questions.' But it doesn't say this. The left brain weaves its story in order to convince itself and you that it is in full control."

Thinking happens after we move, and explanations come after that. This does not discount the role of thought and the significance of ideas, because of course we think about things and adjust our behavior accordingly. From the standpoint of neurons, however, the difference between the perception of things and thinking dissolves. We react in the moment, at the same time as the neurons create patterns that anticipate future perceptions and actions.

— ▪ ○ 8 ○ ▪ —

How We Experience Reality

The brain creates our sense of reality based on the recall of previous experiences. Our eyes and ears work by actively picking up stimuli that make sense, rather than being passive funnels for sensory information.

ONE WAY OF EXPLAINING HOW SOMETHING WORKS is by relating it to other things that have similar functions. For instance, we know that pumps move liquids along a pipe. The human heart moves blood along arteries and veins, so it is easy to think of the heart as a pump. Few of us have seen how a human heart actually works, but many are comfortable with the metaphor that the heart works *like* a pump. Few would say they do not understand how the heart works. We *understand* it.

Similarly, we might associate how the ear functions with the way a microphone operates, or how the human eye works with the functioning of a video camera. If the brain operated like a computer that handles information, these metaphors could seem reasonable. According to this metaphor, the eyes register visual objects by way of the retina operating like the CCD sensors in a camera and sending the images back to the brain via the optic nerve.

But how accurate is the idea that our eyes work like a video camera?

I started wondering about this 35 years ago when I became enthralled by computer graphics and decided to capitalize on the budding technologies and launch a marketing communications company. I invested

$100,000 in a state-of-the-art mini-computer packed with graphics cards and VRAM. Frankly, the whole computer graphics system was a bust. The seemingly powerful computer took minutes to process and display a grainy image. How was it, I asked myself, that the human eye could process images in stunning high resolution in fractions of a second, whereas the computer would take minutes to display a 640x480 image on a big fat monitor?

Consider the physiology of the human eye. It is not possible for the retina to register a perfect full-screen, ultra-high resolution image and transmit information along the optic nerve. Only one spot in the center of the visual field, known as the *fovea,* can register an image at high resolution. The image it registers is small: about the size of your thumbnail when your arm is outstretched. It has receptors, known as *cones,* that are most sensitive to red and yellow light. Surrounding the fovea are cones that are receptive to blue light. Throughout most of the retina are rods, which sense only light and dark. The part of the eye that transmits a quality image is remarkably small; it is the equivalent of looking down a large drinking straw. Outside this area the retina is able to register only large objects or objects in motion. An area in each eye, called the blind spot, does not have any receptors at all. This is where the optic nerve leaves the inside of the eye.

When physiologists look closely at the retina, they do not observe a beautifully engineered device. In fact it looks like a team of demented electricians built it. There is a mat of neurons as jumbled as the filaments in a piece of pressed wool felt. It is organized in three layers, with a tangle of about 50 different types of connection and fibers. Physiologists have described horizontal cells, invaginating cells, midget bipolar cells, flat midget bipolar cells, flat diffuse bipolar cells, centrifugal bipolar cells and amacrine cells. Each cone is directly connected to between 6 and 12 others, and indirectly to thousands more; rods interconnect with up to 70 others.

If the video-camera metaphor for the eye was in part correct, the next question to figure out would be how the brain decodes the impulses. When I was at university in the mid-1970s, neurophysiology lecturer Dr. John Manning described research where electrodes inserted in the brain started firing when specific shapes were projected onto the retina. It seemed only a matter of time before the visual processing system would be explained. Then something peculiar happened: nothing. For 40 years, researchers with increasingly powerful measuring instruments and new ways to peer at the inner workings of the brain have not been able to puzzle out how information gets from the eye to the brain, then how it is decoded.

The reason neuroscientists have yet to decipher how the brain decodes information from the eye is because the visual system doesn't work that way. The brain needs to receive only a mere hint of what is being seen, then it immediately fills out the experience, actively creating the perception of reality. The metaphor of the video camera does not apply. A more accurate metaphor would be that the eye sends file names to the brain, which then opens up files of the corresponding images.

You have probably experienced something similar to this: on a twilight evening, you see a silhouette of someone standing by the side of the road. As you get closer, you realize it is not a person but an object. Your sensation of seeing a person was complete, perhaps for a moment making your heart beat faster, but then, in a snap, your perception changed. The experience is similar for optical illusions, such as the one in many textbooks of the head of a young lady that snaps into the face of an old hag. You can decipher each image at different moments, but not both at the same time.

The fact that our visual perception is created in the brain and not just recorded by the eyes explains a number of conundrums, such as the following: when you see the sun setting in the evening sky, it sometimes looks massive, particularly when it's behind some distant clouds. But oddly, the size of the image of the sun remains exactly the same. You can check this for yourself by extending your arm and covering the sun, wherever it is, with the tip of your thumb.

If your eyes faithfully reported what you see, when someone walks away from you they should appear to shrink. A person who looks 6-foot tall when close by should, at a distance, look the size of a gnat.

Dimensionality and perspective may seem straightforward, but it has taken a long time to figure these out. The ancient Egyptians were accomplished engineers, but they never realized that images in the foreground should be drawn larger than those in the distance. Pictures created by the Egyptians, the Romans and medieval artists appear two-dimensional. In 1435, the Renaissance architect Leon Battista Alberti grasped that parallel lines, such as tiles on a floor, should be drawn as meeting at a vanishing point. Filippo Brunelleschi was the first to represent perspective accurately when he drew a Venetian building with all the parallel lines converging at an imaginary point on the horizon. When Raphael painted *The School of Athens* in 1511, he delighted in accentuating the image's 3D perspective.

We see the world in three dimensions, but the image that falls on the retina is two-dimensional. The usual explanation is that we sense three dimensions because we have two eyes that provide stereoscopic vision. If this explanation were correct, however, when you close one eye your experience of reality would collapse from three dimensions into two, as though you were looking at a giant wall mural.

The way the visual system works is that we *see* things only because we have seen them *before*. Vision is a process of re-creation. It happens because new visual stimuli are matched to previously experienced sensations.

For instance, when you look at a cup, your brain registers that it is similar to other cups you have experienced before. That means each time you see a cup you are instantly recalling every cup you have ever seen. Your brain also notes its various elements: edges, shaded surfaces, colors and textures. If you are briefly shown a white porcelain cup with images of fruit on the sides, even though you have never seen this exact cup before you know the shape of the cup and how it would appear from other angles.

This process also applies to other sensory domains. When you see the cup, you instantly know how the cup would feel if you touched it. You know how heavy it is, how hot it is likely to be and what it smells like. You know that if you stick your finger in the opening at the top you will see your finger disappear from view and meet resistance as it touches the bottom. We are not aware of the process, but the brain creates a fullness of feelings from mere hints transmitted from the eyes. This is possible because when we see the cup we are associating it with every encounter we have had with cups, porcelain, edges, handles, fruit, whiteness, fingers and so on.

The advent of artificial intelligence and machine learning has helped explain how the brain recognizes objects. Before AI, the assumption was that the brain needed to be programmed in some way with predefined rules of logic. AI doesn't work using rules; instead, it needs to be fed lots of instances along with corresponding descriptions and the system learns accordingly. When Google and Facebook categorize images and tag them, they don't need a data engineer to program the system with information that would distinguish a cup from a mug, a cat from a dog or your face from your best friend's. The system teaches itself.

Aspects of this system of re-creation are hard to grasp because we are completely unaware of the process. The eyes take in a lot of information that is blurry, ambiguous and is continuous, but the brain splits sensations apart, so we recognize distinct objects. The brain also links sensations with words associated with them. I'll discuss these points later because they are the foundation of how we understand and communicate.

To reiterate, the brain is not like a computer that handles information, and the eyes are not like video cameras that record data. Likewise, the ears don't work like microphones. In fact, the most important function of the ears is not hearing, but registering balance and orientation, which are necessary to create a dimensional representation of the space around us.

The interior structure of the ear is difficult to investigate because the components are small and encased in thick bone. Deeper than the parts that register sound, is the *vestibular system*, about the size of a sugar cube. Inside three semicircular canals, fluid sloshes around; this enables us to sense angular rotation. Inside each canal are tiny crystals balanced on blobs of jelly that move in response to changes in gravity and movement. This "ear dust" is responsible for the feeling you get on a roller coaster, where your stomach feels like it is in your mouth. When the vestibular system ceases to function correctly, one experiences vertigo. When it is serious, a sufferer will be unable to see properly and will collapse on the floor feeling nauseous. They might be able to crawl, but walking upright is close to impossible. Vertigo feels like being badly intoxicated while moving about on the deck of a boat in heavy seas.

Not only is the vestibular system responsible for balance, but during the past two decades researchers have documented how this system is connected to central parts of the brain, and is responsible for us being able to construct a dimensional representation of the world around us in our head and orient ourselves within that space. The system provides a substructure for consciousness, in that it enables the mind to create a dimensional model of the outside world. It contributes to how we experience the world in three dimensions and, when we close our eyes, we can imagine getting up, walking out of the room and up the stairs.

The vestibular system makes it possible for the eyes to hold steady when the head moves. The mechanism is known as the *vestibulo-ocular reflex*. The system anticipates muscular movements, so when the eyes lock onto something of interest, the ocular muscles preempt the body's movements rather than having to play catch up. The eye's lens adjusts its focus preemptively, and the eyes swivel in toward each other when looking at something close. The system allows us to jump around and still have our eyes register an image that doesn't move.

Watching Roger Federer and other athletes excel in their sport gives us enormous admiration for their skill, but let's reserve total awe for the complexity and reliability of the systems that operate inside our head and point our eyes at things of interest — such as the ball going back and forth. The conscious mind is completely unaware of how essential the vestibulo-ocular system is until an affliction like vertigo incapacitates us.

Genetic evidence suggests that consciousness began evolving in animals about 540 million years ago, when worms evolved and became bilaterally symmetrical. This was the prelude to the Cambrian explosion described by Stephen Jay Gould, when an enormous diversity of creatures became trapped in the Burgess Shale about 508 million years ago. Then, around 450 million years ago, the vestibulo-ocular system developed, allowing early fish to point their eyes toward food and remain locked on it, as their head moved from side to side.

The way the human hearing system functions provides more evidence that the brain does not work like a computer. The ears are not like microphones, although college-level textbooks still portray them as such. The following textbook account sums up how the human auditory system works; it is largely, but not completely, correct:

> Sound waves are gathered by the outer ear and sent down the ear canal to the eardrum. They cause the eardrum to vibrate, which sets the three tiny bones in the middle ear into motion. The motion of the bones causes the fluid in the inner ear or cochlea to move. The movement of the inner ear fluid causes the hair cells in the cochlea to bend. The hair cells change the movement into electrical pulses. These electrical impulses are transmitted to the hearing nerve and up to the brain, where they are interpreted as sound.

Even though hearing is a secondary function of the ears, if the ears worked as just described, we would be nearly deaf and unable to decipher words.

The ability of the ears to detect vibrations is astonishing. To illustrate the point, I'll enlist the help of the princess in Hans Christian Andersen's fairytale, *The Princess and the Pea*. To reacquaint you with this story, the queen placed a pea under the princess's mattress to check whether she was who she claimed to be. The pea was covered by 20 mattresses and 20 eiderdown beds. In the morning, when the queen asked her how she had slept, she replied, "Oh, very badly... I have scarcely closed my eyes all night. Heaven only knows what was in the bed, but I was lying on something hard, so that I am black and blue all over my body. It's horrible!"

In the case of the ear, it can register vibrations the size of a pea, not through a stack of 20 mattresses and 20 eiderdown beds, but through a stack of 100,000 mattresses that is 8 miles high.

The hair cells in the cochlea are unbelievably sensitive, but another mechanism is at work as well. In the 1970s, David Kemp, professor of biophysics at University College in London, was measuring sound waves that echo from the inner ear. He noticed the ear was not just detecting sound, it was *making* sound, which he called *otoacoustic emissions*. When Kemp submitted his research results to the scientific journal *Nature* in 1977, his paper was politely rejected as "most interesting and perplexing... with no obvious explanation." The popular belief at the time was that the ear was a sense organ that *listened* for sounds, not a motor organ that *made* sounds.

Otoacoustic emissions are now routinely used by audiologists to check a baby's hearing. When they play a note into a baby's ears, the ear sings the note back. If there is no responding note, this indicates the baby has a hearing deficiency. But what is the purpose of these otoacoustic emissions?

The established dogma in the hearing profession has been that the ear works like a microphone, taking in sounds and passing the information to the brain. Consequently, until recently, no satisfactory explanation for otoacoustic emissions has been published in professional journals.

Consider that the inside of our head is noisy. When a sensitive microphone is placed in the inner ear, it picks up the sound of blood corpuscles rushing along the capillaries, which are noisier than a rushing waterfall; the sound of the beating heart, like the banging of a kettledrum; and the sounds of breathing and chewing, much like the sound of a hurricane. Despite these background noises, we can easily hear sounds that are significant to us.

The hairs in the cochlea constitute a complex-critical system that is on the verge of oscillating even in the absence of incoming sounds. The neurons in the brain are not the passive receptors of stimuli. Instead, they actively anticipate sounds that are "out there" and likely useful, and they tune up the hairs in the cochlea accordingly. When a baby hears an unusual note played by the audiologist, the neurons in the brain make the hairs in the cochlea beat synchronously so they make the same sound.

Even when we are in a loud restaurant and within earshot of dozens of conversations, we can pick out exactly what someone is saying to us. What happens is our neuronal system takes into account the situation, including the movement of the speaker's mouth. The listener has an expectation of what the speaker is saying and how sentences are structured. The neurons in the auditory areas of the cortex anticipate the next sound and tune up the system accordingly. The process would be like the pre-emptive wordfill on cellphones, except it would be happening in sub-syllable slices rather than whole words or phrases.

Recall the textbook description of the hearing system: "The electrical impulses are transmitted to the hearing nerve and up to the brain, where they are interpreted as sound." I'll correct this statement with the following: The ear and the brain work together to extract meaning from soundwaves. The word *interpret* is misleading because it overlooks that the ear and the brain are mutually active, and it implies that a separate little conscious being presides over the system.

In the same way, the metaphor of the eye being like a camera leads us along a path where the workings of the brain remain a mystery. When a textbook states, "The optic nerve sends these impulses to the brain, which produces an image," this should be corrected to say that the optic nerve sends these impulses to the brain, which produces a fully formed conscious perception. It is not easy to grasp the distinction, but no "image" is produced in the brain.

The muscles, eyes and ears operate together with neurons in the brain. The mathematics of complex-critical systems can describe the system dynamics. It is emergent and self-organizing. And it is nothing like a computer, because each time we see and hear something, the brain is creating new patterns that relate to past sensations.

9

The Neuronal Orchestra

Neurons in the brain's cortex operate like an orchestra, creating our sensation of us in the world. The system acts in a dipolar manner of attraction and avoidance, instantly preparing the body for appropriate action.

NEURONS IN THE EYES AND EARS HAVE CONNECTIONS to different parts of the brain, but mostly to the cerebral cortex. In evolutionary terms, about 300 million years ago, these two wrinkly lobes began to develop from the *dorsal pallium* in groups of animals, long-extinct, known as the *pelycosaurs*.

Most books I've found that describe "consciousness" presume that it evolved recently, and is unique to *Homo sapiens* and possibly other apes. Evidence from geneticists and biochemists, however, indicates it would be impossible for something as sophisticated as consciousness to be bolted onto the brain over the past few million years, like an aftermarket car part. The most astonishing and puzzling aspects of the human brain are to be found in the biochemical processes in each of its cells and how the various systems are emergent and can be described by the mathematics of complex-criticality.

Mainstream scientific accounts about how the human brain works often leave out insights of researchers whose ideas do not accord with the dominant academic paradigm that states the brain manipulates and stores information.

A notable example is Walter J. Freeman III, who was professor of molecular and cell biology at the University of California, Berkeley. As well as being a poet and philosopher, he was a pioneer in the field of computational neuroscience, having published nearly 500 research articles and several books, including one of my favorites, *How Brains Make Up Their Minds* (2001). Much of his research involved analyzing the patterns recorded on the surface of the brain using an EEG machine. He found the signatures of complex-criticality.

In 1990, he published a paper with Christine Skarda titled, "Representations: Who needs them?" In this paper, they state that the brain does not *represent* or *interpret* the world around it. In essence, they argue that the brain does not work by thinking. Freeman notes that biologists make efforts to think objectively about the brain, but "have shown no lack of hubris in pontificating about the properties of the brain supporting mental functions." He wrote, "On the contrary, they have always taken pride in being uniquely qualified to explain brain function to anyone willing to listen."

Freeman explained how the neurons in the brain interact, likening them to the social ritual of a crowd in a stadium watching a football game. The metaphor of an orchestra is, I find, more instructive.

To understand the metaphor of the neuronal orchestra, you need to know about the structure of the cerebral cortex. Most explanations in neurophysiology textbooks describe its divisions into modules. Its structure is, however, more straightforward. The cerebral cortex consists of a sheet of neurons that is slightly thicker than the pressed felt of a Stetson hat. This sheet is referred to as gray matter, or the *neuropil*. Underneath is a layer of connecting wires known as white matter, owing to their fatty insulation. Each of the two neuropil sheets is about the size of a small Stetson hat, and it is scrunched up so it fits inside the skull.

You might expect the neurons in the neuropil to be well organized; otherwise, how else could we think logically? Aside from the fact that they are arranged in layers, they appear to be a complete tangle, with any one fiber cross-connected with thousands of others, through millions of neural junctions, known as synapses. Just like the neural wiring in the retina, the cortex nerves look like they were installed by a team of demented electricians.

Unlike an electrical wire, neurons transmit impulses by firing, and the signals are transmitted along their length like waves along a flicked rope. The neurons fire spontaneously every few moments, with a frequency that increases or decreases according to the rate of firing of those they are connected to. The details of the synapses are beyond the scope of this book because their chemistry is super-complicated; suffice to say, some are excitatory and others inhibitory. All neurons continually interact with others, firing in rhythms. The rhythms can be recorded by electrodes placed on the scalp — that's what produces the squiggly lines on EEG machines.

Think of the neurons in the cerebral cortex as players in a neuronal orchestra. There are about 16 billion of these neuronal players in the cerebral cortex. Now think of the frequency they fire as corresponding to musical notes. Each one plays semi-random notes, but each is sensitive to what other musicians around them are playing. The resulting sound would be a pulsing din. But that changes when patterns of impulses arrive in the brain from the sense organs and the rest of the body.

Suppose the eyes focus, as before, on a cup. The pattern of impulses would be familiar to the neuronal players that had previously joined in playing riffs related to cups. The riffs would relate to what the eyes are registering as well as what the sense of touch and sound have previously experienced. Small sections of the orchestra — after only a few hundred milliseconds — would play a melody called "cup."

Each neuron does not *know* anything, but each recognizes patterns heard before and repeats the tunes it learned. With this concept of the human cortex, there is no hint of information being transmitted from one area to another. There are no circuits, and there is no processing or interpreting of information.

When scientists began to use EEG and fMRI recorders, there was an expectation that different areas of the cortex specialized in different functions. Indeed, different areas are connected to specific sense organs and separate parts of the body. The areas at the back of the head, known as the *visual cortex,* are connected to the eyes. Areas on the left are involved in comprehending and generating speech. The big surprise has been how all areas of the cortex are interconnected and that all the neuronal players play along with everything. If an area of the cortex is damaged or dies, for whatever reason, other areas learn the tunes of the departed players. The ability of the neuronal players to take on different roles is known as "plasticity."

The metaphor of the neuronal orchestra is a radical break from the familiar notion about how the brain works. This perspective requires us to reconceptualize the words we use to describe behavior: for example, *perceive, think, control, behave, input, emotion* and *brain*. Each of these words expresses well-established ideas, but their meaning needs to be reexamined. In ways more profound than I could have ever guessed, *the way we think we think is not the way we think.*

The neuronal orchestra doesn't only play melodies that correspond to what we are experiencing. It also plays melodies that take into account the context and our desires at a particular moment. You might presume that when an animal smells cheese, for example, at different times, the neurons concerned with registering that smell would react consistently and only to that smell. However, according to Dr. Leslie M. Kay, who was a doctoral researcher with Freeman and is now a professor of psychology at the University of Chicago, the neuronal players that are "just one synapse from the nose, respond in a fashion that represents what the animal is doing and what the odor means, not what the odor is, essentially the single neuron representation of meaning is dependent on spatial activity patterns." As Kay concludes, "We have shown that a multitude of factors determine the state of neural activity in the olfactory system. The least of these factors is the odor itself." This means the idea that the sensory apparatus is *objective* is untenable.

Let's return to the era when amphibians were evolving from swamp dwellers to living on dry land — when our early ancestors, the pelycosaurs, were evolving. These early mammal-like reptiles, which evolved from the amphibians, walked on four legs with their bellies raised above the ground. This detail is significant because to walk on four legs animals need to balance themselves and coordinate where to put their feet. The capability of the brain to construct a 3D representation of the animal's surroundings evolved from the earlier development of the remote-sensing system found in worms. The pelycosaurs had the ability to maneuver around objects as well as move quickly to catch prey or avoid being eaten. Their neural system evolved to respond and react as fast as possible to what was happening around them.

The pelycosaurs were early versions of dinosaurs and had large sail-like fins running across their backs. These sails were like solar panels, allowing the animal to absorb heat in the morning and cool off in the shade when it was too hot. A steady, warm temperature was essential for their brain's neuronal players to operate: too cold and the playing would grind to a halt; too warm and the playing would become manic. These animals existed in a world where sluggish amphibians were easy picking for food. Other pelycosaurs, such as the 500-pound Dimetrodon, with its rows of serrated bone-crushing teeth, were making easy meals of slow-moving animals.

These animals were *conscious* — in its consilience meaning of being aware of pertinent details of their surroundings. The purpose of their nervous system was to respond instantly to what might be prey or predator. Their neuronal players struck up different tunes depending on the situation. A vicious adversary would trigger the playing of tunes with titles like "How I need to get away." A small vegetable-eating pelycosaur would trigger tunes along the lines of "Here is a juicy meal."

The evolution of the neuronal orchestra in early reptiles might seem to have little relevance to understanding how human brains work, but it has become clear that, over evolutionary time scales, the cellular building blocks have not changed much. The neuronal orchestra responds to what we smell, see and hear. At every instant, we focus on things that have a *point*. Each of the things we perceive is associated with a corresponding action. The actions are dipolar – like a magnet – corresponding to either attraction or repulsion.

And this is what Kay's research team has been finding. The patterns recorded in nerves that register smell exhibit entirely different patterns according to the animal's situation. For a rat, another rat's smell is experienced differently depending on whether that rat is considered a friend or a foe.

Here is an example of how human beings use these basic mechanisms that began evolving hundreds of millions of years ago. Suppose you expect a family member, whom you love, to walk in the door and you hear a click of the latch. The instant you hear the sound, you experience a feeling of joy. Now picture yourself waking up in the middle of the night. Something isn't right. You listen carefully, and you hear the same sound of the door latch clicking. In that instant, you experience a sharp intake of breath, and your heart starts racing. Exactly the same sound causes a completely different response.

There is another finding that doesn't fit with the data-processing model of the brain, but will not surprise practitioners of yoga who consider controlled breathing therapeutic. The movements necessary for breathing, inhaling and exhaling, have been unbroken through the past 300 million years of evolution, and researchers have confirmed that the neuronal orchestra has adapted its playing accordingly. The neuronal players play slightly differently during each phase of every breath, and these variations can be detected throughout the brain, even in the prefrontal area of the cortex, usually considered to be occupied with higher-level functions.

The neuronal players do not perform specialized functions. Every neuron is only a few synapses away from being connected to every other neuron. The functions of seeing, hearing, smelling, tasting, feeling, speaking and moving are not isolated in different areas of the brain. This neuronal reality likely feels congruent for those who love music, literature, food, art and dance. An illustration of this would be the way we experience an outstanding meal in a restaurant. The combination of the tastes, the food presentation, the restaurant's decor, the aromas, the background music and the conversation make it memorable. Each realm of human experience is enhanced by the others. This fact is certainly not surprising to marketing practitioners such as me, as we routinely deal with these overlapping realms.

Freeman's scientific discoveries about the workings of the neuronal orchestra are not well known. One reason is that he was ahead of his time. He started his research before high-speed computing became available and before AI had been invented. The mathematics of complex-criticality hadn't been developed, so at that time, it was hard to conceive that the complexity of human behavior could arise from systems that are, on the surface, simple.

Another reason is that Freeman was an admirer of the Middle Ages philosopher Thomas Aquinas, whose writings, to this day, are a central point of reference for the theology of the Catholic Church. When Freeman referred to Aquinas in his research papers, he disobeyed the canons of science that disapprove of the blurring of borders between science and religion.

Another factor pushed Freeman's scientific insights to the sidelines. Freeman's great-grandfather, William Williams Keen, was the first brain surgeon in the United States and worked closely with six American presidents. His father, Walter Jackson Freeman II, was a famous physician. One would expect that the professor from the University of California, Berkeley, who was at the forefront of computational neuroscience would have become famous. His Wikipedia entry indicates otherwise. It is a perfunctory half-page.

Although Freeman and Kay's research enables us to reconceptualize how we think and helps us understand the complexities of human behavior, I believe that Freeman's theories have not become well known because his father was an advocate of lobotomies, where a metal spike was tapped through the back of the eye socket into the brain to treat mental illness. More than 300,000 lobotomies were performed in the United States between 1950 and 1965. In some cases, they were performed on individuals who, by today's standards, would not be regarded as ill. The most notorious case was Rose Kennedy, sister to President John Kennedy, who was operated on in 1941 to treat aggressive behavior. The backlash against lobotomies was expressed in Ken Kesey's 1962 book *One Flew over the Cuckoo's Nest,* which was made into an award-winning movie starring Jack Nicholson. In the movie, the clinical psychiatrist, Nurse Ratched, was portrayed as a sinister brain-killer, waging war on the creative spirit of the time. From then on, within the mental health community, the name Walter Freeman was tainted.

10

From the Gut Up

The peripheral nervous system is extraordinarily sophisticated and plays a central role in determining behavior. It operates largely without our conscious awareness.

CONSCIOUSNESS MUST RESIDE SOMEWHERE behind the eyes and between the ears because with a blow to the head you lose consciousness and become incapacitated. Also, because at any moment we might choose to do whatever we want, like touch our left ear, we assume that our conscious mind has control over our body. Indeed, the conception that the brain controls the body like a monarch lording over a kingdom has been well accepted in both science and popular culture. The central nervous system is sometimes pictured as something that an engineer might build to control the various parts of a manufacturing operation.

This chapter describes a different picture, one where the brain receives cascades of nervous impulses from the peripheral nervous system all the time, even when we sleep. One could say these impulses control human behavior, which completely upends the usual portrayal. The notion that a single part of the nervous system *controls* other parts does not, however, align with the view that biology is a bottom-up emergent system. A bottom-up perspective certainly accords with the details of human biology, but this stance is unorthodox. Those wedded to the concept of "free will" might find this bottom-up view disturbing. So I'll explain why I don't believe matters of human control are an issue.

When I was young, I spent several British winters living under the warm sun in Rhodesia (now Zimbabwe) with my mother's parents. My grandmother was an accomplished botanist and an artist. She spent hours painting watercolors of African landscape and plants. She had undergone an operation as a teenager to correct a hearing deficiency. The surgery was botched, so she became completely deaf. She did not learn sign language, so my grandparents lived in a silent, isolated world, but this suited them because they both found solace in their mutual love of nature. My grandfather was a veterinarian and expert on the many parasites that afflicted the livestock and people of Africa.

I recall as a five-year-old watching a chameleon with my grandfather in their lush garden. It was capturing a beetle with its long, sticky tongue. A boy about the same age as me ran breathlessly toward us, crying out. After a brief exchange in the local Shona language, my grandfather took me by the hand and walked briskly to the boy's home where a small crowd of locals had gathered around a young lamb that was lying on the dusty red soil. My grandfather crouched down, looked in the animal's mouth, ran his hands over its abdomen and, after a brief conversation with the lamb's owner, was handed a machete. With his foot, my grandfather rolled the lifeless animal onto its back, and chopped open the lamb's belly and the innards spilled out. He teased the organs apart with the tip of the machete, cutting one of them open and peering at it closely. He returned the machete and, after some brief remarks, we walked back to the garden. He had likely diagnosed the sheep as being infested with the liver fluke *Fasciolosis,* and probably advised the owner to bury the guts and eat the lamb only after cooking it thoroughly.

My grandfather spent his time in the evenings writing articles for various newsletters and scientific journals. He was fascinated by evolutionary theory and the mysteries of the animals he observed living around him and the bees he kept. When he died, I inherited his microscope and dozens of his books, including several about parasitology and others by his favorite philosopher, Teilhard de Chardin. I also inherited his curiosity about science, not just about what is known, but more interestingly what is on the fringes of human understanding and yet to be figured out. From a young age, when I observed under a microscope swarms of noncellular animals with their beating cilia and flagella motoring around in a drop of pond water, I was awestruck by this almost invisible, wonderful world.

And to this day when I read research papers about the tiny worm, *C. elegans*, that has a total of 302 neurons, yet exhibits behaviors that are complex, I do not think to myself how primitive and dissimilar they are to humans; instead, I marvel at how this organism can do so much with such an apparently simple system, and how scientists have so much yet to discover about the mechanisms that result in their behavior. Consider what this worm can do: it can sense gravity and temperature; it has a sense of taste and touch; it moves toward things it likes, such as food, and away from things it doesn't like, such as unpleasant chemicals. Once it has found food, it swallows and it defecates. It learns from previous experience and can remember. For instance, it can be taught to associate salt with the taste of garlic, which it doesn't like, so it swims away from salt even when there is no garlic present. After it matures, which takes about three days, its behavior changes from continual eating to searching for a mate, however tt puts food ahead of sex, so if it is still hungry at maturity, it will continue to feed before seeking a mate. The male will look for a partner of the opposite sex, although an Australian research team found that some are homosexual. Sexual intercourse for such a tiny animal is not easy; in fact, the male has to perform somersaults. After finding a mate, the male runs its back end along the partner's body, turning at the end by arching its back, looping around and swimming up. This continues until the vulva is found, at which point they align and the male enters its two-pronged penis, opening the vulva and locking it in place. The sperm are ejaculated into the uterus, the penis is then retracted and the male swims away.

To my mind, there are two questions that beg to be answered. The first is, How does this tiny worm with a total of only 959 cells accomplish many of the same behaviors that are similarly crucial for human survival? The second is, Why do most scientific accounts presume that conscious reasoning plays a dominant role in human behavior? In my view, believing that humans' neural apparatus is profoundly different from every other multicellular organism on the planet is unscientific.

Scientists have a long way to go before they figure out the answer to the first question. In fact, the more they discover about the complexities of the working of each of the cells in the tiny worm's body, the more the researchers realize how much more there is to discover.

According to evolutionary biologists, behavior can be explained in terms of memes: gene-like codes for each behavior. But like the concept of information in the brain, a meme is a conceptual description, not what actually happens. So the idea of memes conceals much that is unknown about how behavior relates to an animal's genetic code. Specifically, researchers have not yet figured out all the steps that connect the genetic blueprint encoded in DNA with the protein structures in each cell and the various mechanisms by which cells communicate with each other, and interact with their surroundings, that collectively create the patterns of movement we term behavior.

Human behavior is much more complex than that of the tiny worm, but there is little reason to believe that the biological mechanisms are substantively different. Based on knowledge of genetics, cellular chemistry and embryology, it is certain that many of the mechanisms are shared. It is also certain that much of human behavior is not related to conscious thought processes.

To answer the second question about why it is commonly believed that conscious thought processes determine human behavior, let's explore the gap between top-down, mechanistic patterns of thinking and the realities of the human body. To sum it up, the human body is considerably more complex and confusing than described in textbooks.

Modern anatomy got its start when, in 1543, Andreas Vesalius published a massive anatomy text titled *De Humani Corporis Fabrica,* literally, *Of the Factory of the Human Body.* The artistry of the more than 300 original woodcut illustrations were the result of the meticulous dissections of cadavers. Prior to that, the physicians and philosophers of ancient Greece and Rome, most notably Hippocrates and Galen, imagined that the mood and health of humans resulted from fluid substances emanating from different parts of the body, known as the four humors: blood, phlegm, yellow bile and black bile. It should be noted that the physicians of the time had no doubt about the completeness of their theory. The writings of Hippocrates and Galen formed the basis of medicine for more than 1,500 years, and they brim with logic and certainty.

Vesalius pioneered new ways of explaining the processes at work in the body. As well as being passionate about the ideals of classical beauty and the perfect human form, he thought like an engineer: seeing the stomach as a storeroom, the veins and arteries as pipes, the synovial fluid in joints like oil, the skeleton like the beams and joists of a house, and the ligaments working like reins and pulleys.

The artistic, mechanistic and idealized way of conceptualizing human biology was epitomized in Henry Gray's classic book, first published in 1858, *Anatomy: Descriptive and Surgical, Anatomy of the Human Body,* with illustrations by Henry Vandyke Carter. The book has been republished more than 40 times, and remains an essential reference book for doctors and surgeons. The drawings of bones, muscles, blood vessels, organs, the brain and spinal nerve are portrayed with extraordinary clarity, and their style illustrates the human body in a way similar to mechanical and electrical devices. To this day, the diagrams of nerve function appear similar to electrical circuit diagrams that might be used to build a radio.

Early editions of the book emphasize the so-called "central" nervous system and give little account of other nerves, which at the time were termed "sympathetic" nerves. The hormonal system received scant attention, which is understandable because, for example, insulin was not discovered until 1922 and adrenaline in 1950. Through history, reason and emotion have been seen to be working in opposition to each other and, indeed, in contemporary textbooks the emotions are often described as a separate system occupied with various bodily housekeeping functions as well as preparing the body to either engage and fight or take flight.

College textbooks show, in addition to the brain and the nerves of the spinal column, a system of nerves called the "peripheral" nervous system. When Vesalius and Gray were dissecting cadavers, they would not have been able to see much of the peripheral nervous system because those nerves are thin and dispersed. The system is divided into the autonomic nervous system and the somatic nervous system. The autonomic nervous system consists of the sympathetic, parasympathetic and enteric systems. These systems continue to be characterized as "lower" — that is, responsible for reflexes — compared to "higher," equated with the thinking brain.

Similar to the nerves associated with the eyes, ears and muscles, the nerves of the peripheral nervous system run in the opposite direction to what is expected. Only 10% of the nerves run from the brain toward the body. The other 90% go from the body to the brain. Some of the nerves run to a small area in the middle of the brain called the "*basal ganglia*." This structure is critical and, when seriously damaged, results in death.

Since the 1980s, researchers have used new investigative tools to probe deeper into various parts of the peripheral nervous system. The more they discover, the more complex and intriguing it becomes.

More than 50 signaling chemicals operate in cells, synaptic junctions, muscles, organs and the bloodstream. Most cells not only respond to these signals but also secrete them. The hormone-producing glands that make up the endocrine system are known as the pituitary gland, thyroid gland, parathyroid glands, adrenal glands, pancreas, ovaries and testes. The most active producer of more than 20 chemical signals, however, is the gut. Serotonin is widely acknowledged to play a central role in the brain, and is involved in feelings of happiness and depression. But unexpectedly, around 90% of the serotonin in the body is produced, not by the brain, but by the gut.

In the words of Michael Gershon, professor of pathology and cell biology at Columbia University, author of a book about the gut called *The Second Brain*, "The serotonin that's in the brain seems to be involved in everything that makes life worthwhile. For example, it's important for happiness and in fighting depression. It's involved in sex, eating, sleeping and dreaming. I mean, it's wonderful stuff, but, quantitatively speaking, the gut is where it's at." Signaling chemicals like serotonin do different things in different parts of the body depending on other factors, such as the firing of nerves. Gershon goes on, "And inside the gut, it protects the neurons from inflammation, so if any get killed, it helps make new ones from stem cells. So serotonin acts like the sword and shield of the gut."

When discussing anatomy and teaching students it is necessary to distinguish between different types of nerves, but these distinctions are a historical throwback and can be deceiving. The various nervous systems — *central, peripheral, sympathetic, autonomic, parasympathetic* and *visceral* — are interdependent and intermixed with other tissues. In fact, the word *system* is misleading because it infers the causality characteristic of human-made devices.

Scientific understanding of the details of cellular systems that enable the body to maintain homeostasis — that is, a state where all the cells can go about their many functions optimally — is patchy. There is much yet to be discovered. Scientific monographs are littered with phrases such as "it is thought that," "remain to be determined," "have not produced consistent results" and comments such as "central mechanisms of visceroceptor function remain unclear" and "the effect on higher nervous structures of signals originating from [the lungs] is also unknown." In other words, we don't know yet.

Most knowledge about the complexities of various interlinked nervous and hormonal systems of the body has come from the study of health disorders. For instance, changes in gut chemistry are implicated in health disorders that hitherto have been viewed as unrelated to that part of the body such as transmissible spongiform encephalopathies, autistic spectrum disorders, Parkinson's disease, Alzheimer's disease, amyotrophic lateral sclerosis, and herpes-like viruses that cause chickenpox and shingles.

In some instances, knowledge about the effects of gut chemistry on behavior has been discovered by accident. For instance, when gastric bypass surgery is performed to promote weight loss by reducing the size of the stomach, the physical effects are negligible. The operation alters the biochemistry of the gut, however, resulting in significant changes in how patients feel about sweet food and how their bodies handle energy.

The "hunger hormone," ghrelin, was not discovered until 1999. Ghrelin, in the bloodstream, encourages eating and affects taste sensation, but confoundingly, also affects sleep, energy management, fertility, memory, bone formation and lung development.

One way to appreciate the function of the systems involving the peripheral nervous system and associated chemicals is to list the many things that would go wrong if they stopped working. The list would go on for many pages. Here are a few, starting with those that would be catastrophic: the circulatory system would shut down, blood pressure would drop, and the heart would beat erratically and eventually stop. Breathing would cease, and the levels of oxygen and carbon dioxide would drop below the range needed to keep us alive. The volume of liquids and the concentration of electrolytes in the body would become unbalanced. The amount of sugars and other nutrients in the blood would go out of control. Body temperature would fall. These effects would be fatal within minutes.

Many short-term effects would be uncomfortable and, in the long term, serious. For instance, control of gut movements and secretions would be compromised. We would not salivate or be able to swallow or burp to relieve pressure in the stomach, acids would well up in our throat, we would not be able to digest any food, and we'd get constipation that would be fatal. We would not be able to focus our eyes. The iris would not constrict, and we'd be blinded by bright light. Our eyes would dry up without tears, and we wouldn't be able to blink. Males couldn't get an erection or ejaculate, and females would have no vaginal lubrication nor be able to go into labor and give birth.

The peripheral nervous system is also involved in preventing and surviving injuries and illness. Consider that every minute of the day is an opportunity to die. Not in the sense of an heroic death, but death caused by misadventures. Imagine what it was like in prehistory, before we lived in warm homes, with plenty of food and access to health care. There was an ever-present danger of dying from illness, starvation or attack by other humans and animals, both small and large. In this context, minor mishaps become life-threatening. Inhaling a fly and being unable to cough it out could lead to a fatal infection. Bruising a muscle or twisting an ankle and continuing to put pressure on it could worsen the damage, and lead to tripping, falling and being unable to recover. A nick in the skin could become infected and fatal. Eating something that is contaminated or poisonous could be terminal. Organisms in the gut can turn from benign to deadly. In each of these situations, the body systems have a battery of responses that lessen the chance of the condition deteriorating. The conditions we think of as illnesses are, in many cases, responses that increase the chance of survival. During an infection, the body's temperature rises and we feel listless. Both of these responses increase the chance we throw off the disease.

Some neural systems operate fast. Imagine something unexpectedly comes at you from behind. When you hear the noise, you jump. If your head is bumped at the same moment, you jump higher. This is known as the startle response. The mechanism at the level of neurons is well engineered and extraordinarily rapid. It causes us to open our mouth, blink, then open our eyes wide, as well as relax core and limb muscles, then contract them. The movements start in less than one-tenth of a second, then cascade through the body in half a second. The response is tailored to minimize damage from a body blow and prompt evasive action. The reflex is most pronounced when we anticipate trouble and feel scared, but it also happens just as quickly when we are relaxed and even asleep.

There are neural receptors for blood pressure and flow throughout the circulatory system. We are not aware of them at all; however, if blood pressure drops in the main artery from the heart and the one that runs to the brain, it triggers a five-bell alarm that reaches every part of the brain. At the level of consciousness, it is felt as a searing pain running across the chest and a sensation of complete panic. It causes the victim to collapse — which is a clinically appropriate response that lessens stress on the heart and increases the chance of survival.

Body functions and responses to pain, surprise and illness are not often included in discussions of human behavior. Rather, they are simply considered as aspects of being alive. From the standpoint of human biology, however, such functions and responses are indivisible from the neural systems involved in perceiving, thinking, talking and moving.

The most important aspects of human biology have not substantially changed for hundreds of millions of years. The human body needs to maintain homeostasis by taking in liquids and nourishment, and by maintaining a comfortable temperature and protection from harm. And, for the continuation of our genes, we need to procreate. The biological systems that look after these needs operate below the level of consciousness; they are extraordinarily sophisticated, and it will be many years before scientists figure out their mechanisms.

When I scan recent journal articles about the complexities of human biology, I encounter the same feeling that I have about the textbook accounts of marketing. In marketing, there are clearly defined subdisciplines. *Consumer* marketing is separate from *business-to-business* marketing. Creativity is separate from strategy. In practice, however, focusing on the distinctions is counterproductive. Everything in marketing is a subgenre of human behavior, and projects become successful through the cumulative effects of each micro-interaction.

It is the same with textbooks about human biology. They typically show the central nervous system as separate from the peripheral nervous system, and this as separate from the circulatory and immune systems, and the gut as entirely different. Yet when you focus on, say, just a few cells in the wall of the small intestine, all the gaps fuse together. The cells work together not only with each other, but also with the good microbes in the gut to fight damaging bugs and parasites — such as *Fasciolosis*. The cells completely disregard the distinctions between structural, mechanical, chemical and electrical systems. They have been working away perfecting what they do for more than a billion years, changing roles as needed. They pay no heed to scientific categorizations.

— ▪ ○ 11 ○ ▪ —

The Neuronal Conductor

How the cerebellum coordinates repetitive, habitual movement, and introducing the metaphor of the conductor of the neuronal orchestra.

THE PART OF THE BRAIN RESPONSIBLE FOR HUMAN ACHIEVEMENT and civilization — the neuronal orchestra in the cerebral cortex — has a macroscopic structure that is uncomplicated. This part, along with the sense organs, handles consciousness and is mostly straightforward to understand, whereas the so-called reptilian parts of the brain, including the basal ganglia, are unfathomably sophisticated and challenging to figure out. This flip-flop in the ability to comprehend the human brain surely qualifies as an irony of cosmic dimensions.

In earlier chapters, I described how the brain takes in signals from the body and I introduced the metaphor of the neuronal orchestra to explain how muscles, eyes and ears work to represent the world around us. The cerebellum now needs to be brought into the explanation. A pear-sized, wrinkly lump of tissue, the cerebellum peeps out from under the two lobes of the cerebral cortex at the back of the head. Other than the brainstem, it is the only part of the brain that is plainly visible without splaying apart the cerebral cortex t.

The functions of the cerebellum have been something of a mystery and difficult to investigate on account of its small size and tiny neurons. It comprises only 10% of the volume of the brain, yet has six times more neurons than the cerebral cortex: more than 100 billion of them.

If an adult develops a tumor and the cerebellum has to be removed, it isn't fatal. The patient feels woozy, loses fine motor skills and a range of functions are compromised, including the ability to balance, read and speak. Playing tennis becomes impossible. Because the cerebellum is not essential for reasoning, brain scientists describe it as having a lower function and being subordinate to the cerebral cortex.

The cerebellum's role is illustrated by Chase, a baby born in Buffalo, New York, in 2008. From the start, his vision was compromised. His parents noticed he was having trouble with fine motor skills, and MRIs revealed that, for some unknown reason, he was missing his cerebellum. His parents were diligent, helping him learn how to walk and speak. When he turned 5 years old, his vocabulary was around 100 words, and he used a walker to navigate the hallway.

The latest high-resolution scanners, which can register the activities of neurons in fractions of a second, reveal that the cerebellum plays a leading role in the coordination of movement, particularly repetitive motions characteristic of so much that we do. It is also involved in coordinating the movements of the eyes, controlling the vocal apparatus and maintaining balance. As well, the cerebellum is involved in many so-called higher processes: for example, initiating and processing of speech, reading, writing, emotions and memory. It is also implicated in dyslexia, attention deficit hyperactivity disorder and autism spectrum disorder.

How does the cerebellum work? Like the cerebral cortex, it is made of a thin sheet of neurons; however, it is more neatly organized and tightly packed. A cross-section reveals a structure like the flesh of a walnut and the branching shape of a juniper bush. It has a surface area 20 times larger than the neuropil, but one-quarter the size.

The cerebellum operates in a fashion similar to what I described for the neuronal orchestra of the cerebral cortex, except here the neuronal players respond primarily to inputs from the muscles and also from the players in the cerebral cortex. Unlike the cortex, the cerebellum's neuronal players are not linked directly to the eyes, ears and skin.

The cerebellum operates below conscious awareness, yet it is involved in every aspect of thinking and learning. We have no awareness of what goes on during the complex coordination of the 600 muscles in our body, including the repeated, oscillating patterns of motion underlying muscle movement. At every moment, the body is responding to things internally and around us, and does so by carrying out sequences of movements, including looking, breathing, chewing, swallowing, walking and interacting with others. Throughout the day our motions mimic similar movements from the day before: rubbing eyes, standing up, yawning, brushing teeth, getting dressed and so on.

The cerebellum handles mundane repetitive motions, while the neuronal orchestra is occupied with perceiving the surroundings and modeling alternative courses of action.

Seemingly simple actions, such as when I take a few steps on rough ground, emerge from neural and bodily systems that are stunningly complex and remarkable. The brain's neuronal orchestra builds a three-dimensional model of the ground ahead and anticipates what will happen when I step forward. If there is a stone in the way, the orchestra will model the likely consequences of stepping on it, over it or around it. Along with feedback from muscles, my feet will be guided on a path that is the most comfortable, efficient and safe.

This process is happening all the time below the level of consciousness, and it happens extremely fast, allowing us to sprint over rough ground without tripping. It would be impossible to move fast if we had to think about every step we take. Occasionally, however, we arrive at a place where we need to make a choice. Suppose a tree has half-fallen across the path. We might decide to duck under it, walk around it or jump over it. We don't consciously think about such choices, but our neural system quickly plays out each scenario, noting that we might be crushed if the tree falls, so we navigate around it.

This process of playing the scenario forward and modeling the various outcomes forms the foundation for *thinking*. The process involves a three-dimensional representation of our body while it interacts with things around us. At every moment, we are subliminally aware of our surroundings anticipating the results of our movements. The neuronal players perform melodies that foresee what our limbs will feel as we move, touch and talk. Over time, due to repetition, we create a landscape in our mind that is composed of everything we have experienced, all the salient places we have been and their associated feelings.

This finely tuned awareness of our body and the results of our interactions give rise to the feeling that an imaginary knower resides in our heads and controls our actions.

In applying a bottom-up perspective to further understand human behavior, culture and communication, there will be an ongoing challenge to relate the discoveries of frontline researchers with what we already presume is correct.

We will cry out for answers and explanations for many questions: How do we account for conscious versus unconscious experience? What about instinct and also voluntary versus involuntary action? And what about free will, morality and creativity? These are pertinent questions, but instead of getting bogged down in accounting for them, we can consider how to change our frame of reference and step out of the room of familiar modes of thinking — scientific and otherwise — into the new paradigm of consilience.

Recall that in chapter 6 I described how consciousness evolved, as a means of remote sensing, and how the neuronal players in the cerebral cortex relate inputs from the sensory organs to previous experiences. In addition, as just described, the cerebellum handles the fine details of muscular movement. These two structures — cerebral cortex and cerebellum — surround and are connected to other structures called the basal ganglia, amygdala, hypothalamus, hippocampus, striatum, ventral tegmental area and the pituitary. Now I'll describe in simple terms how the parts work together.

These central structures are sometimes referred to as the reptilian part of the brain because the various components can be traced back to structures in reptile brains, and because their functions are not considered part of conscious behavior. But dividing brain function between conscious and unconscious processes is not helpful. Also reptiles are conscious: for example, a chameleon can place its feet precisely on the stems of plants and swivel its eyes toward a beetle on a neighboring flower, then nail it with its sticky tongue. To accomplish this, it needs to be conscious of its surroundings and the position of its body.

Tracking brain structures back across evolutionary time scales does not simplify explanations of their functionalities. When amphibians ventured onto land, the area of the brain called the *dorsal pallium* started growing to become the cerebral cortex. So the *dorsal pallium* of the early reptilian brain is analogous to the neuronal orchestra — but not exactly because the areas dealing with the sense of smell and the amygdala that were part of the *dorsal pallium,* while closely connected, are set apart.

To provide a completely new frame of reference for understanding the human brain, I'll give the so-called reptilian brain structures a new name — the neuronal conductor — and I'll describe the organization and functioning of the brain as a relationship between the neuronal orchestra and the neuronal conductor.

The neuronal conductor structures are in the middle, surrounded by the neuropil of the neuronal orchestra. The neuropil is darker in color, hence the term *gray matter.* These gray-colored neuronal players sit on top of a mass of neurons that are covered in whitish insulation, hence the term *white matter.* Some of this white matter includes interconnections between different areas of the cortex, and the rest connects the gray neuropil to the neuronal conductor in a configuration like the radiating struts of an umbrella. The cerebellum rides along, shotgun style, with nerves connecting it to the neuronal conductor.

By way of example, I'll describe how these various parts interact and what the neuronal systems are doing when I feel hungry and decide to eat a cookie.

The neuronal conductor is the collection point of all the inputs from the peripheral nervous system. The feeling of hunger comes when sensors in the body detect that sugar levels in the blood are falling. Ghrelin is released into the bloodstream and detected by the neuronal conductor. The neuronal orchestra plays snippets of many different tunes, including ones associated with walking into the kitchen to find the cookie jar. When the neuronal conductor starts tapping out that particular beat, other neuronal players start playing the same tune, until a good number play the melody called *Walk to the kitchen.*

The *Walk to the kitchen* melody biases the neuronal players in the cerebellum to start playing their part, which is to initiate the tune called *Stand up.* The muscles signal *We're okay with stand up,* so that's what they do. Then many of the players in the neuronal orchestra join in and I walk to the kitchen. A few of them start playing the next verse, called *Reach for the cookie jar.* The neuronal conductor recognizes that it has previously delivered pleasing sensations from the stretch receptors in the walls of the stomach. So it continues tapping along with the unfolding song.

In preparation for what is coming next, my salivary glands kick into action. The neuronal orchestra visualizes the steps toward the kitchen and the act of reaching to open the cupboard. The cerebellum looks after the important details of muscle coordination as I step into the kitchen, reach up and take down the cookie jar.

When I start eating, the visceral and autonomic nervous systems continue to handle the matters of breathing, swallowing and stimulating the flow of gastric juices needed to start digesting the cookie. Perhaps the conscious mind is playing an active role, but saying it is in control misses the point that everything is working together. But when it comes to chocolate chip cookies, my conscious mind likely starts playing another melody — *That's the last one!* — and the peripheral nervous system sends impulses to the neuronal conductor, saying *We are not done yet; go on, reach for another one.*

Psychologists have traditionally viewed the conscious mind as being in control of human behavior, along with occasional interference by the subconscious mind, with its suppressed memories, anxieties and a vipers' pit of sexual urges. It is natural to imagine I went to the kitchen because my conscious mind "felt hungry." The reality is that body systems that operate below the level of consciousness encourage us to move toward the kitchen and reach for the cookie jar.

The players in the neuronal orchestra know untold numbers of tunes, but they don't *know* what each tune is for. Nor is the neuronal conductor in control. It is not like a typical conductor. This conductor is blindfolded, deaf and does not *know* anything. It certainly is not conscious. From the time of birth, the neuronal conductor matches up tunes from sensory inputs that lead to inputs from the peripheral nervous systems that move the body to homeostasis and safety: in other words, which tunes lead to less pain, the right foods, the right amount of liquids, the right bodily temperatures, the right amount of sleep and all other matters that are necessary for everyday well-being.

An imaginary knower in our head that seemingly directs activities is riding along, but our behavior results from the cumulative cooperation of every part of the human organism; however, that imaginary knower has a vital role. Its purpose is to play out different scenarios, especially social ones. It allows us to run through alternative courses of action, much as when we navigate around a tree that has fallen across the path ahead. We can preemptively rehearse how to interact with the people we encounter.

Suppose I have my hand in the cookie jar and I hear my partner approaching the kitchen. I'll visualize what she is likely to say and start modeling forward: Should I put the cookie jar back and pick up a cup instead? Or alternatively, I'll act nonchalant and get ready with a diversionary comment.

The way the imaginary knower works is similar to AI computers that play games against themselves. A demonstration of the power of this approach is provided by a match between AlphaGo and the world champion, Lee Sedol from South Korea, playing the ancient board game, Go. The game had long been regarded as too strategic for computers to master; yet in 2016, the computer prevailed in a match against Lee by winning four games out of five. The computer had, in effect, taught itself by repeatedly playing games against itself. And with each iteration, it had become smarter and smarter, until it was smarter than the very best human player.

The imaginary knower can move around in a virtual space that has been constructed over time through repeated experience with kitchens, cookies, cups and people. A key aspect of consciousness in humans is this imaginary knower that constantly models scenarios in the arena of social life.

Its function is demonstrated by how we like to occupy ourselves. Everyone has different preferences, but, on the whole, we like entertainment that involves people interacting with each other. We like to watch comedies, thrillers and dramas. We enjoy binge-watching multipart dramas on Netflix with exciting characters and intricate plotlines. The most popular genres of fiction are romance and crime/mystery. Males in particular like watching sports, and teenage males like playing combat video games. In all of these instances, the neuronal players are taking in the relationships between the characters and anticipating how the narrative will unfold. In all these forms of entertainment, relationships change from moment to moment, and we are never sure what is going to happen next.

Our *feelings* relate to our experiences and urges. The word *feeling*, in the pre-consilience paradigm, has connotations of emotionality and being indecisive, as in "I feel like eating a cookie, but I am not sure." Knowing the complexities of the peripheral nervous and sensory systems that continually keep us safe, we can see that feelings occur when unconscious processes bubble up into the conscious arena. When we say something along the lines of, "I feel hungry," "...tired" or "...irritated," the feeling is the result of biological urges. The power of these urges is betrayed by addictive substances, such as nicotine. When a smoker says they feel like having a cigarette they are articulating an urge to smoke that is nearly impossible for their entire system to resist.

Historically, reason and emotion have been viewed as distinct systems. There is, however, no evident demarcation between these two in the biological structures of the nervous system. Everything we think and do involves some degree of emotional salience; otherwise, we wouldn't notice or respond. The fight-or-flight reaction, used as an example of an emotional response to danger, is just the visible tip of a neuronal and physiological iceberg. The neuronal players become tuned up and start furiously playing out scenarios: What if I run? What if I freeze? What if I physically engage? What if I act cool and negotiate? Some of these scenarios become conscious and can be manipulated using logic. We only become aware of the many processes that prepare our body for action as we feel our skin flush and our heart pound.

In pre-consilience terms, *thinking* refers to everything the brain does other than instinctive responses. With an understanding that most neuronal system functions occur without the imaginary knower playing an active part, we can redefine *thinking* as a specialized function that plays through scenarios and uses causal logic to make sense of things we care about.

Although we might believe the imaginary knower is fully in control, it is more of a bystander in the dynamic business of ongoing survival. It is like a child riding a galloping horse. The child does not appreciate that the horse is being kept alive from second to second, minute to minute and hour to hour by a system that is instantaneous, sophisticated and so invisible that scientists have only recently begun to understand its complexity. Nor does the child appreciate that the system controlling the placement of the horse's hooves from millisecond to millisecond is more remarkable than all the supercomputers on earth combined.

12

Neuronal Melodies

The neuronal orchestra arranges the tunes of sensations into melodies to make sense of the complexity of everything around us. Melodies are arranged into narratives and metaphors that relate nonmaterial ideas to physical things and actions.

I DESCRIBED HOW THE NEURONAL ORCHESTRA OPERATES in chapter 9, by recognizing patterns and playing tunes that correspond with ones learned previously. In this chapter, I'll explain how the neuronal players handle the constant stream of impulses from the sense organs and create order from the immense volume of sensory input.

When I glance out my window, I see a few trees, some grass, and now and then several birds. I can discern what I am looking at within a fraction of a second. That might not seem remarkable, but my brain is taking in a jumble of impulses from the eyes and providing a sensation that what I am seeing is comprehensible and can be easily categorized.

If I spend a moment longer and look at the details of the trees, I can differentiate between thousands of twigs, millions of leaves and uncountable numbers of other things. Every single leaf and blade of grass is unique, yet my brain is not overwhelmed.

We don't notice it, but the brain takes shortcuts to make sense of our surroundings. In just a fraction of a second of seeing an object, we know a lot about what we are observing based on prior experience, and we can sum it up with a word, such as *tree* or *leaf*.

What each of us sees depends not only on our surroundings, but also on prior experience with similar things. When my grandmother observed the plants in her garden, she noticed distinctions that will never be apparent to me. When geologists look at a rock face, they notice the different strata. Each shape and shard of rock has meanings of which nongeologists are unaware.

The same process happens with sounds. Listening to a popular song we might be aware of the words and melody, but not notice the drums. However, an experienced drummer told me, "I can't listen to music at home that has drums in it. I hear nothing else but the drums." He can pick out the kick drum from the snare, the toms, the hi-hat and the cymbals, which is disconcerting to him, so he prefers listening to classical music.

The brain also categorizes the actions we observe. When we see a person walking, we do not treat their every step as a unique event. We make a generalization and call the action "walking." Experts in human locomotion, as well as professional dancers, note details about human walking that others miss. Similarly, with a forehand shot in tennis, most people see only the swing, but an experienced coach notices the position of the head, shoulders and feet, as well as the trajectory of the racquet head.

The neuronal orchestra plays tunes that correspond to everything we experience, including objects, sounds and patterns of movement. It also plays forward potential scenarios at every moment. The neuronal conductor tilts the playing toward tunes that lead to desirable outcomes. It also enables us to think logically and create new ideas as far as our imagination wishes to go.

To help explain how the neuronal orchestra handles the immensity of the incoming and previously experienced sensations, and how the system organizes tunes and creates new ones, I'll extend the metaphor of tunes to musical elements of all sorts, including chords, refrains, stanzas, melodies and symphonies.

Each of the neuronal players — the neurons — happens to be more versatile than human musicians as they can play any number of different genres of music from jazz to orchestral to rap, using a variety of instruments, including their voice. Along with the players around them, and those they are connected to via the white matter, they play chords to make a never-ending variety of melodies. Neuronal melodies are associated with sensory experiences and also with melodies that make *words*. The neuronal orchestra can string together melodies in unlimited combinations.

The neuronal players don't have sheet music, but instead constantly improvise as they try to synchronize with as many other players as possible. At every moment they come up with new compositions. Dissimilar melodies that become synchronized result in metaphors. Melodies become strung together to make a performance, producing a narrative. Melodies, including those that are metaphors and narratives that are broadly applicable, we call *ideas*.

The capacity to create melodies and arrange them in many different ways is highly significant. This points to a neural mechanism that enables people to organize their beliefs into a meaningful whole. Each piece of known information has a context, or frame, and is experienced as an arrangement. In turn, these form larger compositions that are symphonies of understanding.

The interrelationship between different melodies of experience helps account for why literature, poetry, music and other experiential domains are possible and meaningful. Recall the example of how your neuronal orchestra starts performing tunes associated with cups when you see a teacup. These melodies will be similar for many different types of cups, including coffee cups and paper cups; however, the neuronal orchestra arranges the experience of a teacup with other things that are similar but different, such as egg cups, prize cups and the cup on a golf green. It goes further. This melody is used for the verb *to cup*, as in "she cupped the baby chick in her hand," and also for a quantity, as in a cup of flour, whether or not a physical cup is involved.

From the standpoint of a neuronal orchestra, both the tunes within melodies and the melodies themselves are never static. When a cup is touched, it engenders tunes associated with touching and drinking. The word *cup* is a succession of sounds and, when written, our eyes experience it as a sequence of letters.

At a subliminal level, the melodies pertaining to particular experiences are associated with contextual feelings. For example, cups are generally associated with drinking, often in a social setting, so a cup generally engenders some positive feeling. But the metaphorical associations can go further. Barbra Streisand in *Don't Like Goodbyes* sings the following verse:

Now that your future is looking up
Forget the past and go fill your loving cup

Her song tells a story — from a musical, penned by Truman Capote and Harold Arlen — of Ottilie, who has fallen in love with a young man she has to leave. In the context of the musical, the loving cup is a sexual metaphor for Ottilie's vagina. In this instance, feelings associated with the word *cup* have an emotional poignancy that extends beyond its regular meaning as a large ornamental drinking vessel with two handles.

The use of the term *metaphor* in the context of the neuronal orchestra is more than a literary device; it refers to things that are in many cases clearly dissimilar. A cup is not much like a vagina, but neuronal players make the association.

The ways in which neurons create and connect melodies has yet to be figured out. The tight synchronization between widely separated parts of the brain is remarkable. The smell, touch, sound and visual experience of a cup occur in different parts, and yet they hit the notes at the same instant.

Scientists are now getting glimpses of the sophistication of single neurons. Their many branches perhaps act like self-contained mini-computers, more analog than digital, helping account for the almost endless number of experiences we can recall.

Over the past few years, neuroscientists have been discovering that the neuronal players are adept at playing and remembering all sorts of melodies. For the system to avoid getting clogged up with melodies of little significance, most need to be forgotten. Perhaps that is why we need to sleep. It gives the neuronal conductor the time to instruct the neuronal players which tunes they should erase.

The notes the neuronal orchestra plays for both sensation and movement, as far as we can tell, are identical. Their functions, however, are different. To highlight the distinction, I'll introduce another metaphor, one that associates tunes related to movement with paths created in a landscape.

A mental landscape is a suitable metaphor because human behavior, contrary to how we perceive ourselves, consists of a series of small, stereotyped, repeated motions. Beginning early in our life, we build a landscape of behaviors that become progressively harder to change. You can visualize it like this: at birth, the terrain of the neuronal orchestra is completely smooth, and each experience is like a raindrop falling on the surface. Over time, the falling raindrops combine with others to form rivulets — a narrative of movement. The neuronal conductor through repetition makes deeper channels, sending the water along progressively larger streams. Over the years of our life, the streams form rivers — the habitual patterns of experience and behavior that allow us to perceive and respond within an eyeblink.

The mental landscape we create is our worldview or personal paradigm. Once our paradigm has formed from countless experiences with other people who share a similar landscape, it becomes nearly impossible for us to change. If you use a spade to create a new channel it will not alter the course of a long-established river. Max Planck's joke that new scientific truths take hold only when their opponents die is closer to the truth than supposing that people change their mind easily. Later, when I discuss the formation of tribal journeys, I'll refer back to the metaphor of well-formed landscapes.

The process of arranging similar sensations together is a core mechanism required for consciousness. It evolved long ago so organisms could move toward food or away from danger instantaneously. The same mechanisms are at work in the human brain. Things that have some pertinence, or a *point,* have an instant association along the dipole of either attraction or repulsion. As soon as we experience something, our neuronal mechanisms respond. If things have no *point* we do not notice them.

Even when two objects look almost identical, the neural system reacts to them according to melodies of prior experience and ideas. For instance, I might step over something that looks like a short length of brown garden hose and hardly notice it. A similar shape that wriggles will make me recoil instantly and my heart pound. My neuronal orchestra plays different tunes for "snake" and "garden hose."

Similarly, if someone used the metaphor of a snake to warn me to be careful of a certain individual, my systems would be primed with a splash of adrenaline when I encounter that individual. The sensation of wariness happens before I have a chance to think about the situation.

The key point is that neuronal systems work "in the moment." There is no information uploading and processing like a computer. Instead, the sensory systems and neuronal orchestra register patterns of sensations and constantly play the situation forward, anticipating what could happen next. Hormonal and muscular systems prepare responses in real time, and feed options for movement back to the neuronal orchestra. When necessary, the body will move fast — about half a second faster than our ability to think.

Much of what we experience in politics and interpersonal behavior is polarized. We respond *yes* or *no*. We *agree* or *disagree*. Information is *correct* or *incorrect*. In movies and books, there are *good guys* and *bad guys*. In sports, there is *our team* versus *our opponents*. This yes–no and us–them has its roots in a neuronal system that is dipolar, like a magnet. The neuronal system deals with the world in a simplistic manner: either attracted to or repelled by different things, people, situations.

Knowing how the neuronal system operates, it becomes evident how television advertising works. For example, when I see a product on TV that I've never encountered before, along with images of people using it and liking it, my neuronal orchestra creates a melody for this product and associates it with positive emotions. If the "positioning" of the product is clear, which in marketing jargon is the *purpose* of a product, my brain will place this new melody with others that include other products of a similar type or function. TV advertising works like magic because it happens at a subliminal level. Suppose the product is a box of cereal — the next time I'm in a supermarket, I'll know where it is likely to be shelved, and my eyes will readily pick out the particular product from among the thousands of others that I don't notice. When the advertisement is well made and believable, the product will arouse positive feelings. In this way, short TV advertisements have little do with persuasion, logic or thinking; rather, it is a matter of in-the-moment recognition with favorable feelings. This account fits with all the data I have come across relating to advertising effectiveness. However, I've never seen the neuronal mechanisms explained in any textbook.

A quiet revolution has occurred in the field of neuroscience over the past 40 years. Metaphors are now recognized as a foundational concept in how the human brain works. George Lakoff, a retired professor of cognitive science and linguistics at the University of California at Berkeley, has written 11 books on the role of metaphor in the mind and in public discourse. His ideas, along with those of fellow academics, overturn the idea that the mind is a computational device similar to a computer that handles information.

How we create and arrange melodies is necessary to understand because it helps account for how ideas affect human behavior. We create lower-level melodies based on sensory inputs, with examples being everything we see and touch, including cups, leaves and trees. We create melodies related to common characteristics, such as the color blue and the sensation of hot. We also create a group of melodies related to movement through space, including movement forward, backward, up, fast and so on.

When it comes to more abstract concepts, such as time, love and purpose, we make use of lower-level concepts, particularly spatial ones, to convey their meaning. For instance, we might say time moves forward or backward, or love is a journey, as in "look how far we have come, but now we go our separate ways."

Language is built at every level metaphorically in the sense that words can be conceptualized as symbols that represent things. Every word is metaphorical, because words are representations of sensations, and sensations are representations of matter; sensations are not the matter itself. Words are meaningful because they engender feelings.

Consider these examples: we relate temperature to relationships, as in "she has a warm personality, and he is as cold as ice"; we relate loudness to direction, as in "turn the volume up"; and we relate debate to war, as in "you shot down my argument and won."

What does the word "understanding" actually mean? One way to make sense of this word is by relating it to a physical action or position, such as standing or seizing, which are physical actions one can visualize. The word comes from the Old English word *understandan*, which meant to "be on one's feet in the midst of." In another sense it can mean to grasp an idea. *Grasp* has roots in Proto-Germanic as *begreifen*, and meant "seize with the mind."

Comprehend is derived directly from Latin, where it meant to grasp something physically.

We build up a landscape of metaphorical associations that enable us to arrange ideas and communicate with each other. One knows instantly whether a turn of phrase makes sense or not. Here are some examples:

- Life is a journey — makes sense. Life is a series of colors — does not.

- We want to get ahead in life — that is understandable. Life is a liquid — does not make sense.
- I'm at a crossroads in life — that's meaningful. My life is arithmetic — does not mean much.
- Politics is a dogfight — okay. Politics as a growing plant — doesn't make sense.

The domains of time and space are different, yet we talk about time and movement as though they are identical. We might say, "October is coming and Joe is coming here." This means that Joe will physically transport himself through space; October, however, will not arrive in the same way. October gets closer not in terms of space, but in terms of how we view time as coming toward us or us approaching it. When we reach October, it passes us and leaves us behind. The words we use that refer to time describe movement through space: for example, *close, reach, pass* and *behind.*

We effortlessly apply concepts from one realm to another. Because this cross-domain convergence is instantaneous, natural and pervasive, we lose sight of the distinction between what is real and what is a concept. "October" might seem real and exist as a thing, but it is a concept that exists only in the mind. "Joe" on the other hand, exists outside our mind and is real, even though his name is simply a representation of him. As mentioned earlier, we assume temperature, science and memes are real, when in fact they are ideas.

Metaphors we take as givens reveal the peculiarities of cultures and personal viewpoints. For instance, consider a neuronal melody labeled *money,* which comes into play when we see dollar bills. This melody is positioned within a higher-order melody that, depending on a person's situation and prior experience, is labeled *security, wealth, status* or *freedom.* When you stop to think about it, to associate a dollar bill — a piece of paper with ink on it — to these other domains requires an extraordinary metaphorical leap.

The metaphorical leaps hardest to grasp are the purely mental constructs, especially mathematics, which does not exist in the world as a thing. Take the example of adding two things together. The math couldn't be simpler: 1 + 1 = 2. But where do the numbers exist? If you speak the numbers they exist as sound waves in the air. If you see them written on paper, they exist as squiggles of ink or dots on a screen. But the numbers exist only in the mind — as metaphor melodies.

Let's now turn our attention to how we learn the meaning of words, because when we understand the realities of language, a new picture of human social behavior comes into focus.

13

Learning to Communicate

Communication extends beyond language, is learned socially and is a bottom-up emergent system. Treating language as symbolic supports a modernist philosophy, but is misleading.

SCIENTIFIC BREAKTHROUGHS HAVE PROPELLED OUR UNDERSTANDING of the human brain forward. One example is Luigi Galvani's discovery of animal electricity. At the same time, some ideas have led up blind alleys. For example, the pineal gland is no longer considered the principal seat of the soul. Another is that the brain works by transmitting *information* — a nonmaterial concept — between different people's brains via symbols. This idea persists in part because of the digital revolution, where information, memory management and symbolic notation are invaluable.

In the paradigm of consilience, *everything* we interact with is a form of communication. Our neural mechanisms are picking up the *point* of everything around us and deciphering their potential salience during every waking moment. The meaning of sounds changes with context, as illustrated by the sound of a door opened by a family member during the day versus an identical sound heard from your bedroom in the middle of the night.

That the mind is a repository of information acquired through use of symbols and taught by parents and teachers is the underlying presumption of mainstream textbooks. The gap between theory and reality is illustrated by the difference between learning a language in a classroom and the way growing babies acquire language.

At school in England, I was taught Latin by Mr. Boyd, an enthusiastic and patient teacher. I was not an enthusiastic pupil. The line drawings in the textbook of Romans strutting around in kilt-like tunics looking imperious were of little interest to me. Instead, I spent my time looking out the classroom window and observing a robin building its nest, carefully placing each strand of straw with its beak, then shaping it with its body. After the chicks hatched, I was captivated by how their little yellow beaks quivered when their mother stood above them with a worm as if considering which one deserved it most. After two years of being taught Latin's grammatical rules and how to conjugate verbs, let's just say I didn't become fluent in speaking Latin. My current Latin vocabulary is *amo, amas, amat* (I love, you love, he or she loves) and *veni, vidi, vici.* (I came, I saw, I conquered). That's it.

And yet, by the time children reach school age and head to kindergarten, most will have a vocabulary of around 2,000 words. Without being explicitly taught grammar, they use pronouns; express the past, present and future tenses; and ask questions and understand answers.

The learning process starts before birth, with the baby's neuronal orchestra players sending out tunes and listening for echoes of tunes from elsewhere. After birth, the neural self-programming continues as inputs from the eyes, ears, skin and mouth become synchronized. Each of the neuronal players starts to get a sense of how to play tunes that result in things happening, such as leg-kicking and thumb-going-into-mouth. The baby's neuronal orchestra starts to get the hang of which tunes result in being hugged and fed. Each time mom speaks, the baby's eyes focus on her lips, noting the details of how they move and marrying them with the impulses picked up by the baby's ears.

As soon as babies are born and feel the cool air, they make a noise like *waaahuhhuhwaaaahuhu*. Crying signals distress, and over time it develops into more distinctive sounds. Priscilla Dunstan, a former mezzo-soprano who was featured on the Oprah Winfrey Show, reckons babies make five distinctive sounds relating to what they want. *Neh* means "I am hungry." This sound is produced when the sucking reflex is triggered, and the tongue is pushed up on the roof of the mouth. *Owh* means "I'm sleepy" and is like an audible yawn. *Heh* means "I'm experiencing discomfort and want to be changed." *Eairh* means "I have lower-tummy gas." She states, "The sound is produced when trapped air from a belch is unable to release and travels to the stomach where the muscles of the intestines tighten to force the air bubble out. Often this sound will indicate that a bowel movement is in progress, and the infant will bend its knees, bringing the legs toward the torso. This leg movement assists in the ongoing process." And lastly, "Eh" means "I need to be burped."

Every baby is different, so a universal language of baby cries is unlikely. Over the eons, moms would have figured it out if there was. The point is that the baby's language starts forming in concert with what's happening in their body. The cries of the first few months evolve into gurgling and then into playful interactions with the adults looking after them.

A groundbreaking book written by Horst Hendriks-Jansen in 1996, *Catching Ourselves in the Act,* mentioned in chapter 1, describes how his research team used slow-motion video to observe the micro-behaviors of mothers and their infants.

He explains how mother-infant exchanges in the first few years of life allow the mind of the infant to program itself by "bootstrapping" — that is, by learning in tiny increments and developing complex behaviors by putting them together from simple constituents. The mother plays an active but unconscious role in this process. Interactions that might appear to be trivial are the precursors to more complicated behaviors. For instance, to encourage a baby's feeding to continue, a mother suckling her infant jiggles the infant each time the baby stops. In fact, the infant is just taking a breather and would start suckling again without being jiggled. Nonetheless, this interaction of suckle-rest-jiggle-suckle is the precursor for turn-taking in adult conversation. "Thus," he writes, "the 'dialogue' between a suckling infant and the mother who jiggles him whenever he pauses in feeding constitutes a recognizable interactive pattern that emerges from low-level reflexes and centrally generated rhythms and establishes a habit of turn taking on which later, face-to-face exchanges will be built."

Behaviors that we think of as discrete events, such as smiling, reaching and grasping, suckling and kicking, when carefully analyzed using slow-motion video, are made up of smaller micro-behaviors that we are largely unaware of because we group them together and label them as intentional acts. One researcher commented that the actual movements of human beings, as opposed to the intentional acts that we perceive, were as difficult to observe before the invention of video as were the planets before the invention of the telescope. Movements that we hardly notice are the precursors of sophisticated, intentional actions. Kicking is the beginning of walking.

I'll describe what happens in the baby's brain by using the metaphors of the neuronal orchestra and the developing landscape. As the baby's eyes, ears and sense of touch provide stimuli, the neuronal orchestra learns the associated tunes and melodies. Feedback from the peripheral nervous system via the neuronal conductor encourages the playing of melodies where the associated movements contribute to homeostasis. Inputs from the baby's muscles create melodies in the cerebellum that relate to small, stereotyped movements, such as sucking, reaching, grasping and crawling. There is no sharp division between sensing things and movement. It is like learning to dance. The neuronal orchestra plays the music, and the muscles learn the corresponding movements.

Also, there is no sharp distinction between the movements of the mother and the baby. It is like they are dancing together, building a shared landscape and constantly anticipating each other's next move.

The baby quickly learns the mother's dance steps have a point. From the baby's view, each move she makes sets her on a little journey to do something somewhere. Mother might be going to provide food or go to sleep or to return with a toy to play with.

At around six months, the infant learns to make sounds in response to the mom. It will pump its arms down, clench its fists and expel air, making the sound *heh*. Mom will mimic it, and they'll take turns, smiling at each other. This will develop into repeated sounds, like *ma ma ma ma* and *ma da da da*. At this point both mom and dad will spend hours, mom saying, "moma moma moma" and dad saying, "dada dada dada." It is a serious contest. Everyone knows that dads are the favorite parent, but mom generally wins because saying "dada" requires the tongue to tap the gum right in front of the teeth at the same time as the infant's vocal folds contract. Saying "mama" is easier, requiring the vocal folds to contract while the lips open and close — similar to eating — so saying "mama" is likely to happen first.

We think of noises like *mama* as being simple words. But from the standpoint of the baby's neuronal orchestra in the cortex and the other finer grained one in the cerebellum, hearing and saying "mama" is a remarkable, acutely timed and extraordinarily complicated series of movements. Saying mama involves, wait for it... the breathing muscles in the chest, diaphragm and core; the movement of a series of muscles in the larynx, which loosen and tighten the vocal folds as well as raise and lower the whole apparatus; the shaping of the pharynx, including the opening and closing of the valve that funnels air into the nose; the movement of the tongue so it either taps the roof of the mouth at the back, middle or front of the mouth where it touches the teeth; and also the opening and closing of the lips.

The growing baby's neuromuscular systems marry together what mom does with her lips, the sounds she makes and the corresponding sounds the baby makes. The cerebellum plays a major role in this complex and intricate process that is invisible to us.

Learning to understand the word *cup* begins when the baby first sees a cup, then touches it. Its neuronal orchestra starts playing tunes and marrying those with the sensation of grasping the cup and, with mom's help, guiding it to its lips. The neuronal orchestra recognizes the similarities between seeing mom's mouth and lips move when she makes the sound *cup*. After thousands of tries, the dozens of muscles needed to micro-coordinate the movements will perform a recognizable dance and the baby will be able to utter, "cup."

The word *cup* becomes a melody for a variety of different types of cups, including sippy cups and play cups. The neuronal melody for *cup* includes how the cup feels, and the dexterity required to hold it, raise it to the mouth, touch it with the lips and swallow.

Over time, mom and dad, with a smile and the repetition of words such as "aren't you a clever little thing," teach the infant the difference between a red cup and a blue cup. The infant learns that cups, regardless of their color and texture, are all cups. Unless of course, the container is made of glass — in which case, it is not a cup.

As we advance in years, we expand our lexicon of dances through our interactions with parents, friends, teachers and everyone else with whom we communicate. It is a dynamic, ongoing and mostly reinforcing process. We learn the dances of life and where they lead.

The above explanation of how language comes into existence as an emergent system is fundamentally different to the idea that language is a system of symbols. For consilience, we need to be clear about the distinction between things that materially exist and ideas, which appear to be real, but exist only as conceptual melodies in the mind. The difference in the two views — the emergent versus symbolic — has far-reaching consequences and is illustrated by how modernist thinkers explain the definition of words. You can define a word's meaning by looking it up in a dictionary. A *cup* is defined as an open vessel. Then you can look up the meaning of *vessel*, which is defined as a *container*, and so on. You could carry on defining words until you have a network of meanings. This way of defining meaning is associated with the Enlightenment movement where human society advances forward by employing reason.

The implications of this approach are evident at interpersonal and societal levels. The intelligentsia can derive satisfaction from presiding over the meanings of words and cataloguing human knowledge. With more precise definitions, people can understand one another better and social interactions can have more clarity and certainty. Once the meaning of words is locked-in, legal statutes can be defined precisely so the law can be applied consistently and fairly.

Also, teachers can command respect and keep order in the classroom when language is conceived as a network of factual definitions and grammatical rules. Teaching is more challenging when you admit that the meaning of language is emergent, ever-changing and dependent on the state of the people involved. I'll return to this matter in chapter 29.

Inconsistencies between the modernist understanding of language and how humans actually communicate are revealed in the discipline of linguistics as expounded by Noam Chomsky and Steven Pinker. In the book *Words and Rules* published in 1999, Pinker, with impressive literary flair, takes a small subset of language, regular and irregular verbs, and devotes the entire book to explaining algorithms — the "rules" that govern their use. The reader might expect to find a list of rules in the book; however, the problem with the underlying assumption becomes apparent when in 287 pages, no rules are listed, except perhaps one: if people say something in a certain way to mean something, that is the way it is repeated and understood.

An online search for scientific papers concerning linguistics mostly turns up competing theories described with alien words, such as *nativist, interactionist, pragmatics, morphology schemas, iconicity, morphemes* and *transitivity*. I have tried to relate these concepts to my world of marketing communications and have not been able to figure out their utility. Orthodox linguistics appears to live on a different continent than the one everyone else inhabits — where we greet each other, play sports, take dogs for walks, cook, eat together and play with babies.

A word, noise or mannerism can take on new significance during the course of a lecture, and mean something different at the end than it meant at the start. Words such as *lockdown, isolation, bubble* and *mask* took on different meanings during the COVID-19 pandemic, and their meanings continue to change.

If anyone needs to be persuaded that communication does not require words, they need only look at a popular genre of videos called "animal reunions." In these videos, dogs are reunited with their owners after long periods apart. Sometimes, at first the dog creeps forward, unsure of who the person is. When they get a whiff of scent, they launch themselves into the arms of the owner, licking their face, pedaling their legs and wagging their tail.

Videos of primatologists being reunited with baboons and gorillas after a long period apart show a sequence that often goes like this: the primatologist and the ape start looking at each other from a distance. Neither is sure what will happen. A miscalculation could be deadly. They get closer and closer until only a few feet are separating them. Then the ape reaches out and touches the primatologist's face. You see their bodies decompress. The primatologist smiles, and they hug. Baboons bare their teeth and pant. Gorillas emit a love gurgle similar to the purring of a cat.

There is never any doubt that this communication is rich and meaningful, yet it does not involve words or information. Chimpanzees, orangutans, baboons and gorillas don't have a human-like ability to speak. Nonetheless, primatologists, including Kinji Imanishi, Jane Goodall, Dian Fossey, Frans de Waal and others, have shown they exhibit many human-like traits. As Goodall has observed, they show "jealousy, empathy, compassion and considerable manipulation of both the environment and others... in order to get their own way." They use a rich lexicon of nonverbal forms of communication to achieve their goals.

A discussion of the realities of interpersonal communications unavoidably becomes entangled with the touchy matter of personal characteristics. Let's explore the topic by looking at what happens when two people approach each other.

First of all, the context is crucial. Is the location isolated? Is it dark? Is the country at war with a foreign power or a deadly virus? Second, the characteristics of each person dictate how they react. What is their age and gender? What is their appearance? How are they dressed? Do they look as though they are from different social groups? Are they members of rival gangs or threatened minorities?

As they approach each other, their gait and how they direct their gaze will indicate the tenor of the interaction. At this point not one word has been spoken, yet much has been communicated. Then, as soon as one person says, "how do you do" or "g'day, mate" or "hey up" or "how ya' doing," it is likely clear what country the person comes from, down to the region and their social ranking.

Where I grew up in England, living on the outskirts of an industrial town in the Midlands, there were clear differences even between people living close by. A plummy "good afternoon" would indicate the greeter had been educated at a fee-paying school. "Howya luv" would mean they were from the town. And the accent of a working farmer — "howeryew" — was clearly different from a landowner's greeting — "afterrrnoon" — as he touches his hat and glances away. It would have been instantly clear if the speaker was from further afield: say, Yorkshire, "ow up"; Northumbria, "alreet pet"; or from London, "awreet."

Languages are defined by the people who use them, and they evolve rapidly. If I had been brought up in Britain when the Romans were living there, building roads, growing grapes and relaxing in communal baths, I would have likely, with an appropriate level of deference, been able to understand Latin and talk with them. But if I were transported back through time with my current linguistic knowledge, I wouldn't be able to understand a word being said. It is also unlikely I would understand the English that Chaucer spoke when he wrote *The Canterbury Tales* in 1387. Nowadays, it is hard enough to understand Shakespearean plays when they are performed with perfect modern diction. If I were teleported back to a seat at the Globe Theatre in London in 1600 to see a *Comedy of Errors*, I doubt I could follow the plotline.

Rather than considering language as being symbolic and uniquely human, it is more productive to view language as a bottom-up, emergent aspect of culture that has evolved in lockstep with the human propensity to live and work in groups.

— ▪ ○ 14 ○ ▪ —

Origins of Human Culture

Communication is a physical act linked to movements of the fingers. The human capacity to communicate, cooperate and plan ahead evolved on shorelines.

THE MELODIES FOR HUMAN ACTIVITIES such as *discussing, writing, eating, dancing, wrestling* and *making things* are obviously different and don't overlap. However, take a look at humanity from the perspective of someone who hasn't grown up learning the categorizations we take for granted.

Imagine being an alien who has arrived on earth from a planet circling Gliese, a red dwarf star that is nearby in the Milky Way. Your planet, Gliesan, is completely different from Earth. It is bigger and has no water or atmosphere. You would not look like Spock from *Star Trek* or have the stereotyped almond-shaped eyes of aliens. You perceive your surroundings as a bat does, by sending out pulses of radiation that are reflected back. Unlike a bat that uses high-pitched sound, you use a broad spectrum of electromagnetic radiation, which allows you to see what is happening inside the human body, something similar to the way a radiologist uses MRI.

You embark on a long-term ethnographic study of Earth's inhabitants and observe the humanoids interacting, taking turns moving their mouths, reacting to each other. You see them looking at books and tablets, and notice this sometimes changes their behavior. You observe that they have the ability to manipulate their fingers as well as the muscles in their chest, larynx and mouth. With sophisticated sensing equipment, you detect that these creatures use sound waves and light waves in their interactions. You note the humanoids are in communication with each other all the time, and with other species, through the use of gestures and movements of their eyes, limbs and bodies.

As a Gliesian, you would see no reason to classify human communication in a category separate from movement. Speaking, writing, dancing and wrestling all result from muscular activity. Speaking involves the muscles of the vocal apparatus. Writing utilizes the muscles in the fingers and hands. Different sets of muscles are involved in wrestling and speaking, but these are two forms of interpersonal interaction. To humans they look different, but to a Gliesian they are essentially the same.

The Gliesian perspective is becoming easier to comprehend owing to some surprising developments on the frontlines of research into the genetics and biology of language. For example, the use of language by birds and humans has considerable similarity, even though the two lineages diverged 300 million years ago. Whereas previously the thought was that bird song has little in common with human speech, there is now evidence at a genetic and cellular level that the singing of birds is closely related to how we speak. The brain of a parrot is small: about one-fifth the size of a chimpanzee's brain, but with the same number of neurons. Nevertheless, parrots can form sentences and understand them with a surprising level of sophistication.

The mice and rats that scientists worked with for years and thought were uncommunicative are far from silent. Their vocalizations are ultrasonic and need to be processed by computers so they are audible. Mice and rats, much like birds, make more than 20 different sounds — for courting, to locate pups and as warnings. They even giggle when tickled.

When scientists probe how communication takes place within certain species — for example, songbirds, mice, whales, dolphins and elephants — they uncover details that lead to the conclusion that humans' ability to communicate is not as unique as we thought. In an odd twist, our closest animal relatives, the chimpanzees and apes, are laggards in their ability to communicate using vocalizations.

How is it that *Homo sapiens* developed the capacity to communicate using speech, while the chimpanzees did not? How did we evolve from being speechless apes to having the full-featured languages used today, and do this in an evolutionary eye-blink of several million years?

All the evidence points to early hominids evolving in the rift valleys of Ethiopia and East Africa. The apes possessed an essential prerequisite for the development of speech. Unlike four-legged animals, they had mobile shoulder girdles with arm sockets that enabled them to hang from trees similar to today's chimps and other apes. When our forebears ventured down from the trees about 7 million years ago, they had the body architecture for an upright gait that freed up their front hands, which developed flat palms, long fingers and a thumb that can be moved independently of the other fingers to hold and manipulate things.

Early hominids survived in a precarious ecological niche in the zone between forest and savannah. In the deep forest, our forebears would have been easy prey for tree-dwelling apes that have powerful jaws. On wide open grasslands, they would have been unable to protect themselves from large carnivores, packs of hyenas and wandering elephants. This ecological zone would not have been an easy and safe place to live. They would have needed to seek out caves and strategic locations for protection.

Caves formed from wave action on the shores of lakes and the ocean were appealing sites for living. Early hominids developed an affinity for water, likely for a number of reasons, including the availability of water for drinking and bathing, succulent plants, seaweed, fish and shellfish. These early humans would have been able to evade predators by retreating into the water. They would have also been able to feed off the parade of animals that need to drink. The affinity for waterside living has not been lost. To this day, people enjoy the seaside and waterfront cottages and cabins.

There is some controversy among anthropologists on the matter of whether hominids were savannah or waterside dwellers. In my view, the evidence is overwhelming that our forebears developed anatomical features that are adaptations to spending time in water. Most importantly, they lost their body hair, which meant they could move through the water faster, clean themselves and dry quickly. Fossilized skulls show bony protrusions, called "exostoses," in the ear canals that would have protected the eardrums from water pressure. Modern humans who swim or surf in cold water also happen to develop the same distinctive protrusions — hence the name, surfer's ear. Significantly, early humans evolved large lungs and a nose that points downward, so when they were submerged, water did not flow into the nasal cavity. A larger nasal cavity made their vocalizations sound richer, and swimming required them to control their breathing.

The habitat along the shores of East African lakes had benefits for each family, or troop, of hominids, but whenever their lake flooded or dried up they would have moved to another location. Climate change is often portrayed these days as a consequence of human activity, but over much longer time scales human evolution was stimulated by constant, often abrupt, changes in climate. In the region of equatorial Africa, the climate changed repeatedly and completely. Sometimes the land was covered in lush forest; at other times, only seasonal rains would fall, and the land would turn to savannah, then desert.

A changing climate not only put stress on each troop of hominids, but also put pressure on other animal populations. A warming and wetter climate crowded savannah-living animals into smaller areas. When the cycle reversed and became dry, the forest turned to scrubland, causing tree-dwellers to retreat and hang on to life in the remaining islands of woodland.

Hominid troops living on the shores of lakes and oceans likely remained small, and they competed with each other for living sites and food. During periods of favorable weather, their numbers would grow; during periods of drought, the weaker troops would succumb. Situations like this, with small, semi-isolated populations and changing conditions, would have created evolutionary fast-breeder reactors — similar to the Galápagos Islands.

Within groups of early hominids, individuals learned from each other, looked out for each other, foraged cooperatively and protected themselves from competing troops. These groups were more likely to survive than those who didn't develop these abilities. About 2.6 million years ago, our ancestors started making rough stone tools, which paleoanthropologists unearth today. Other artifacts of their daily life that were undoubtedly crucial for survival have disappeared, such as, implements for collecting and preparing food, receptacles for carrying water, skins for clothing and bedding, and protective animal corrals and shelters.

By learning to copy each other's movements, they could pass on skills from generation to generation. Sharing waterside habitats rich with crocodiles, hippos and thirsty carnivores encouraged them to vocalize warnings. While hunting, they learned to stay quiet and gesture to each other with their arms and hands.

Over many generations, early hominids developed into *Homo erectus* and became increasingly dexterous, able to make and effectively use many types of tools. Whenever they used a stone to bash a nutshell to share the food with family members, coincidentally, their neuronal orchestra created narratives. There was a subject, the stone; an object, the nut; and a verb, bash. The three parts of speech became hitched together in a sequence of cause and effect. The proto-narrative resulted in behaviors that strengthen social bonds, as well as their ability to speak and understand. Not coincidentally, proto-languages, from which all the world's languages evolved, have the same sentence structure.

The parts of the brain involved in controlling the hands and fingers became larger over time. These same parts in the modern human brain are adjacent to, and partly mixed with, the parts involved in speaking and writing.

Although details of how speech developed are not known, early human speech was most likely tied to the ability to make and manipulate the many items needed for daily living in a habitat that was precarious. The neuronal players associated with the hands and fingers would have become linked with those associated with controlling the chest, larynx, tongue and lips. The outcome would have enabled troops of individuals to bond with each other, protect each other, plan hunting trips and organize themselves. The vocalizations would have been part of courtship rituals, raising children, preparing food and eating communally.

How humans evolved the ability to work peacefully in groups has been described by Richard Wrangham, British primatologist and professor at Harvard University, in *The Goodness Paradox*. He terms the process "self-domestication." As hominids lived together in small hunter-gatherer groups, individuals who exhibited behavior that was "emotional, hostile, impulsive, uncontrolled and reactive" would either be kicked out of the group or not selected as a mate. Individuals who behaved positively would have been selected preferentially.

The process parallels the domestication of animals such as dogs and farm livestock, where animals that are easy to handle are selected over unpredictable and aggressive ones. The process was demonstrated in a breeding study conducted on silver foxes in Siberia, where a team of Russian biologists led by Lyudmila Trut, "the Jane Goodall of the fox world," picked "the sweetest and calmest 10 percent of each generation" to breed. As Lee Alan Dugatkin, professor of biology at the University of Louisville, describes, the breeding study involved "turning wild animals that fled from humans, attacked when cornered, or both, to foxes that begged for belly rubs, wagged their tails when Trut approached and whined when she left." This was achieved after just six generations.

It took our ancestors millions of years to make the transition from "troops to tribes" — to use the expression of professor of anthropology, Stanley H. Ambrose, a leading researcher in the field. One can envisage how these hominids spent hours crafting finely knapped tools; carrying an arsenal of weapons on expeditions, both for hunting and combat; reacting to threats; and changing plans as they went. Members of the tribes learned to think ahead and plan progressively longer sequences of actions, such as selecting stones, making arrowheads, attaching them to sticks, putting them in carriers, setting off as a group, killing adversaries, tracking game, bringing meat back, cooking it and eating communally. Each action became married with the making of sounds, which became words, and the words were strung together into narratives. The narratives could then be rearranged and used to plan the next defensive encounter or offensive excursion.

It seems reasonable to suppose that the development of language occurred as a result of an increasingly tight coupling within the neuronal orchestra between areas that control the hands and fingers, and areas involved in hearing and generating speech. The skills needed to make tools, yarn, clothes and shelters coincided with the development of neuronal melodies of increasing length and subtlety. Over many generations, individuals who created longer sequences of neuronal melodies — narratives — could anticipate more scenarios and plan ahead. The size of the neuronal orchestra would have grown accordingly and also taken longer to become functional in newborns. The bare-skinned little infants could no longer cling to their mother's fur like savannah-dwelling baboons; instead, they needed increasingly long periods of suckling and care.

When a living site became crowded, food sources ran short or weather patterns changed, members of a tribe would have needed to get together, make a plan, pack up their belongings, fill skins with water, sling their babies onto their backs and move to another area, then select a site, build shelters and construct barriers against predators and rival tribes.

The capacity to communicate about the next step for the tribe and plan journeys would have conferred a powerful evolutionary advantage. Tribes that did not think ahead, could not communicate with each other or had poor social cohesion were wiped out.

Through the several million years it took for apelike hominids to evolve into *Homo sapiens,* the neuronal orchestra — the cerebral cortex — tripled in size. Recently, geneticists have shown how the cortex grew. It was not simply a matter of growing bigger, but rather neurons associated with specific areas connected to the muscles involved in speech and the hand muscles needed for tool manipulation and writing, grew in number. Referring again to the metaphor of the drum circle, the stem cells in this area of the developing brain, generally on the left side, drummed longer and louder, causing the neuronal orchestra to become far bigger than, for example, the areas of the brain connected with the sense of smell. Consequently, relatively simple changes in the ways genes are expressed, from the bottom up, have given us the capacity to speak, write and communicate.

The growing brain happens to need the nutrients that are relatively plentiful at waterside locations, including salt, iodine, zinc, selenium, vitamin B12 and fish oil fatty acids. Another essential nutrient, vitamin D, was made in the skin from the bright tropical sun. Through this period of evolution, the neuronal capacities required to play, make things, hunt, eat, fight, plan ahead, discuss, select mates, raise children and migrate would have been interwoven. It was during this time that the human ability to communicate and think creatively took shape, along with our social dependencies.

15

Inseparably Social

Humans are profoundly social. Being part of groups is an ever-present need, and the neuronal mechanisms have roots deep in our evolutionary past.

I'VE ALWAYS ENJOYED SOLITUDE, but the feeling of being completely alone is disquieting. I realized how we are rarely, if ever, entirely and absolutely alone when I went on a solo hike along the north shore of Lake Superior shortly after I first arrived in Canada — at a time before cellphones and satnav. It was mid-October and my car was the only one parked at the trailhead. After hiking for two days I had encountered no one else on the trail and was at least 80 kilometers (50 miles) away from the nearest human being — the distance to the closest road or dwelling was lengthening. These days with uncommon exceptions, we can at all times, access a phone, get to a road, or walk toward a light in the distance where we can find help. But this was different. I was truly by myself and help was well out of reach. As I climbed up a small crag high above the lake and looked down, I sensed an unfamiliar knot in my stomach. I realized that if I slipped I would tumble onto partially submerged rocks and die. No one would know. Normally, if I'd been hiking with friends, none of us would have given the matter a moment's thought. We are social in ways we rarely appreciate.

Saying that humans are social beings brings to mind people living as families, working in organizations and, perhaps, drinking coffee with friends. Over the past few years, however, frontline researchers have been studying many different aspects of human social nature, including the harmful effects of loneliness on well-being. As well, their investigations of the neuronal foundation of our social dependencies have uncovered some surprising and sobering details. They have been revealing that our social nature is emergent from several basic functionalities that originated hundreds of millions of years ago.

The most basic neuronal functionality is the capacity to model situations forward, with anticipation of what is likely to happen next. When you see something in motion, such as a bird flying, your neuronal system anticipates the continuation of the movement. Indeed, if the bird happened to freeze in mid-air it would cause your head to snap with surprise. This capacity of neuronal systems enables all animals to anticipate the movements of predators, prey and others of the same species.

Many animals not classified as social nonetheless live in groups, variously referred to as swarms, flocks, schools, colonies, herds, bands and packs. The tuning of neurons to pick up on the behavior of other individuals of the same species is a basic functionality that underlies our ability to live together socially.

The second basic functionality is imitation. The biologist Lee Alan Dugatkin, in the book *The Imitation Factor: Evolution Beyond the Gene* describes his research on guppies, also known as rainbow fish, which are popular with owners of aquariums. Female guppies are attracted to males that have bright orange flashes of color. They are also sensitive to how other guppies are behaving. Dugatkin found he could change the preferences of female guppies so they were attracted to drab-looking males. He did this by orchestrating an "evolutionary soap opera" where he made the drab male look more sought after. The drab male guppy who was made to look popular became the one that most attracted female guppies. This shows that the ability to imitate behavior is a functionality deeply plumbed into the workings of a basic nervous system. We shared common ancestors with guppies around 450 million years ago: an epoch not commonly considered to have much relevance to modern culture. However, imitation is a rudimentary aspect of culture, as Dugatkin observes: "What matters is not brain size so much as the ability to incorporate what others are doing into one's behavioral repertoire."

The ability of animals to imitate others has been documented by animal behavior researchers across many animal groups. One example is blue tits in the U.K. In the 1920s, a few birds learned how to peck holes in the silver foil tops of milk bottles and, by the 1950s, the behavior had spread to every blue tit across the country. Another example was a female macaque on the Japanese island of Koshima, who figured out how to remove sand from wheat by throwing handfuls of the mixture into the sea and scooping the wheat off the surface. Soon the entire troop learned this trick, and it became part of their behavioral repertoire passed from generation to generation. The ability of neuronal systems to imitate other individuals' actions is not unusual and not a recent evolutionary invention.

A third neuronal functionality — evident in newborn babies through to adults — is gaze-following. Without being fully aware of the behavior, we tend to look where others look: shifting our attention in harmony with the people around us. Say we are in a stadium watching the World Cup and a few people start looking intently at something over their right shoulder, we would also look in the same direction, and the behavior would spread quickly through the crowd. The same behavior has been observed in most primates and dogs, as well as horses, reptiles and birds. An even broader array of animals, including birds, fish and reptiles, become jittery if another animal starts looking at them intently. Their attentional systems would be preparing for fight or flight.

Two other functionalities that are foundational to social living are parenting and attachment. The parenting instinct — where mothers and sometimes fathers protect their offspring — is one of the most widespread instincts in the animal kingdom. Ducks, swans, geese and chickens can become vicious if you get near their chicks. Elephants, buffalos, lions and just about every sizable mammal will become aggressive if their young are threatened. Even domesticated dogs and cats will bite if provoked. Humans as well are highly protective of their young. The biochemistry of this behavior has been well researched using various tools, including brain scanning. The hormone oxytocin plays a starring role, and large areas of the neuronal conductor light up during parental responses of nurturing and protecting offspring. Oxytocin can also have a powerful effect when injected into a female animal without offspring; it immediately triggers mothering behaviors.

The attachment instinct among infants is powerful. When separated from their mothers, infants become panicky. In mice and rat pups, researchers have found that the changes in brain chemistry are widespread and persistent after being kept apart from their mothers for extended periods. Social isolation in adult animals provokes the same chemical pathways, causing them to become antisocial, and when reintroduced to groups they behave aggressively. A big surprise is that the same chemical pathways operate in distantly related animals, including fruit flies.

The biochemistry of separation anxiety involves a neuropeptide called Tac1, which is released widely in the neuronal orchestra. Tac 1 works differently than neurotransmitters that operate in the synapses: the nanometer scale gaps between the neurons. Synaptic neurotransmitters operate and reset almost instantly, whereas the larger molecules of the neuropeptides spread widely and change the tempo of the playing across large areas of the neuronal orchestra.

The necessity of parental love for the well-being of offspring was shown in some heartbreaking experiments performed by Harry Harlow in the 1950s. He separated newborn rhesus monkeys from their mothers, supposing that their affection was merely because they needed their mothers' milk. This was disproved when the young monkeys clung to cloth surrogate mothers rather than ones that were wire mesh that provided milk. When deprived of the cloth surrogates, the young monkeys ceased to be able to handle any stress, stared fearfully, circled their cages and engaged in self-mutilation.

It does not feel self-affirming to admit that human sociability is a consequence of parenting and attachment instincts. This realization is not sticky, and is unlikely to become prominent in portrayals of human accomplishment and the rise of civilizations.

Social belonging is essential for overall health. Persistent feelings of social isolation and loneliness are directly linked to higher risks of depression, anxiety, heart disease, high blood pressure and premature death. As well, loneliness hyperactivates the immune system, contributing to a range of chronic diseases that older adults in particular are more vulnerable to developing.

The COVID-19 lockdown caused widespread distress, particularly among the elderly and others already suffering from loneliness. Consequently, a spotlight became focused on the work of researchers who are documenting the effects on the brain of social contact. Neuroscientists Livia Tomova and Rebecca Saxe and their MIT colleagues scanned the brains of 40 adult participants who underwent two 10-hour sessions: in the first they were deprived of food, and in the second they were denied social contact. Their conclusions, simply put, are that the human need for social connection is as compelling as the need for food.

A young human cannot survive without adult protection well into adolescence and beyond. The psychological necessity of belonging to a group begins at a young age. Nothing is more petrifying for a child than being ostracized or bullied by their friends and schoolmates. Children who are singled out and isolated become terrified going to school. They have difficulty concentrating, they cannot sleep and the resulting anxieties can last a lifetime.

Likewise for adults, few things are more anxiety-inducing than the suspicion we are being left out of something that concerns us. Whether at work or home, one becomes deeply troubled to learn that colleagues or friends have been talking about you behind your back, keeping you in the dark or excluding you from an activity.

Our social functionalities and need to belong result in the addictive power of social media described in the Netflix docudrama *The Social Di-*

lemma, which spells out how the algorithms used by tech firms have the unintended effect of amplifying social vulnerabilities, particularly of teenagers, and causing mental health problems.

In our evolutionary past, the consequences of someone being excluded or treated as an outsider by their community would inevitably have been fatal. Researchers studying a troop of chimpanzees in Senegal described the type of scenarios that early humans might have encountered. They observed the horrifying outcome of an individual chimp being ostracized. A male chimp, Foudouko, was the alpha leader, supported by Mamadou, the beta male. When Mamadou became injured, Foudouku fell from power and was forced to leave the troop. After living alone for a few years, he attempted to rejoin his former family. One morning the researchers heard a commotion and immediately observed that Foudouko was dead and his corpse was being flung about by five young males who had turned on him. An older female started cannibalizing his body before the researchers, shell-shocked by what they had witnessed, stepped in to bury him.

Humans and chimpanzees do not behave alike, and the differences are telling. Humans are drawn to be part of different groups, and overt acts of aggression are rare. Researchers have documented that, on average, even when you include wars, humans are 1,000 times less violent than chimpanzees.

Groups are so much a part of people's lives that it is easy to miss how ubiquitous they are. They include families, neighborhoods, nonprofits, charities, religious groups, industry associations, institutes, sports teams, schools, colleges, universities, hospitals, media organizations, regulatory bodies, police forces, armies, unions, utilities, government, businesses, music bands and online collectives. Everything of significance that we do is related to a group in some way.

For many, there is little in life more satisfying than being a member of a high-functioning team where everyone gets along, values each other and is productive in whatever ways their members choose.

Often the dynamics of groups are overlooked because they are taken for granted — like the air we breathe. Every time a group comes together, the participants form ways of interacting that are specific to each one of them and their interests: for example, by jamming together as musicians, dancing together, making art, playing sports or conducting scientific research.

The functionality of groups is facilitated by processes that happen at a subliminal level. The neuronal orchestra picks up on the behavior of everyone around and learns what constitutes normal behavior. This happens unconsciously, as we observe what others are paying attention to or worrying about. Neuronal mechanisms continually register the point of everything that is happening around us, then pattern our behavior accordingly.

Groups quickly build a common vernacular. Teenagers develop phrases that seem like a foreign language to their parents. Professional groups build a jargon that helps them work together efficiently, coincidentally differentiating group members from outsiders. Specialized jargon is a hallmark of many professional groups, including lawyers, medical practitioners and academics. Sometimes specialized words are used instead of ones that are widely understood. For instance, when I suffered a bout of extreme vertigo after climbing a mountain in the freezing cold, a neurologist diagnosed my condition as *idiopathic neuropathy*. Although that may sound insightful, what it really means is "nerve damage that we don't understand."

Humor and sociability go hand in hand, and people smile, chuckle and laugh all the time. But what humor is and why we find it so appealing has remained something of a mystery. Comedians and writers know how to inject humor into their art, but there is no easy formula. People laugh when something is funny, but there is no telling exactly why it is funny.

From the standpoint of the neuronal orchestra, every joke involves something that doesn't make sense or is inappropriate in some way. So the really funny jokes are ones where the neuronal orchestra is following one narrative path and suddenly there is a jump to another path that is unrelated. It is akin to seeing a bird freeze in mid-flight. The orchestra could react with confusion, triggering anxiety and hostility, but instead it signals, by laughing, that all is OK. Laughter is a quick neuronal reset and a form of mutual affirmation and bonding. A laugh communicates, "I understand that what you have just communicated makes no sense in the usual way. But that is OK, we are aligned and still members of the same group."

How we interact and form bonds with others can be observed, but much of this process happens below the level of consciousness. Advances in genetics and neuroscience are revealing profound effects of social interaction.

For example, the advent of social media over the past two decades has changed society in ways that were simply not anticipated. Social psychologist Jonathan Haidt likens the effects of the internet to changing one of the 25 physical constants of the universe: "Imagine if God one day said let's double the gravitational constant just for fun." He explains, "Everything would go totally haywire in the physical world and planets would change their orbits and planes would come out of the sky. It would be bizarre and disastrous and I think that is what has happened in the social world. Connectivity is generally good but we're now hyper-connected and that is changing a basic parameter of the universe."

A neurochemical connection between the effects of social isolation during the COVID-19 crisis and the violent behavior seen in many cities around the world is hinted at in research published in 2018 by Moriel Zelikowsky, a neuroscientist at the University of Utah School of Medicine. Her team found that a messenger protein called Tac2 became active throughout the brains of mice that were socially isolated for two weeks, which increased their aggressiveness. Likely, the same mechanisms are at work in the human brain.

The human instinct to be social forms our patterns of thinking and has enabled the many marvels of modern societies, but they also have a dark side.

— ▪ ○ 16 ○ ▪ —

Instinctive Tribalism

Tribalism is a foundational aspect of the brain's biology and responsible for the noblest aspects of humanity as well as its depravities.

WHEN I FIRST ARRIVED IN TORONTO, I attended a meeting where our advertising agency J. Walter Thompson was presenting a script for a new television spot. It went something like this: Creative director Marlene Hore begins, "The Pepsi truck draws even with the Coke truck" — she pauses, then adds — "and then *overtakes.*" She beams, and my colleagues smile back, knowing this competitive symbolism would be appreciated throughout the Pepsi organization. "Then you'll hear the jingle." She hums the refrain familiar to us, then chants the words, "Look who's drinking Pepsi now," repeating it, "Look who's drinking Pepsi now." She beats the rhythm on the boardroom table. "Look who's drinking Pepsi now. You see a girl in profile chugging." She mimes the motion of drinking and concludes, "The camera pulls back, wide-angle shot... you see the girl is in a crowd... the crowd begins to roar."

As the most junior person on the team, I commented on the spot first, then it was my boss Colin Moore's turn. With a level of confidence that impressed me, he declared his approval by saying, "The script is on strategy and creative."

That level of decisiveness about something so multifaceted was new to me. Only a few days before, I had left the genteel culture of the United Biscuits marketing department in London, where my colleagues would have mused over the TV spot's many details. Here, my colleagues were more matter-of-fact and making references to *Leave It to Beaver* and *Archie Bunker,* TV programs I had never heard of. They used sports metaphors all the time, referring to "the winning team," and pre-selling rival managers to get them "onside" or "doing an end run." I felt disoriented.

At dinner with my workmates, I ordered a rum and Pepsi. When the waiter informed me that they "did not have Pepsi; would Coke be OK?" I answered, "Sure." Everyone around the table froze. That was the last time I committed that fireable offense. I quickly learned that I was part of a tribe that was energized by delivering knock-out punches and overtaking the evil red enemy.

Humans have neuronal mechanisms that make working in groups not only possible, but also enjoyable and productive. We naturally gravitate toward being part of social groupings, identifying with them. But the flip side of that is we draw away from people outside the group.

Take any group of people, and split them randomly into two groups, then give them a goal where they are in competition, and they will instantly coalesce into two teams. This scenario plays out in sports venues around the world all the time. The competition between teams of professional athletes transfixes billions of their supporters every day. When fans pour into the stadiums sporting team colors and painted faces, it is clear to everyone to which tribe each individual belongs.

The instinct to split groups of people into "us" and "them" is instant and intuitive. This behavior has roots in how early organisms exhibit taxis, and are drawn toward something or repelled. Similarly, our forebears needed to react instantaneously to move either toward food or away from predators. This dipole aspect of neural systems explains why we answer "yes" or "no," or say certain things are "right" or "wrong," or that people are guilty or not guilty, or that political parties are left wing or right wing. In most situations, reality is somewhere between the dipolar extremes, but neural systems are biased to operating simplistically.

As already described, chimpanzees live in troops and are violent. They routinely murder members of their own troop as well as mount organized skirmishes against rival troops. They hunt and wage war, not always to gain territory or because they need food, but just for sport. We did not evolve from chimps, but we do share common ancestors. The question about the similarities and differences between human and chimp behavior is often framed as a matter of competing philosophies. Some believe we are human apes that can barely contain the promptings of our violent genes and others believe human behavior is cultural and we have long outgrown our apelike tendencies. Which position is closest to the truth?

With the perspective of consilience, we can address this age-old question of biological essentialism versus social constructionism — nature versus nurture. First we should note one technical detail: there is no sharp distinction between genes and culture. Genes are part of, and cannot operate outside, the cellular environment, and, in turn, each cell cannot exist separated from others. And human offspring cannot survive without their mothers; moreso, we cannot survive without each other.

A sanguine way of addressing the question is by seeing how our ability to cooperate and protect ourselves evolved within an environment of competition with troops of extremely violent, aggressive and physically powerful apes and apelike hominids.

When the human genetic makeup is analyzed, more genetic variation is found among individuals living in a single African village than among all humans living around the world, from Australasia, through Asia, Europe and the Americas. A genetic bottleneck occurred 70,000 years ago. It is impossible to be sure what happened at that time, but it coincides with the depths of an ice age after Mount Toba blew its top in Sumatra.

The Toba supervolcano ejected 2,800 cubic kilometers of material into the atmosphere. The eruption was 1,000 times larger than Vesuvius and 70 times larger than the 1815 eruption of Tambora, the most powerful in recorded history — the results of which poet Lord Byron described as "the icy earth swung blind and blackening in the moonless air." The Toba eruption coated India and Southeast Asia in ankle-deep white ash. In Africa, the remnants of forests were obliterated, the trees on the savannahs turned to brittle skeletons. A few tribes of *Homo sapiens* clung to life on the shores of East African lakes and along the coast. These tribes spread back into Africa, whereas others crossed into Asia, and radiated east, west and north.

Anthropologist Stanley Ambrose writes, "Disastrous environmental degradation at the beginning of the last ice age may have been the catalyst for forcing the expression of this capacity for cooperation at this crucial transition in the archaeological record of the evolution of modern human behavior... The troop-to-tribe transition may have been essential for the few survivors of this disaster." *Homo sapiens* made finely crafted stone tools and clothes, used fire to cook food and stay warm. In their DNA and habits, they carried the ability to form tight-knit social groups, cooperate and intermarry with other groups and, when necessary, coalesce into defensive or offensive units. They expressed ideas visually on the walls of caves and engaged in trade, which is clear from tools that have been unearthed, some of which were made of materials from far away.

Tribes of Neanderthals and other hominid species already living in Asia and Europe also survived the ice age. Their patterns of behavior were not as sophisticated as *Homo sapiens*. Their tools and beads were rougher, they did not trade or intermarry with those outside their tribe and they engaged in ritual cannibalism. *Homo sapiens* prevailed over subsequent millenia, developing the widely diverse cultures of the world. As Ambrose states, "In the risky environments of the last ice age, regional cooperation and reciprocation were probably better adaptive strategies than territorial defense and selfishness. Loving thy neighbors had greater long-term advantages than eating them."

Knowing the conditions under which *Homo sapiens* evolved makes it easier to understand not only our ability to work productively in groups but also to immediately differentiate friend from foe. When early humans went on expeditions to trade the glasslike material, obsidian, and flint to make into tools and likely other items of value, including food and ornaments, they would have been vigilant about who was an ally or a potential aggressor.

Tribal behaviors that are the currency of modern life — as witnessed at sporting events, in politics and in rival companies — were hewn from millions of years of tribal life: groups residing in settlements and continually watchful for threats, such as disease, ecological collapse and carnivores, as well as incursions from rival tribes that might also be undergoing hardship, needing land and food, or simply envious.

Evidence for the need to rally together for the survival of the tribe remains today in the honor bestowed on military personnel and medals awarded for valor. The obverse is readily apparent in the connotations of words such as *coward, traitor* and *turncoat.*

The human instinct to form teams and work together against outside threats is ingrained in the human psyche, but there isn't a suitable word or phrase to sum it up. The closest expressions fall short, but include *rally together, step up, close ranks, man the barricades, batten down the hatches* and *circle the wagons*. The idioms from sport include *play as a team* and *we can win*.

In the terminology of consilience, the word *tribalism* applies to all the tribes people belong to, including family groups, businesses, religious groups, professional groups and nations. The instinct to see outside groups as threats can be seen in people's behavior day to day, yet few psychology textbooks refer to and account for the human characteristic of instant us-and-them tribalism.

An example is the famous Stanford prison experiment run by Philip Zimbardo at Stanford University in 1971. To summarize, a group of Stanford University students were recruited through newspaper ads to participate. They were the picture of West Coast middle-class normalcy and randomly assigned to take on the role of either prisoners or guards. The Palo Alto police arrested the prisoners and dropped them off at the mock jail in the basement of the psychology department. "Our planned two-week investigation into the psychology of prison life had to be ended after only six days because of what the situation was doing to the college students who participated," recounts Professor Zimbardo. "In only a few days, our guards became sadistic and our prisoners became depressed and showed signs of extreme stress."

This matter has been recounted in *Quiet Rage*, a 50-minute documentary, as well as in the 2015 docudrama, *The Stanford Prison Experiment*, directed by Kyle Patrick Alvarez. It is also a staple of psychology textbooks, and variously portrayed as pioneering, insightful, unethical, bad science and verging on fraud.

The reason why otherwise normal students in just a few days could devolve into behavior reminiscent of gulags and concentration camps has been hotly debated. Words generally used to explain such behavior are *conformity, group norms, peer pressure* and *obedience*.

A more basic way of understanding this behavior is that deeply plumbed into human makeup is the appeal of being part of a group, as well as, not far below the surface, the fear of being made an outcast. The propensity to become part of a team and treat outsiders as a threat is instinctive and immediate. When any sort of danger is perceived, the dynamic of us-and-them tribalism gets triggered; small irritants can escalate and sometimes lead to violence and worse. In the context of waging war, inhumane behavior is expected and can lead to depths of evil that are shocking not only to the victims — if they survive — but also to the perpetrators.

A new genre of academic literature is producing compendiums of research papers that list the discoveries of archeologists and paleopathologists who unearth the remains of massacres, where most skulls show evidence of blows that either healed or were immediately fatal. Everywhere the researchers look, they find defensive works, military camps, the remains of battle-related rituals, and symbols of violence on cave walls and in graves.

The view that human beings are essentially peaceful is appealing, but the evidence is not supportive. The narrative that early farming communities were making pottery, clearing the land and living amicably in the wilderness is not proving true. Evidence from the Bronze Age in the northern German valley of the Tollense shows that around 4,000 warriors fought a battle and about one-quarter of them perished. At Els Trocs, a site in the Spanish Pyrenees, rival tribes, perhaps migrating farmers, collided violently with hunter-gatherers, leaving their smashed bones. At Asparn/Schletz in Austria there are the remains of 67 people who died from blows of stone axes. Tellingly, there were no children aged 9 to 16 or young women among the dead.

Dr. Rick Schulting, now at the School of Archeology at the University of Oxford, has studied bones predating the Bronze Age at museums in the U.K. and found that Neolithic people had a 1-in-14 chance of getting a cracked skull. One is left to speculate how many among the other 13 deaths resulted from a slash, arrow or spear in soft tissues, which would have left no trace in the archeological record.

Prehistoric hunter-gatherers did not record their battles, and all evidence was quickly swallowed by nature. A few sites have been discovered, such as the 10,000-year-old remains of 27 people at Nataruk, near Lake Turkana in northern Kenya. Ten of the skeletons show war damage from arrows and clubs. One pregnant young woman was left to drown with her hands bound behind her back.

In the recently published *Cambridge World History of Violence*, Steven LeBlanc, former director of collections at Harvard University's Peabody Museum, writes, "Lives in the past were those of fear, war, worry and hunger." Among lowland South American tribes, an estimated 15 to 25% of males and about 5% of females died due to raids and occasional massacres. "This is a rather shocking conclusion to many," he states.

The sometimes horrifying details of war and violence that characterize human history are not a consequence of modern society because small egalitarian clans are also violent. Anthropologists have variously portrayed hunter-gatherer communities as pitiless warriors, gentle foragers or victims of Western exploitation. Now, based on ever-expanding evidence, the causes of violence can be seen to vary according to the situation. They include revenge, irritation, envy, prestige, sorcery, narcotics or a shortage of resources. The most prevalent, underlying causes of violence, however, are threats of some sort and the tribal narratives created to address them.

— ▪ ○ 17 ○ ▪ —

Understanding by Pointification

With the view of consilience the word *understand* takes on new meanings. Pointification is the process whereby related ideas are summed up by a single word that becomes a symbol of tribal practice.

THE ACT OF PERCEIVING SOMETHING as simple as a cup, from a neuronal standpoint, is an act of extraordinary complexity. Having learned the word *cup* and having encountered cups of many different sorts over a lifetime, a person knows its purpose and reacts appropriately the instant they see it. If someone hands you a cup of black tea, you immediately understand what the object is, but also, at a subconscious level, you understand the point of the interaction. The point changes according to the object, the context and the people involved.

Here's an example to describe what occurs in the sensory systems during an interpersonal interaction and why knowing the *point* of something is necessary for system functionality. Suppose you are occupied with walking toward the kitchen and you pass several people talking to each other; your eyes and ears do not lock onto any person or conversation in particular. The various parts of the neuronal orchestra play different tunes with little coordination, so you neither notice nor remember anything. But when a close friend, Sam, whom you haven't seen for a long time, steps in front of you and smiles, the players immediately start playing tunes related to other times you saw Sam. When Sam says, "Hi," auditory players strike up that tune and vocal players start up, and you exclaim, "Oh, hi Sam." Immediately, the point of the interaction is clear. You are both expressing a mutual bond.

Suppose a stranger, Pete, approaches you and offers you a glass of dark, bubbling liquid. Immediately, the neuronal orchestra kicks into tunes, such as *Who is he? What is that stuff? Why is he offering it to me? Do I trust him? Am I thirsty?* The orchestra looks to unite on a single melody. The players try to settle on *What is Pete's point?*

Pete appears unthreatening and, in concert with the visual players registering the movements of Pete's mouth, the auditory neuronal players hear, "Hi, I'm Pete; do you want a Coke?" He speaks in the same manner as your friends and has a cordial voice. At that moment the point of the interaction becomes clearer, and immediately your level of anxiety drops and you smile.

Neuronal players search for the point of interactions with others and in the same way they search for melodies that settle on the point of objects. This foundational aspect of how the brain works shows that every interaction is goal-directed; that is, our interactions with people and objects are concerned with attaining some sort of benefit. This notion doesn't feel good because it implies everyone is selfish. That is not the case however; it is simply how the neuronal orchestra operates.

In this context, what is the meaning of "benefit"? From the standpoint of evolutionary psychology, benefit refers to fulfillment of basic human needs. Human needs vary according to a person's age, gender and circumstances from moment to moment. They can, however, be summed up with a truncated Maslow's hierarchy of needs: most critical are food and hydration, then warmth and security, then social and tribal factors.

The nature of what constitutes a benefit is not always straightforward to figure out. Take the 1980 TV ad for Pepsi that I described in chapter 16. The benefit for the Pepsi bottlers, who were daily scrapping over store-shelf territory with the Coke bottlers, was the tribal symbolism of Pepsi's market share, as represented by the Pepsi truck overtaking Coke's.

The benefit to consumers was social and unspoken, along the lines of "if you drink Pepsi you are joining a growing tribe of sexually appealing young people." This strategy contrasted with Coke's approach that targeted the main purchasers, who were middle-age mothers. In our creative strategy, we labeled the social aspects as popularity, which went under the heading of nonfunctional or emotional benefits. As strategists, we believed the "functional point of difference" was Pepsi's superior taste: meaning the consumers' rationale to drink Pepsi was that it tasted better than Coke, and consumer research corroborated that claim.

With the perspective of consilience it is naive to suppose that *taste* is the driving benefit. Benefits that rank ahead of taste are hydration, which is communicated through the chug shots of glistening, back-lit bottles being gleefully polished off by fresh-faced models. But moreso, the combined kick of sugar, caffeine and carbon dioxide on the peripheral nervous system makes the product semi-addictive. Of course, it would have been corporate death to admit that we were selling a semi-addictive product using psycho-sexual innuendo and, what's more, a product that with hindsight is far from healthy.

The stickiness of the words *Coke* and *Pepsi* relate not only to the meaning of the words but also to their linguistic structure. It is a lot easier for people to remember names that begin with consonants that then roll off the tongue, because the muscles required to form the sound need to be coordinated between the abdomen, chest, larynx, tongue and lips. Coca-Cola and Pepsi-Cola are good examples of brand names that are sticky. They start with an explosive sound, with the neuronal players needing to be tightly focused, and are then followed by a rhythm. Brand names that start with vowels are more like a puff of breath, where the tongue and lips remain passive. In this case, the neuronal players don't need to be closely coordinated, so the words are less sticky. Apple is one of a handful of top brands that start with a vowel. Apple as a brand is sticky because of the hard-edged, visual symbol of the Apple logo and its immediate association with the physical fruit.

—— ▪ ○ ● ○ ▪ ——

In the process of making sense of the world and remembering experiences, complex matters become distilled into simple concepts. That is what constitutes a brand. Most people the world over know what Coca-Cola is, but other categorizations work in the same way. When I say, "I'm a Canadian," you would experience a momentary "got it." When I say, "I was born in Worcestershire," you might nod with understanding because you are familiar with the sauce. But that momentary feeling of confidence is illusory. Obviously, I have no relation to the sauce. In fact, my characteristics could map anywhere on the universe of English-speaking people, including the United States, Australia and New Zealand. Neuronal systems work by mapping different concepts together; but this leads to generalizations that verge on self-deception.

Confidence in one's level of understanding is affected by social relationships. Groups of people are united by their shared understanding of diverse and complex subjects. Nutritionists understand nutrition. Psychologists understand psychology. Medical doctors understand health. Scientists understand science. Politicians understand politics. Economists understand the economy. Marketing experts understand branding. However, if a nutritionist was speaking with a group of associates and said, "I understand nutrition," the colleagues would view this statement as an empty claim and ask, "To what aspect of nutrition are you referring?" However, if one of their clients asks, "Do you understand nutrition?" the question would sound impertinent, because, of course, a nutritionist understands nutrition.

Is it reasonable for anyone to claim that they *understand* human nutrition? In the 1960s, it seemed to be a straightforward matter of science. The body needs energy, protein building blocks and certain amounts of nutrients such as vitamins. This view was dubbed "nutritionism." At that point, the laws of thermodynamics about the conservation of energy were applied to the human body, by saying body weight is a matter of balancing calories being eaten with calories burned. Fat is particularly calorific and doctors could see that plaque buildup in the arteries clogged them — like hard-water deposits in domestic plumbing. Therefore it was logical to advise everyone to cut back on the amount of fat in their diet — particularly cholesterol.

Then waistlines started growing and cardiovascular disease became prevalent. In 1972, Dr. John Yudkin, a British physiologist and nutritionist, published *Pure, White and Deadly*, stating that sugar was a major cause of obesity and heart disease. At the time, his ideas were not welcome in the communities of health experts, and he was accused of having motives that were commercial rather than scientific, so he was forced to give up his professorship in 1971 and leave the doctors' college.

In 2009, Yudkin's ideas gained attention because of a video called *Sugar: The Bitter Truth*, posted on YouTube by Dr. Robert Lustig, a pediatric endocrinologist. He argued that too much fructose and not enough fiber are the main reasons for the obesity epidemic, due to the effects of fructose on insulin.

Since then, Gary Taubes and Michael Pollan have written books that describe further complexities. Pollan maintains that the very act of cooking for a family is itself a necessary aspect of good health. "Cooking," he writes, "is one of the most interesting and worthwhile things we humans do." Jamie Oliver, the celebrity chef, added his voice to a growing health movement that recognizes that human nutrition is complex and multifaceted. It has become clear that a narrow scientific understanding of nutrition has been the cause of much poor health.

The history of science and medicine — and other areas of expertise — shows there has been undue confidence in the human ability to understand and explain complex matters by applying science-like theories. Theories are productive when applied in physics, chemistry and human-made systems, but when applied to complex biological systems, inevitably they fall short.

This account is not intended to disparage professional expertise. An expert's knowledge built on study and multiple observations is clearly superior to the hunches of nonexperts. Expertise that is arrived at through top-down generalizations and rule-following, however, needs to be treated with caution.

Each scientific and academic community is made up of individuals who are motivated to contribute to the well-being of those around them. They think up ideas, then through experience and experimentation they become experts. They lecture and write papers and books that detail the complexities of their ideas, along with nuances, caveats and distinctions. Over time, however, their principal ideas become distilled into simple narratives that collectively have a well-defined point.

Visualize the process like this. Experts forge a path over rocky and unmapped terrain, making note of the paths of practical solutions as well as the obscurities and uncertainties represented by boulders, potholes and cliffs. In the case of the development of nutritional science, early researchers were clear about their goal, which was to find the causes of diseases such as scurvy and beriberi in order to prevent them. As the discipline developed, subsequent researchers followed the same path to a broader goal of promoting overall health. The path became worn in and easier to follow, with less need to worry about the boulders, potholes and cliffs. It was clear that vitamin C and vitamin B_1 are necessary for human health. Nutritionists then applied the approach more broadly, giving rise to nutritionism, and a belief that a handful of vitamins and other nutrients are adequate for good health.

The same process happens in other disciplines. Complex ideas are distilled, then combined with others and arranged into seemingly coherent bodies of knowledge that collectively have a point.

Consider the ideas and practice of psychology over the past 150 years. An early contributor was the Russian researcher Ivan Pavlov. A medical doctor and pharmacologist, he wrote papers on many subjects relating to nerves and the effects of stress, and he developed some breakthrough techniques. His career was long, and his personal life full of tragedy. History has condensed all of this down to Pavlov's discovery of the conditioned reflex of dogs salivating. It is the same with B.F. Skinner, the

American psychologist, behaviorist, author, inventor and social philosopher; he published 21 books and 180 articles. All of that has now been condensed to the punishment-reward model of learning and the theory that free will is an illusion. Sigmund Freud likewise was a prolific, lucid writer and lecturer. His name is now associated with sexual fantasies and psychoanalytic therapy.

The ideas of these thinkers along with many others are distilled into the practice of psychology. Psychology might be thought of as a straightforward discipline that collectively has a point. Psychology "is the science of mind and behavior," according to Wikipedia. Its point is the "assessment and treatment of mental health problems… and understanding and solving problems in several spheres of human activity." The community of psychologists incorporate these ideas into a broader narrative that "ultimately aims to benefit society."

A markedly contrasting view was advanced by the French philosopher Michel Foucault. In the 1961 book *Madness and Civilization: A History of Insanity in the Age of Reason*, he placed the treatment of mental disorders into a historical context, where the poor, morally lax and nonconforming were locked up and subjugated by "the man of reason." In a poetic, meandering style that became characteristic of postmodern philosophers, he was critical of "the language of psychiatry, which is a monologue by reason about madness," and divorced from "the secret heart of madness, at the core of so many errors, so many absurdities, so many words and gestures without consequence, we discover, finally, the hidden perfection of a language."

Contemporary commentators are also skeptical of the motivations and practice of the profession. Robert Whitaker, a journalist, wrote *Mad in America* and, more recently, *Anatomy of an Epidemic: Magic Bullets, Psychiatric Drugs, and the Astonishing Rise of Mental Illness in America.* His view is that the point of psychology is to medicalize mental traits and prescribe drugs that in the long term have not only been harmful, but also have created epidemics that didn't previously exist. He maintains that the explanation that drugs correct "chemical imbalances" in the brain is an unscientific myth that has been conceived to serve the needs of the practitioners themselves and big pharma.

In my view, psychology is founded on the idea that it is productive to extend metaphors used in physics and chemistry to understand the human mind. The discipline tried to be scientific long before the tools became available to enable researchers to probe the gelatinous substance of the brain. Really, in writing about psychology I should be careful. Which aspects of this complex subject am I referring to? Am I choosing to refer to the historical science-like theories that in hindsight look bizarre? What about evolutionary psychology, which is often sidelined in university courses? Am I unintentionally dissing the many clinical psychologists who provide people with badly needed therapy? When speaking face to face with someone, the meaning of the word *psychology* would depend on its context at a particular moment and on my understanding of their knowledge — and on our respective tribal allegiances.

Over time, groups of diverse ideas, initially practical and far from simple, become summed up by a single word or phrase. In my profession of marketing, we practice this when building brands; a single word or symbol is used to represent an organization that's composed of many individuals and multitudes of brand experiences. Political operatives do this as well, when they formulate simplified talking points and mold language to suit their purpose in a press release.

I have not come across a term that sums up this process, so I've coined the term *pointification* to mean the process whereby useful and complex ideas become simplified over time, distilled into a single word or phrase, and representative of the motivations of members of a particular community. In the process, the context, nuances and caveats are forgotten. The single word becomes the summation of a shared tribal goal and, when used by competing or opposing tribal groups, the word is often used pejoratively.

Visualize how this occurs in the neuronal orchestra by relating it to the process where a landscape is formed through the repeated action of raindrops falling and forming rivulets. These flow together forming streams and then rivers; over time they erode the earth to form valleys. Initially, different ideas are disconnected and collectively don't have a recognized point, but through repetition among tribal members, ideas coalesce into rivers of meaning.

In chapters 23 and 24 I'll describe how academic disciplines, including sociology and economics, have become pointified. The process also applies to religions where practical concepts, over time and with many retellings, become pointified as beliefs that become summed up by a single word. The quintessential example is the word *God*. Other examples of words that have become pointified are *liberal, conservative, socialism, evolution, creationism* and *climate change*. Each encapsulates many diverse ideas that have become tribal banners. The meaning of these words differs according to each person's tribal allegiance, so the words are immediately polarizing.

Fundamental to a person's social disposition is an instinctive need to figure out tribal loyalties. Is this book about science or business? Does that person believe in science or God? Do they believe in evolution, or are they creationists? Are they left or right wing? Do they care about social justice?

I'm hoping that everyone who becomes familiar with consilience will recognize words that have become pointified, and be more likely to ask: "Precisely what do you mean by that?" And then listen, with genuine curiosity, to the answer.

18

Tribal Journeys Divide Us

Three dominant frames of reference, or tribal journeys, prevail in the Western world, and the rifts between them have been widening.

OVER MY CAREER OF WORKING WITH MANY DIFFERENT COMPANIES, I've noticed that the single most important factor determining success are the minute-to-minute habits of each team member. In successful companies, one can feel the intangible buzz conveyed in the alertness and optimism of everyone involved. In meetings, the meaning of what people say seems to be less significant than how they react to each other. Sometimes this feeling is termed *culture*, but I'm referring to something that runs far deeper.

The dynamics relate to what everyone feels at a subliminal level is acceptable behavior. It is expressed in how clearly team members talk and write. Most particularly it is demonstrated when something goes wrong. How do members of a tribal group react? Do they hang back wishing not to be associated with the issue or step forward regardless of formal job descriptions? It is also manifested in how everyone feels as they walk in the door each morning. Do they believe in their shared mission? Are they turning up to collect their pay, or are they looking forward to spending their day as a member of a high-performing team? The feelings are contagious. Once I have gotten to know a company, I can feel the difference in my stomach as I enter their lobby.

People are associated with many different tribes depending on their particular circumstances. In my case, during a typical day I converse with family members, colleagues in my company, clients in various businesses, members of professional tribes including lawyers and accountants, members of my tennis club and various interest groups. In each case, the words I use and also the purpose of my interactions are different. For example, my goals in my business interactions are not the same as when I play tennis doubles, where my goal is to win with whomever happens to be my partner during that particular set.

Psychologists refer to the change in how people speak and relate to each other as *code-switching*. The term arose in linguistics to explain how the mannerisms and attitudes of people change according to the language they are speaking. Code-switching happens whenever people speak with members of different groups or in different situations. A lawyer addressing a judge in court speaks very differently than when she's addressing her teenage son at home. When someone's social life and personal beliefs are not congruent with their work environment, the necessary code-switching becomes stressful, and they feel inauthentic.

Code-switching is foundational to how we perceive and think — and it relates to *framing*. The different codes are like the compositions the neuronal orchestra plays that vary according to the context. Each player can use many instruments and play different genres of music. Each genre, say jazz or rap, is associated with a different frame of reference. The melodies created in our mind and through our actions and social interactions determine how we perceive reality — our unique mental landscape. This is a confusing matter because we are unaware of what the neuronal orchestra is doing. We can get a hint of the significance of framing by looking at how earlier civilizations represented their world.

For example, the drawings of ancient Greeks depict large sea creatures as a dragon-like mix of features, such as the tail of a lizard, the face of a dog, the tusks of a wild boar, the scales and fins of a fish, and the teeth of a shark. They did not see a clear distinction between whales, dolphins, tuna, sawfish, sharks, seals and giant squid. Romans categorized dolphins as sea monsters and depicted them with human eyes and demonic teeth. Were they wrong? They wouldn't have believed so. Compared to today, many more large animals would have been swimming in the Mediterranean, and sailors would have witnessed how wounded soldiers falling in the waves would get devoured by indistinct monsters in the frothing darkness. The classical ways of depicting sea creatures persisted for a long time and did not start changing until about 500 years ago when commercial whaling began. Today, perched in a small boat on the ocean, we would likely smile and feel lucky if we see a dolphin. If we see a whale, we might grab a cellphone and try to take a photo; .however, if we see the dorsal fin of a shark slice the surface, our reaction would be different.

To sum up — contrary to intuition — our mental frames of reference affect what we see and how we behave.

In the Western world, mass media has been a powerful creator of shared frames of thinking. For 50 years after the end of the Second World War, national newspapers, radio and TV stations represented the world in ways that became widely held norms. Tens of millions of people went home in the evening and watched identical newscasts, documentaries and sitcoms. Everyone acknowledged that the West was engaged in a Cold War against the Soviets. The goals for politicians could be summed up as increased wealth and security for their citizens. People held differing views about social fairness, but it was possible to easily spell out the different positions. The meanings of words such as *right wing, science, religion, truth* and *environment* were, on the whole, clear.

Since the advent of the internet and social media, a common understanding has weakened. As a result, differences between frames of reference have widened. Events are interpreted using different frames. For instance, a police shooting will be seen by one tribal grouping as a systemic failing, and by another as much-needed law and order. Tribes and sub-tribes have begun forming and picking issues, such as immigration, freedom, racism, sexism and climate change, to use as tribal banners.

In later chapters I'll lay bare the philosophical and educational underpinnings of some of the sub-tribes. For now, I'll name three frames of reference that prevail in the Western world. They are not synonymous with political groupings and so I'll coin these descriptive names: *Climb Higher, Hold Firm* and *Gather Together.* These frames of reference, that I term them *tribal journeys,* each have a point that is implicitly understood by their members.

The Climb Higher tribal journey has evolved based on scientific frames of reference and the ideas of Aristotle, Plato, Descartes, Newton, Poincaré, Stuart Mill, and many others who contributed to the accepted practices and beliefs of scientists.

The second tribal journey, Hold Firm, has roots in the Abrahamic faiths of Judaism, Christianity and Islam. The fundamental view is belief in piety, and respect for the cultural heritage and religious practices of their respective tribes.

The third tribal journey, Gather Together, has developed based on concern for ecological harmony and equality. Underlying beliefs can be traced to the writings of Jean-Jacques Rousseau, who, in the mid-1700s, popularized the view that man in the "state of nature" lived peaceably and inequality was "almost null." This tribe is mostly aligned with postmodernist philosophies.

Recall the metaphor of the landscape fashioned from countless raindrops merging into streams and rivers, and carving out valleys. The neuronal orchestra develops landscapes from our experiences and interactions with others. New experiences and ideas find their place on a unique, personal landscape.

As people search for the point of their journey in life, they find meaning in relation to their own neuronal landscape. Today, communication in the Western world conforms with one, or two, of the three tribal journeys. A political statement, blog post, newspaper article, TED Talk or scientific article rarely deviates. If it does, it is sidelined.

The objective of naming these journeys is not to judge them, but to help explain the rifts encountered daily in politics and the media. Each tribal journey caricatures the followers of the other tribal journeys. With tongue-in-cheek I'll summarize the beliefs and adherents of each one.

Climb Higher is grounded in science, logic and reason. Adherents believe that Darwinian evolution has resulted in progressively more sophisticated organisms. Over the past few million years, our forebears made the transition from instinctive behaviors to consciousness and civilized social behavior. Transformative leaps were made during the Renaissance and the Age of Enlightenment, and the pace is speeding up with the digital revolution. Humanity is overcoming religious and tribal differences to reach a world of natural morality, empathy and altruism. If we manage technology wisely, we will continue to progress. The defining unit for this tribe is the individual.

The Climb Higher tribe can be caricatured as caring intellectuals and bureaucrats dressed in sensible shoes scurrying through halls of academia, the United Nations, the World Health Organization and the European Parliament, making speeches and figuring out ways to nudge the less-enlightened populace to good behavior. Cognitive psychologist, linguist and popular science author Steven Pinker, and biologist, author and staunch atheist Richard Dawkins are the rational sages of this group.

The Hold Firm tribe provides a stark contrast. Believers are marching toward heaven, which can be reached through observance of their tribes' dictates. They value faith, patriotism, valor, chastity, law and order, community, hierarchy, and tradition. The defining unit is husband, wife and family. They see faith as timeless and defer to the wisdom of God rather than ever-changing and fallible scientific theories.

Countless popes, clerics, preachers, rabbis, imams and spiritual gurus have defined the beliefs and behaviors for this tribe. Modern-day secular spokespersons for this group are the psychologist and author Jordan Peterson and political commentator Ben Shapiro.

In the United States, this group can be caricatured as families eating BBQ ribs outside a football stadium or raceway, leaning against their F-150 trucks, drinking Bud Light. It is a world where women can be girls and boys can be men. This group tends to vote for conservative and Republican politicians.

The Gather Together tribe believes that the forces of history, the tyranny of the minority, capitalism and the excessive exploitation of natural resources have upset the natural balance. Adherents are associated with the social justice movement, where it is considered honorable to speak out against slights, insults and inequalities. They are moving toward a society of equality, acceptance and sharing where everyone lives tranquilly with each other and Mother Earth. The defining unit is the community and pan-national bodies such as the United Nations that ensure that countries act responsibly.

The group is represented by writer Naomi Klein; Kate Raworth, economist and author of *Doughnut Economics*; and journalist George Monbiot, who envisions "private sufficiency and public luxury" in the forms of "wonderful parks and playgrounds, public sports centers and swimming pools, galleries, allotments and public transport networks."

This tribe rallies behind the climate change movement, with the International Panel on Climate Change providing scientific support. They vote for socialist and green parties. The Gather Together tribe can be caricatured as communities tending to their shared organic vegetable plots, surrounded by windmills turning in a steady breeze without any need for fossil fuels.

The beliefs of each tribe are evolving. Hold Firm, for instance, in earlier eras was associated with honor cultures that valued demonstrations of bravery. This has given way to dignity culture, where virtue is demonstrated through quiet stoicism.

People tend to gravitate to a spectrum of news outlets that coincide with their tribal beliefs. Roughly speaking, Climb Higher follows CBS, NBC, *The Wall Street Journal*, *Financial Times* and *The Economist*. Hold Firm follows Fox News, Breitbart, Drudge Report, *New York Post* and *The Washington Times*. And Gather Together follows BBC, CBC, ABC, NPR, CBS, CNN and the *Guardian*.

The most significant aspect of these three tribal journeys is that each of them is in its own right a self-sufficient paradigm or metalandscape. Each is composed of constituent melodies of theories, ideas and histories that can be arranged into coherent metanarratives. And each provides a *point* for the lives of their adherents. The Climb Higher tribe is moving toward a society of technological progress and higher reason. The Hold Firm tribe is moving toward a place of personal meaning and salvation. The Gather Together tribe is journeying toward a society of equality and peace.

On the surface, the Climb Higher and the Hold Firm tribes appear to be moving in opposite directions. You believe in science *or* you believe in religion — it is unusual to believe in both at the same time. Both, however, ascribe to the belief that society is advancing from states of primitivism to enlightenment. The Climb Higher tribe is achieving it through technological progress and an improved standard of living. The Hold Firm tribe advances through the virtues of productive work and growing families. Both these views can be termed modernist, and both contrast with a traditional Eastern viewpoint that life is cyclical.

The Gather Together tribe is moving in the opposite direction. It aspires to go back to a time of innocence when humanity lived in small communities at peace with nature.

At a collective level, all three tribal journeys share many similarities however the members of each immediately sense their loyalties and how they are apart from the others. By adopting the perspective of consilience, we can see that the three tribal landscapes include a multitude of different ideas contributed by notable thinkers through the ages, as well as by journalists and other influencers of contemporary culture. We can look at the merits of the constituent ideas of each tribal journey and explore how each emerged and continues to mold humanity's collective consciousness.

We can also see that our neuronal orchestras conflate different realms. Personal journeys are not the same as societal journeys. Perhaps if we understand the realities and quirks of neuronal systems, it will be possible to spark dialogue about how tribal narratives might evolve that are more compatible and realistic.

— ▪ ○ 19 ○ ▪ —

Moving Beyond Childhood

The transition from childhood to adulthood is a phase of development that happens at both neuronal and social levels, where individuals formulate their personal journeys.

THE PRE-CONSILIENCE VIEW OF THE HUMAN MIND is something like this: As children grow up, they are taught information and acquire skills, including writing and arithmetic. When they reach adulthood, they are equipped with a mind that enables them to apply reason to make decisions and earn a living. If they have a high IQ, they can make superior decisions and earn more money than those less intelligent and less motivated.

This picture doesn't match with research into how children learn. For example, researchers have observed that babies as young as six months are more responsive to noises made by their peers than by their mother.

Judith Rich Harris, author of college textbooks on child development, recounts in *The Nurture Assumption: Why Children Turn Out the Way They Do* that, "one day it suddenly occurred to me that many of the things I had been telling those credulous college students were wrong." Having had children of her own, she realized that they learn from their peers more than from their parents. "Adolescents are not aspiring to adult status — they are *contrasting* themselves with adults." She noted how adolescent children of immigrants don't end up sounding like their parents; they have the same accent, vocabulary and mannerisms as their peers:

"They adopt characteristic modes of clothing, hairstyles, speech, and behavior so that, even though they are now the same size as adults, no one will have any trouble telling them apart." She continues, "If they truly aspired to adult status they would not be spraying graffiti on overpasses, going for joyrides in cars they do not own, or shoplifting nail polish from drug stores. They would be doing boring adult things, like figuring out their income tax or doing their laundry."

From the perspective of consilience, the brain is one part of a dynamic system, constantly absorbing new experiences, picking up on other people's behavior, and coming up with new ways to organize ideas into a coherent mental landscape so each individual can live their life.

Late adolescence and early adulthood is a critical period when youths settle on their own personal journey and things to care about. It is a time when the neuropeptides involved with separation anxiety become less active, and individuals switch from being a protected child to having self-dependence. In terms of animal behavior, particularly among males, in this phase of life individuals look for new territory away from their home and have an increasing urge to associate with new social groups, find sexual partners and ultimately become protective parents.

This period of transition is a distinct phase of mental development that manifests in many different ways. Often it is associated with feelings of angst and confusion. Early last century, the respected psychologist William James lectured and wrote about the characteristics of this period of life, linking it with spiritual awakenings and conversions. "The further limits of our being plunge into an altogether other dimension of existence from the sensible and merely 'understandable' world," he wrote. "It plunges into a realm of spiritual agents, with whom we come in contact, at certain points of our being, and from whom 'higher energies' filter in."

At this time, a section of the neuronal orchestra — the prefrontal cortex — at the front of the brain just above the eyes starts maturing. This is the only part of the neuronal orchestra not directly concerned with the senses and muscles. Think about it like this: up to the age of 19, this part of the orchestra hangs back, waiting for the other parts to learn their melodies. After that, the prefrontal players start searching for tunes that fit together into higher-order arrangements. Researchers have linked this part of the brain to personality expression, decision-making, moderating social behavior and the desire to be productive.

The neuronal conductor causes all the players to become more sensitive to cues from around them. A book, a teacher, a professor, a friend, a movie, a poet, a song or an inspiring event can trigger the neuronal players to discover new patterns. The patterns might focus on academic work, making money, music, art, science or a social cause.

During this post-teen period of development, individuals look to organize what they have learned into a coherent metanarrative that gives meaning and direction to their existence. As James wrote in *The Varieties of Religious Experience,* "Knowledge about life is one thing; effective occupation of a place in life, with its dynamic currents passing through your being, is another." Ideas become arranged accordingly and classified onto a landscape of *agree, unimportant* or *disagree.*

This time of life is associated with questioning, rebellion, exploration and creativity. The neuronal orchestra may end up arranging the melodies of experience into unique symphonies of meaning inspired by whatever maestro fits: Beethoven, Brubeck, Davis, Armstrong, Houston or Jackson. These symphonies are sometimes accompanied with vivid dreams and described with words such as *watershed moment, turning point, transformation, awakening* and *a deep shift in core values.* The feeling might last minutes or weeks, and when it quietens down, angst is replaced by a determination to forge ahead with a new purpose in life.

In this post-teen period, the prefrontal cortex neuronal players exist in a heightened state of criticality. At each moment the system can tip in any direction. Sometimes the result is spiritual in nature, with a feeling that the mind has merged with the universe, completely free of boundaries. Occasionally, the experience brings feelings of messianic power. Sometimes individuals become withdrawn and feel possessed by demons. In certain cultures, such experiences may be viewed as a normal part of spiritual development, and are helped along by shamans and spiritual teachers. In Western culture, these tendencies have tended to be viewed as the work of the devil and more recently as pathologies that need to be treated with drugs.

Loving family members, caring friends and teachers are sometimes able to direct the young adult's anxiety toward a productive goal. In some cases, individuals can be attracted to join religious groups, cults and adopt extremist positions where they see dark forces conspiring against them. Others find meaning through sports, dance, yoga or meditation. Some find fulfilment in artistic endeavors or skills such as computer coding or scientific research. Newton's resulted in the invention of the laws of motion; Einstein's resulted in the publication of four scientific papers that were revolutionary.

The outcome of this transitional period of life can be remarkably productive or, conversely, sad. The neuronal orchestra in the prefrontal cortex can tip toward a spectrum of manias and paranoias. When genetics, disease, drugs or trauma cause the neuronal system to break down, the consequences can be depression, psychosis, schizophrenia and suicide. It is no coincidence that the prefrontal cortex is the part of the brain disrupted by lobotomies.

Many people in this stage of life come up with transformative new ideas that can spread to become symbols of a generation or even an era. In the 1960s, feelings of rebellion, creativity and rebirth fused to give rise to the hippie movement. For the youth of the day, it was the start of a new era, the dawning of the Age of Aquarius, with some people adopting religious traditions of Asia, including transcendental meditation, and others experimenting with cannabis, LSD and mescaline. The ideas of that time were spread by artistic figures such as Ken Kesey and rock bands, including the Grateful Dead, and eventually defined a widespread, unstoppable, social movement. The ideas permeated a whole generation in North America and Britain. In the United States, when combined with the human rights movement and opposition to the Vietnam War, the hippie movement became political. Those who in 1969 experienced Woodstock — billed as "An Aquarian Exposition: 3 Days of Peace & Music" — participated in the synchronization of 400,000 neuronal orchestras among a growing tribe of individuals united on a journey that would set the Western world on a trajectory that rejected the conformities of suburbanism.

Each generation finds its voice, often through music, sometimes through dance and social gatherings. When Beyoncé headlined the 2018 Coachella Valley Music and Arts Festival in California, 125,000 concert-goers along with millions of others who watched the Netflix documentary *Homecoming* participated in a tribal happening that celebrated female confidence and the exuberant swagger of Black college marching bands.

At the neuronal level, the close relationship between perceptions of reality, artistic and social creativity, and profound experience about one's personal significance is illustrated by the effect of drugs. Hallucinogens and amphetamines were foundational in the Beat Generation, expressed in the writings of Allen Ginsberg, William S. Burroughs and Jack Kerouac, and later in the hippie movement. Convinced of the profundity of their experiences, authors of the time wrote detailed accounts of hallucinations and commentaries on their artistic and spiritual significance. They described how their trips were not only indistinguishable from reality, but that they *were* reality. The experiences felt so real, so vivid, that they were convinced they were just that — alternative realities. Carlos Castaneda wrote in *The Teachings of Don Juan* how his experiences while taking the hallucinogen peyote with a Yaqui Indian shaman introduced him to "an astounding realm outside the bounds of everyday life." The book was believed to be an accurate account of Central American native culture and it has been on the syllabus of university anthropology courses.

The sensitive state of the neuronal orchestra can tip suddenly from feelings of sublime omnipotence to experiences where everything, in the words of Aldous Huxley, "is unspeakably sinister or disgusting; every event is charged with a hateful significance; every object manifests the presence of an indwelling horror, infinite, all-powerful, eternal."

Sensory deprivation can induce similar effects. Imagine being suspended in water close to body temperature in the quiet and dark. You can see nothing, and all sound is muffled. After a while you start to feel disconnected from reality, and may experience feelings of tranquility, unease or panic. Soon hallucinations begin when you start to see objects and lights, which feel real, not dreamlike. The players in the neuronal orchestra, robbed of their normal stimulation, start concocting melodies under their own freewheeling initiative. One can only imagine what would happen if the neuronal orchestra was entirely deprived of sensations from skin and gravity. It might very well feel like hell.

The ways in which post-teen experiences crystalize into different tribal journeys is illustrated by Sam Harris and Jordan Peterson. Both have documented how their personal quests took shape. Harris built his personal landscape following a transformative experience with MDMA, which led to trips to India and Nepal, and a commitment to meditation. Peterson became anguished over the writings of Aleksandr Solzhenitsyn, Fyodor Dostoevsky, George Orwell and others. He needed to account for the "insidious, subtle and damaging force of evil."

Both men needed to settle on the nature of truth and virtue, but when they debated the matter in 2018 it became clear their mental landscapes were incompatible. Both are highly intelligent and articulate and in the debate were steelmanning each other's position, yet they were unable to arrive at a common understanding of what it means when something is or is not *true*. Harris could hardly contain his exasperation when, after hours of debate, Peterson refused to say that some things are self-evidently true.

Nearly everyone understands the difference between telling the truth and telling a lie. In most situations, telling a harmful lie results in a feeling of guilt. Harris takes this as a starting point, then extrapolates that feeling to a broader philosophical position, saying that certain ideas are evidently and morally true, and others are evidently false and sometimes destructive. "We are doomed to talk past each other with every sentence," he stated, "if sane and reasonable people cannot differentiate fact from fantasy."

Referring to the certainties of science, Peterson countered, "Imagine for a moment that the invention of the hydrogen bomb led to the outcome which we were all so terrified about during the Cold War, with the total elimination of human life... the science would be true enough to generate a hydrogen bomb but not true enough to stop everyone from dying." Peterson concluded, "And therefore from a Darwinian perspective in some fundamental sense it would be wrong."

This question is like a rivulet on the continental divide between two landscapes. Either the water flows in the river of modernist rationality of the Climb Higher tribal journey followed by Harris or it flows toward the river of human vulnerability and transcendent reality characteristic of the Hold Firm tribal journey espoused by Peterson.

From the standpoint of consilience, we can see and accept both landscapes. The word *true* exists because it communicates an idea, whose meaning is unavoidably subjective and therefore depends on mutual understanding. We can acknowledge Harris's position that truth is an objective category that has utility in the day-to-day dealings of people. Peterson's position, on the other hand, that no one should get overly cocky about their own convictions, also has utility.

In the Harris–Peterson debate, each made slightly different points, both of which are useful, and each could have yielded a little on how they expressed themselves without letting go of their convictions.

Most people aspire to reach a place where they can live comfortably, without stress, surrounded by family and respected by members of their tribe, and they look to leaders to help them get there.

Leaders of all sorts — business leaders, educators and politicians — express their desired destinations and the obstacles in their own way. Elon Musk's dream is to relax among thick greenery with other visionaries bathed in golden light as they watch tiny Earth slowly rise over Mars' horizon, no longer bothered about the U.S. Securities and Exchange Commission, and Tesla's share price. As they sit together in their Martian greenhouse, they would undoubtedly start discussing how much better life would be on Venus.

That is a modern-day version for what transpired on the shores of the Indian Ocean 70,000 years ago. Our forebears would have gathered around a fire watching sparks fly heavenward, hearing the pulsing cicadas and the crescendoing cackle of hyenas that had been driven to the coast by years of drought. Drawing maps in the dirt and recalling their parents' stories — about trudging from where the crimson sun sets and muddy lakes thick with crocodiles, with only a few gulps of water left in the skins slung around their shoulders, then arriving at the salty waves — they would have been dreaming of a more secure life somehow, somewhere else. And making sure everyone was committed to the same journey.

In the post-teen years, each of us in our own way search out role models, find our tribe and sub-tribes and set off on a personal journey.

20

The End of the Road

History shows that tribal behaviors, along with stressors, trigger unrest, war and can lead to the collapse of civilizations.

MY GRANDFATHER, HENRY BEAKBANE, died of a heart attack before I was born. My father told me that he was a quiet man and, like my maternal grandfather in Rhodesia, he was fond of gardening and beekeeping. At the start of the First World War, he enlisted in the Royal Artillery. That would have been normal and patriotic at the time. He could have, however, easily stayed home as he was 35 years old and running a large tannery whose products were needed for the war effort. His decision was surprising because his parents and eight generations before him were devout Quakers for whom the testimony of peace is a foundational belief. He was posted to the Western Front close to a Flemish town called Leper; its French name is Ypres. It marked a line of trenches that hardly moved from the start of the war to the end, and yet witnessed five battles and the death of 1.3 million soldiers and civilians. He manned the 16-pound field guns – serving until the armistice was signed. Somehow he was lucky enough to not be among the many who were shot, gassed, burned, blown up, executed or caught in the shelling that by the end of the war had flattened the town.

He never once spoke to his family about those four years near the frontlines. Before the end of the war he married a vivacious Parisian lady, Camille Renault, and they had four children. But he never breathed a word of his experiences to any of them.

At Ypres, the Germans had first experimented with mustard and chlorine gas. It was more effective than they had expected: it seared the lungs of everyone and every animal downwind of the lead pipes snaking out from the rows of steel cylinders. The Germans hadn't amassed enough troops to follow the clouds of gas across the trenches, and so the frontline on those Flanders fields remained bogged down. Why would my grandfather speak of this? He knew that each of the 16-pound shells he loaded had killed people much like himself. He had returned fire with shells filled with poison. A number of those many muddy, mutilated bodies killed during the four years at Ypres would have been etched in his memory. He had friends who were German. Also, he likely understood that the war was no simple matter of good versus evil. He had survived and was no hero.

Around 20 million people died in the First World War. Who was to blame for this destruction? The immediate cause was the assassination of Archduke Franz Ferdinand of Austria-Hungary and his wife, Sophie. Was it because of the Archduke's carelessness, or does the blame lie with the Serbian nationalist, Gavrilo Princip, who fired the shots? Or was Austria-Hungary to blame for annexing Bosnia and Herzegovina in the first place, and declaring war on Serbia? Or was it because Russia began mobilizing its forces to defend its alliance with Serbia? Or was it the Germans because they declared war on Russia? Or was it the web of alliances between countries that made their involvement unavoidable?

None of these reasons explain why the citizens of Britain were so quick to enlist and fight alongside the French who had been on-again/off-again enemies since the collapse of the Roman Empire. Was it because the British were becoming fearful of the buildup of the German military? Or because Britain and Germany were competing on the chessboard of world imperialism?

There is truth in all these reasons and, considering the major powers, it is clear that every party was anxious about their future. The Germans were concerned that France would take back the resource-rich territory of Alsace-Lorraine. Bosnian Serbs and Croats, both Muslims and Christians, felt vulnerable as a southern appendage of the Austro-Hungarian Empire. The Russians were concerned about the growing armies on their western flank. And Britain was concerned about their weakening hold over the British Empire.

Layered onto these anxieties were the intellectual movements of German romanticism and anarchism, and the writings of Fyodor Dostoevsky and Friedrich Nietzsche, as well as an increasingly pervasive modernist mindset. Science was transforming agriculture and manufacturing as well as being used by Karl Marx to apply the "laws of motion" — as he termed them — to the capitalist system, including its origins and inevitable evolution. His book *Das Kapital*, published in 1867, took hold in Russia with consequences that were not foreseen and yet ultimately fatal for the last tsar of Russia, Nicholas II, and his German-born wife, Tsarina Alexandra.

To plan an invasion of France and Belgium, the chief of the German Army General Staff, Field Marshal Alfred von Schlieffen, applied scientific thinking to enable the swift movement of troops and artillery by train. Because of the Schlieffen plan, the German military had confidence they could attack and eclipse the French army within the six weeks before Russia had time to mobilize troops on the Eastern Front.

What caused the war? Look closely at all wars and revolutions, and you find the same motifs. Anxieties, either real or imagined, become spun into visions of a future that is more appealing than the one that exists. At the turn of the twentieth century, the writings of various intellectuals illuminated visions of the future, which politicians and journalists put to use. The tribes involved in the First World War quickly grouped together into improbable alliances. There was no mastermind moving the pieces on the chessboard, nor deep conspiracies. Everyone was behaving as humans do, moving forward with their lives, looking after themselves and their families and, on the whole, doing their best. No one planned it. No one could have foreseen the carnage. The dynamics of human groups were at work and what transpired — the biggest conflagration in human history — emerged from all the many interactions. My grandfather, brought up as a pacifist, was swept along and enlisted in the British military.

Was the "war to end all wars," as the Great War was called, an aberration of history? If the little town of Ypres is representative of history, the answer is a clear "No." Julius Caesar's army passed through the area in 55 BCE on his way to wiping out two Germanic tribes, the Tencteri and the Usipetes, who had migrated from the east. They begged for asylum, but Caesar's troops slaughtered them entirely, including the women and children. Archaeologists have uncovered the remains of between 150,000 and 200,000 people near the Dutch city of Kessel. Caesar reported 450,000 killed.

Since Caesar's time, Ypres has seen a string of tribal conflicts, including the Battle of the Golden Spurs, the Battle of Mons-en-Pévèle, the Peace of Melun, the Battle of Cassel, the siege led by the English bishop Henry le Despenser and conquest by the forces of Louis XIV of France. The town remained under French control until the Spanish took possession, then it was handed over to the Habsburgs and became part of the Austrian Netherlands. The French recaptured the city after a siege in 1794.

After the Great War, did humanity come to its senses, reason prevail, with everyone living happily ever after? Of course not. Several decades later, one of the most educated and cultured countries in the world unleashed terrors that resulted in the deaths of 85 million people. I will not recount the details here.

The usual explanation for World War II is that one evil man bullied and manipulated reluctant citizens into committing atrocities, which haunt our collective conscience. This explanation, however, absolves us from acknowledging a truth about our species: that we fall into line according to our tribal allegiances and rarely feel the need to speak out against prevailing norms.

Societies result from the behavior of individuals. That is, they are built from the bottom up. Members of organizations and citizens of countries want to be led. We look to leaders to help us collectively arrive at destinations that are better than where we are. The dynamics of tribes can result in war irrespective of what is reasonable.

Can academics help us understand the realities of human psychology and social dynamics? This doesn't appear to be the case. The current, dominant narrative is that if people suppress voices that do not conform we will collectively make progress toward a desired destination of peace and harmony: a narrative common to the Gather Together and Climb Higher tribal journeys.

This perspective is captured in a new genre of nonfiction books that has been dubbed "new optimism." The names of the books are self-explanatory: *The Better Angels of Our Nature: Why Violence Has Declined* (2011) and *Enlightenment Now: The Case for Reason, Science, Humanism and Progress* (2018), both by Steven Pinker; *Factfulness: Ten Reasons We're Wrong About the World – and Why Things Are Better Than You Think,* by the late Swedish physician Hans Rosling, written in conjunction with Anna and Ola Rosling; *It's Better Than It Looks: Reasons for Optimism in an Age of Fear* (2018) by Gregg Easterbrook; and *Abundance: The Future Is Better Than You Think* (2012) by Peter H. Diamandis and Steven Kotler.

The metrics for both the eradication of poverty and disease, and many achievements since the end of the Second World War, are truly impressive. To extrapolate this trajectory into the future and imagine that everything will continue to improve, however, is a logical stretch not evidenced by history.

The modernist philosophies espoused by the Climb Higher tribe and the postmodern philosophies of the Gather Together tribe do not take into account that humans will never be free from our biological roots. While science and technology will likely progress increasingly rapidly, the same cannot be said for human nature.

The current trajectory ignores lessons of history that show repeatedly how mighty, seemingly invincible, civilizations inevitably disintegrate. It has happened many times.

The situation in the Western world is unusually precarious for many reasons: most pressing are economic and the anxieties of young people, who cannot find jobs and feel, with good reason, that older generations are blocking their opportunities. In part, this is a result of automation and 20 years of shortsighted trade deals and currency imbalances that have hollowed out the Western world's manufacturing capacity. Companies can readily buy services from workers without hiring them, resulting in the growth of the gig economy. Young people have to compete in a flattened, globalized world, where the wages in many countries are a small fraction of what they need to live on in the West.

So-called blue-collar jobs that involve physical labor, including agriculture, extractive industries and manufacturing, have disappeared particularly fast. Earlier generations valued these types of jobs, but now they are regarded as anti-environmental. White-collar jobs, part of the fast-growing digital economy, are more abundant and often well paid. The adverse outcomes are particularly noticeable in large cities. Cities attract young people because of the buzzing social scene, but the white-collar economy inflates the cost of accommodation. Few opportunities exist for blue-collar work and, as a result, groups of young urbanites, mostly young males, cannot get a secure foothold; they feel the system has conspired against them. The educational system has not provided them with the confidence and skills they need to start businesses of their own.

Young, well-educated urbanites with white-collar jobs don't feel secure either. Sometimes they are weighed down by university education debts, and jobs in law, finance and consulting appear increasingly vulnerable to the advances of AI. Climbing on a professional career ladder is no longer a ticket to long-term security.

As well, among the younger generations, rules of engagement between the sexes have become full of contradictions. Gender categories once considered an unambiguous matter of biology have blurred. Internet pornography — only a click away — shows graphic and willing sex, yet in real life an unwanted glance may be characterized as microaggression. The rules are not uniform. A class of hot, wealthy extroverts get a stream of right-swipes on dating apps and, apparently, do not have to abide by the same rules as everyone else.

As each generation comes of age, young people are justified in feeling anxious about their future. Currently, however, society is undergoing unprecedented shocks. Just 30 years ago, the internet hardly existed, no one carried a smartphone, electronic games were not part of everyday life, social media hadn't been invented, many people watched the same TV shows, the mass media was profitable, and journalists could spend time researching local and international stories. The manufacturing sector provided jobs, and wholesale outsourcing to low-cost jurisdictions hadn't begun. Thirty years ago prospects for the future were positive. Trade and travel were increasing. Pan-national organizations, such as NATO, the European Economic Community and The World Bank, appeared to be functioning well. The Berlin Wall fell in 1989, and people in Eastern European countries looked forward to enjoying the lifestyles they had seen in the movies and on television.

Along with massive social changes, the details of people's lives have been transforming at rapid speeds. The generation now coming of age has spent a large proportion of their waking life looking at a digital screen. They have been taught that education is a matter of remembering facts and answering multiple choice questions. They have not been trained to be skeptical about the pronouncements of experts, nor have they had the freedom to build the resilience needed to fend for themselves.

Many individuals suffer from mental health issues, loneliness, depression and despair. And at this time, we have to contend with the reverberations of the COVID-19 crisis and a rapid growth in the money supply that is unprecedented — certainly in times when there are no major wars.

Science and technology have been advancing rapidly, but discourse about current political and social issues has become mired in tribal battles. Many hope that people in authority will somehow work things out for everyone. But authority figures are immersed in their day-to-day challenges. They need to project certainty and are unable to break free of the established patterns of thinking.

21

Battlefield of Ideas

Many ideas that constitute the tribal journeys take shape in academia. Some are unavoidably controversial. Study of the genetic nature of human behavior encroaches on the social sciences.

CONSILIENCE IS FOUNDED ON THE IDEA that it is beneficial to be honest about the true nature of human beings, including the fallibilities of the human mind, whether or not the facts are self-affirming. The subject is, however, inherently controversial no matter how it is explained.

The subject is controversial because to understand human beings one must venture over the well-trodden ground of various academic disciplines. In the process of saying something that is both new and useful, one trespasses on the territory of experts, whose career motivations have included building academic status, progressing along their life journey and helping others do the same.

There are mountainous divides between the three tribal journeys. For those passionate about their chosen path, it is easy to recognize emerging rivulets of ideas flowing in an incompatible direction that potentially undermine their beliefs and status. These days, tribal battles are being fought in the press, on social media and in schools across the Western world.

To begin, let's visit the frontlines of intellectual development occurring in lecture theaters, cafeterias and campuses of universities. Outwardly, universities are revered and majestic institutions with centuries-old, ivy-clad buildings, and great halls with Renaissance-style oil paintings of deans and chancellors. They are places that wealthy parents, at least in most cases, can send their beloved children to come of age among the modern-day likes of Newton, Galileo, Einstein, Curie, Faraday, Franklin, Kant, Nietzsche, Wittgenstein, Darwin and Hawking.

But these institutions are composed of real people. First, there are the students, who appear to be full of confidence but they need to find friends, fit in and deal with anxieties about the journey on which they are embarking. At this stage their future lies before them, but they cannot see over the next hillock and are fearful of what might be on the other side. Second, there are faculty members, who fit into a hierarchy — from research associates hoping to gain a toehold on the climb toward a tenured position, up to the heads of departments aiming to consolidate their power, spread their influence and eclipse weaker disciplines. Third, there are the administrative staff, in separate hierarchies, whose job is to safeguard the institution's brand and keep it functioning.

A mixture of authority, ambition, enthusiasm, uncertainty, fear and hormones is combustible, and at every moment liable to explode into something like a combination of the reality shows *Jersey Shore, Too Hot to Handle* and *Survivor*. Students and faculty are intoxicated with ideas or alcohol, or both, but are also vulnerable to being voted out of the tribe. Every interaction between faculty members and students is potentially incendiary. A humorous comment or a flirtatious touch can flare into accusations of favoritism and sexual exploitation. The authorities have to keep a balance between the need to keep order and the need to encourage discussion and freedom of thought, and this takes place at a time when everyone on campus walks around with a device in their pocket that gives them dizzying knowledge, instant porn, social connectivity, and access to wisdom and craziness that is borderless. Plus the devices can capture unguarded and embarrassing moments that can be twisted, then broadcast to millions.

This is a battlefield never experienced before, where a word spoken in anger or a dangerous idea can set off a tussle that within days can develop into a media conflagration that is global. Institutions need to safeguard their reputation and, therefore, the path of least resistance is to catch skirmishes early, smother the alleged perpetrator and quietly bury them.

Many students and faculty work away in laboratories and libraries, preoccupied with the joy of research and discovery. Bewildered by the commotions around campus, they stay quiet, hoping that intelligent debate and decorum will at some point gain the upper hand.

Even nonpolitical books, written in the spirit of personal achievement, expose the rifts between contrasting tribal journeys. For instance, Tara Westover's *Educated: A Memoir*, published in 2018, was a bestseller from the start. For many readers the book was about the triumphs of education: "An exhilarating account of how she liberated herself from a strict Mormon household who taught her to reject the government, the school system, science and books other than the Bible, and then ending up with a Cambridge Ph.D." The online reviews reveal the schism. Although the book validates the Climb Higher tribal journey, reviewers espousing the Hold Firm perspective interpreted the book as a betrayal of her family and a misrepresentation of her upbringing, stating the book is "pure fiction," "a very public charade" and by "an excellent writer, who takes you as a fool to believe this is true."

Each tribal journey has deep roots in competing philosophies, and with the perspective of consilience we can see their shortcomings. Climb Higher is rooted in the dreams of modernist thinkers who believe we can progress toward a realm of higher reason. This philosophy imagines that through science-like theories we can understand how everything works and take control — including taking control of human nature and society. The shortcomings of this approach include that it blocks a realistic understanding of human behavior and does not account for the capriciousness of life. The Gather Together tribal journey is energized by postmodern thinkers who argue that modernist conceptions of science and society are constructed with language dictated by those in power. Their philosophy can be seen as a validation of personal journeys and the dynamics of the social sciences, rather than being about time-proven truths. The Hold Firm tribal journey is rooted in the virtues of scriptural practice and the writings of saints, priests, rhabbis, imams and mystics. One does not need to look far to find examples of corruption and depravity carried out under the cover of religion.

The predominant tribal journeys in academia are Climb Higher, with its upward journey of increasing rationality and knowledge, and Gather Together, with its narrative of inclusivity, tolerance and equality. Taken together, the idea of leaving behind the injustices of the past and moving toward a place of higher reason, personal fulfillment and social justice has appeal. It points to a time when environmental challenges are solved and right-wing extremism is eliminated, bringing society to a place of stability and contentment. Increasingly, the voices arguing for these progressive, secular, humanist tribal journeys have become overpowering. They characterize their opponents as anti-intellectual, anti-science and alt-right, a movement intent on taking humanity back to an era of religious crusades and medieval social inequalities.

The progressive, combined movement of Climb Higher and Gather Together has given rise to a new form of vigilantism, one that labels opposing views as sexist, racist and anti-reason. Those holding nonconforming views are prevented from speaking on campuses because of concern about the mental health and safety of students. In its milder form, this response is referred to as political correctness. In its activist form, this is known as call-out culture, cancel culture and woke. Anyone who is male and white, irrespective of their behavior, is viewed as occupying the top of a hierarchy of sex, race and privilege.

The hotbed for progressive activism is the social sciences, including feminist studies, sociology, psychology, politics and teacher education. A subculture of professional associations and academic journals hold conferences and publish papers that are unintelligible to outsiders and don't illuminate the day-to-day realities of most people's lives. The culture of social justice has seeped into mainstream academic journals. Researchers whose findings contradict progressive outlooks are shut out.

If progressive activism was restricted to academia it would be of little concern to everyone else. It has, however, taken hold among graduating students, and they are teaching it to subsequent generations. The three tribes are becoming increasingly irritated with each other. Fortifications are being built; intellectual and real ammunition is being stockpiled.

The divide between tribal narratives is instantly discernible in the everyday press. A few decades ago, the mainstream news outlets had the financial muscle to pay journalists to investigate local and challenging subjects. Journalists could spend weeks or months exploring unorthodox perspectives and explain unfolding current events from new angles. With declining advertising revenue, journalists are now expected to create short articles that can compete with the clickbait that continually pops up on mobile devices. Longer articles that go deeper than the dominant tribal narratives cannot compete in the "race to the bottom of the brainstem," to borrow the words of Tristan Harris, Google's former design ethicist.

Presumably, scientific findings should be beyond the reach of social extremists. Science is founded on the belief that facts are facts. Good science should be immune to the biases of race, gender and politics. There are, however, well-established trenches and barbed-wire demarcations between disciplines. Particularly vulnerable are scientists dealing with the science of human behavior.

An early casualty is the bookish Harvard University professor, Edward O. Wilson. He is an unlikely victim because he is a gentle soul and an arch environmentalist, whose first love is social insects — ants in particular. Social insects, including honey bees, wasps and termites are fascinating because, even in colonies of millions of individuals, they are wonderfully well organized. A well-defined division of labor exists within each colony, and, curiously, they are organized without an organizer. The queen does not reign over her subjects; instead, she is not much more than an egg-laying machine. Wilson studied how the insects signal to each other by using about 20 different pheromones and through touch. It is indisputable that their behavior is programmed by their genes rather than arising through learning.

Wilson realized that many of the principles he observed in the colonies of social insects were likely at work in other animal societies. He published a book in 1975 called *Sociobiology*. A large textbook, designed for biology students, it summarized research into animal behavior, especially its genetic basis. The book was written for an academic audience and was largely uncontroversial. At the end of the book, almost as an afterthought, Wilson included a short chapter on human behavior that drew parallels between animal behavior and human social organization. In it, he summarized what was known at the time about aspects of human behavior, such as communication, barter, division of labor, bonding, culture, religion, war, ethics, esthetics and tribalism. Although the book was written by a scientist with a deep commitment to measurement and observation, as well as a humanistic love of nature, the author had strayed into the territory of the social sciences.

Social studies have adopted modernist, top-down, scientific ways of thinking. With this perspective, human society can be conceptualized as a cultural system with hierarchies and power. Society can be pictured in a way that's reminiscent of how physicists and chemists use the periodic table to arrange the elements.

Wilson's approach challenged the underpinnings of the discipline of sociology, and his book *Sociobiology* was the short end of a very big wedge. At a symposium on animal behavior, protesters tipped a jug of ice water over his head, chanting, "Wilson, you're all wet!" The incident might have been explained away as the reaction of a political fringe had there not been intellectual attacks by his Harvard University colleagues, led by Gould, the paleontologist mentioned earlier, and Lewontin, a leading geneticist. Their arguments spilled over into *The New York Review of Books,* and became public and political.

Wilson had given birth to the fledgling discipline of *sociobiology,* but it was snuffed out before taking its first breath.

The border between the life sciences and social studies is marked by the question of nature versus nurture mentioned in chapter 16. How much of human behavior can be explained scientifically?

In a 2018 debate, professor Bret Weinstein asked Dawkins about the connection between natural selection and the behavior of the Germans and Russians in the lead up to World War II. Dawkins, author of *The Selfish Gene,* responded, "I'm not sure that it's actually very helpful to talk about [nationalism] in Darwinian terms. I think perhaps this might be a case where we need to defer a little bit to historians and nonbiologists, and think about it in other ways." Coming from a standard-bearer of scientific rationalism, this response is startling. If Dawkins is correct, it means that geneticists and evolutionary psychologists cannot throw light on the most important questions that confront societies.

During the debate, Bret Weinstein made the point that "the belief structures that cause people to step onto battlefields and fight were clearly comprehensible as adaptations of the lineages in question." Weinstein, an evolutionary theorist, also made it clear that the reasons for the evolution of tribal behaviors are readily understandable. The previous year, as a professor of biology at Evergreen State College, a liberal institution in Washington State, he had spoken out against a racist Day of Absence. He had written: "On a college campus, one's right to speak — or to be — must never be based on skin color."

Although he was standing up to racism, he was labeled as a bigot — succumbed to the forces of political correctness — and was thrown out.

If the sociologists are correct and pitiless behavior occurs because, for example, Hitler used ideologies spelled out in *Mein Kampf* to subvert German society, then it would be reasonable to conclude that freedom of speech should be curtailed to guard against the reemergence of extremism. On the other hand, if societies are emergent from the behaviors of their members, the current state of discourse is reminiscent of the early days of social conformism in Germany in the 1920s.

To understand these matters we need to fly higher to see the entire landscape and disregard the boundaries between academic disciplines.

22

Consilience in History

Summarizing the historical development of consilience and a philosophical divergence that resulted in an intellectual chasm between the sciences and the humanities.

IN 1998 I PICKED UP A COPY OF *CONSILIENCE: The Unity of Knowledge* by Wilson. Bruised from his tangle about sociobiology with his fellow academics, he wrote, "If history and science have taught us anything, it is that passion and desire are not the same as truth." He dreamed of the day when truth would prevail, uniting science with the humanities.

I was intrigued because I have never believed that science, the arts and human culture exist in disconnected domains. Nor have I believed that faith and science are incompatible. When I learn about different religions and cultures, I attempt to understand them historically and experientially. In my marketing communications discipline, we have to deal with the real world and real people, whatever their beliefs. It would be counterproductive and frankly insulting if we discounted large sections of the populace who hold viewpoints different from our own.

Perhaps Wilson was on the brink of a new way of understanding, and the flourishing disciplines of evolutionary biology, paleontology, neurophysiology and genetics would enable the unification of the sciences, the humanities and social sciences.

Consilience is arriving, but not in the way Wilson imagined. It is happening because of breakthroughs in many different fields.

Advances in mathematics and computing have shown that systems of unbelievable beauty and complexity can be derived from repeated calculations of extreme simplicity. Physicists have discovered that the universe and everything in it, even when particles do not exist, is quantum in nature.

Historians have documented the complexities of the world and humanity's alarming lack of understanding of our vulnerabilities. Philosophers and linguists have described the significance of metaphors, providing abundant examples of how people have made sense of the world through the ages and how that understanding has, on occasion, changed dramatically and unpredictably.

Anthropologists, ethologists, primatologists and ecologists have uncovered details about how *Homo sapiens* evolved, and how our social dispositions and language are inescapably tribal. Economists and psychologists have realized that humans, even in aggregate, don't behave according to simplistic, science-like laws. Yet, paradoxically, statistics helps expose patterns of human behavior that are indistinguishable from those seen in nature.

The work of geologists, paleontologists, archeologists and climate scientists has revealed the course of evolution over long time scales as well as the effects of climate change. The work of neuroscientists and physiologists have been figuring out how human neuronal mechanisms work, notwithstanding the mainstream belief that the brain functions like a computer that stores and processes information.

Scientists have probed the workings of cells using extremely powerful technologies that allow them to see molecules and how they interact, which has led to the fusing of the disciplines of chemistry, physics, biology and genetics. This has revealed that the magic that enables human ingenuity — the workings of cells and their power to organize themselves into organisms — evolved a billion years ago and are shared with every other multicellular animal on the planet. Consciousness evolved because of the practical necessity for organisms to build a picture of the things around them and react preemptively. Consciousness is not a recent miracle.

— ▪ ○ ● ○ ▪ —

Consilience is happening because courageous individuals are exploring new ways of making sense of the social trends we have been witnessing and they have been encouraging open debate. Many others have followed their own personal journey and created threads between disciplines that were previously disconnected. In some cases their breakthrough ideas have been the result of nontraditional career progressions and grit spurred by personal adversity.

One example is Erich Jarvis, currently an associate professor of neurobiology at The Rockefeller University. Growing up in Harlem, Jarvis studied ballet at the High School of Performing Arts and became a professional dancer before switching to science. "I found it quite natural to transition from being a dancer to a scientist," he states, "Both required discipline, creativity, hard work, and often you have to accept failure before something works."

Jarvis is employing the new tools of science to draw the family tree of various families of birds and to probe the expression of genes involved in comprehending and generating speech. He has shown that areas in a bird's brain that allow them to sing are, at a genetic level, similar to areas in the human brain responsible for speech. In birds, these areas are close to the part of the brain that controls hopping, which is why parrots can bop along to music. By contrast, in chimp brains the neurons concerned with moving their limbs are not interconnected with those controlling their vocal apparatus. Chimps cannot talk, and it is not a coincidence that they cannot dance either. The neural connections exist in humans — so we both speak and dance.

Jarvis's personal journey to uncovering the evolutionary connections in the brain between speech and movement was spurred by challenges and tragedy, which he recounts to inspire others. His father suffered from drug-induced schizophrenia and was murdered in a gang initiation ritual.

Generations before and born on a different continent, the inventor of the word *consilience*, Whewell, also followed a noteworthy journey from a humble Lancashire household, where his father was a carpenter and his mother a poet, to the highest echelons of British intellectual society. He became Master of Trinity College, Cambridge, and was an Anglican priest, a poet and a mathematician. He wrote extensively on diverse subjects, including mechanics, mineralogy, geology, astronomy, political economy, educational reform, international law, architecture and the nature of scientific discovery. He thought up words that we use to this day: including *scientist, physicist, linguistics, electrode, anode, cathode, ion, catastrophism* and *astigmatism*. The words *genius* and *polymath* when used to describe Whewell are understatements.

He mused about consilience at a time before battlelines had formed between religion and science. In the mid-1800s, public intellectuals viewed religion and science as mutually affirming domains. In his extraordinarily articulate and logical way of thinking, science and theology were aligned: "[Belief] grows stronger by an actual study of the details of creation," he wrote.

He could see how the disciplines of mathematics and astronomy were fertilizing each other and that physics was merging with chemistry. He was cordial with Darwin, and realized the characteristics of animals might one day be understood scientifically. When a scientist conceived a theory, or as he termed it, an *induction*, unrelated observations were united together. He believed the same thing would happen with different arenas of human knowledge. He expressed this "jumping together" of knowledge thus:

> The Consilience of Inductions takes place when an Induction, obtained from one class of facts, coincides with an Induction, obtained from another different class. This Consilience is a test of the truth of the Theory in which it occurs.

Whewell's explanation of the process of scientific discovery, the nature of ideas and human society are aligned with the ideas in this book, although, as you can note, the terms used are markedly different.

In the mid-1800s, a philosophy very different from Whewell's gathered momentum. Its chief proponent, John Stuart Mill, was a British philosopher, political economist and civil servant. He has been called "the most influential English-speaking philosopher of the nineteenth century." He believed that logic and reason existed independently from language and that ideas conform to the "law of the three stages," where every field progresses from religious superstition, then to the metaphysical and finally to the scientific.

Mill's philosophies underpin the Climb Higher tribal journey. A contradiction is, however, embedded in his logic. On the one hand he dismisses religious superstition, but on the other he continues to employ ideas of Descartes that suppose there is a realm of logic and reason that stands apart from the human brain and the stuff of life — a realm of pure disembodied thought where ideas exist like angels.

During their lifetime, Whewell and Mill debated their contrasting philosophies, but after their death Mill's ideas eclipsed those of Whewell. A crack had developed in the prevailing view of the world: on one side, the humanities, arts, religion, and the delights and challenges of everyday social interaction; on the other, and seemingly unrelated, secular, logical positivism, set apart from emotion and subjectivity. The realm of pure reason, both appealing and highly functional, paved the way for mathematicians, physicists, chemists and engineers to build the infrastructure of modern life.

Since Whewell's death in 1866, the sciences have progressively taken over territory previously the concern of religion and the humanities. Science has become pointified, with scientists routinely caricaturing religion as belief in the supernatural and the humanities as merely entertainment.

In 1958, a British scientist and novelist, C.P. Snow, published *The Two Cultures*. He observed that "the intellectual life of the whole of western society" had become split into "two cultures." He noted how scientists don't care about Shakespeare and nonscientists don't have any interest in the second law of thermodynamics.

—▪ ○ ● ○ ▪—

Consilience is a new way of thinking because it makes a sharp distinction between the material things of the universe — that is, the particles that physicists describe that constitute matter — and the ideas the human mind employs. I term the material things *reality,* whereas mental conceptualizations I broadly term *ideas.* By employing this sharp distinction, we can reason more objectively than before, yet at the same time recognize the value and power of ideas.

Consilience does not mean the same as *third culture,* a term coined by the New York-based scientific publicist, John Brockman, who presumes the sanctity of science, particularly ideas emanating from the northeastern universities.

Also, consilience should not be confused with the *Theory of Everything,* which is the dream of physicists and cosmologists to describe everything in the universe, including quantum effects, dark energy, black holes and gravity, with a single mathematical theory. Nor is consilience the same as *singularity,* a hypothetical point in time at which technological growth becomes uncontrollable and irreversible, resulting in unforeseeable changes to human civilization.

It would indeed be pleasing if consilience could be equated with higher states of consciousness and the forward progression of human civilization; however, I believe that conception would be dangerous. Instead, consilience forces us to recognize the fallibilities of the human mind, the fragility of society and the value derived from different domains of human existence, including spirituality and religious practices. While consilience can sensitize us to the complexities of human ideas, it also makes it easier to recognize statements that are unjustifiably dogmatic, wherever they come from. In my case, I have become less tolerant of them.

Religion and spirituality continue to play a treasured part in many people's lives. While attendance at church has decreased, many people celebrate religious holidays, and births, marriages and deaths are presided over by religious officials. Over half the adults in the world say religion is "very important" to them. Religion isn't going away, but some members of the Climb Higher and Gather Together tribes portray religion as a throwback to an age before the ascendancy of reason. For example, the late Christopher Hitchens, author of the bestseller *god is not Great,* has argued that organized religion is "the main source of hatred in the world"; and Dawkins, a fellow Oxford University intellectual, claims it is "one of the world's great evils."

Dawkins states, "I am against religion because it teaches us to be satisfied with not understanding the world." He appears to be unaware that the neuronal label *religion* was invented within the past 500 years, more than 1,000 years after people began to pattern their lives according to scriptures. For clarification, we need to ask him, "What do you mean by *religion*? Do you mean Christianity, Judaism, Islam, Hinduism, Buddhism, Confucianism and Taoism?" They are not the same, and the last four have nothing much to do with God. "If you mean Islam, are you referring to Sunni, Shia or Kharijite? And which aspects in particular? Do you mean the social aspects and unifying beliefs, which are, to some degree, logical? Are you referring to humility, a hallmark of Islamic practice?" If so, Dawkins would benefit from a dab of it.

By *religion,* perhaps he means institutions that have faith in a supernatural power. If so, what sort of power is he discounting? As a scientist, Dawkins presumably believes in *entropy*. But since he has never seen or been able to directly measure it, why doesn't he count that as supernatural?

What does Dawkins understand *science* to be? He would likely relate science to his personal experiences at Oxford University, where faculty members have a tradition of engaging in highly ritualized bouts of intellectual fencing, thrusting, parrying and scoring points for humor and cultural erudition. The player with the idea that withstands the cuts of Occam's foil wins.

To explain science, Dawkins would most likely refer to the *ideology* of science, where ideas exist independently of the human mind and can be arrived at through discovery and reason. But the ideology of science is a belief, not reality. Dawkins would likely *not* refer to the reality that scientific journals must cater to their markets, and the peer review process is sometimes a ritual of mutual affirmation and back-scratching. He would likely not refer to the many scientific ideas that were accepted wisdom for long periods, but with hindsight are clearly nutty, a few of which are alchemy, aether, phrenology, geocentric Earth, bloodletting, radium treatments, lobotomies, Lysenkoism and, perhaps, string theory. Another is the four humors — blood, phlegm, yellow bile and black bile — that physicians believed governed human health and were the basis of mainstream Western medicine for over a thousand years.

The advent of consilience along with a recognition of how neuronal systems work allows us to see that thinking exhibits biases and forms misleading concepts. One such bias is that *facts* are unrelated to *beliefs*. At the level of neurons, however, sensations are not separated from emotions. If a sensation has no utility it will not stick. Therefore, every categorization, fact and belief has some degree of emotional salience. By arranging sensations and ideas together, the brain is using a shortcut to deal with the constant impressions we receive from the complexity of the world around us.

The word *brain* itself is a shortcut. Does it refer to the high school science textbook definition of a discrete organ set apart in the human body? Yes, it probably does. But that is a misleading concept. A more accurate conception of the word *brain* is a living mass of cells existing on the edge of criticality, perfused with a broth of nutrients and neurochemicals, that cannot function without the steady stream of impulses from the peripheral nervous system and the senses.

When I started to examine the concept of consilience as it relates to human behavior, I felt that every word I used should be put in quotes. When I write the word *science*, do I refer to science as a brand representing logical, rational investigation — a perspective held by many? Or do I refer to its consilience meaning, which is the real-life, often messy collection of disconnected ideas that the tribe of scientists stands guard over in the pursuit of certainty?

When nonscientists stray into scientific territory, some see this as a threat to scientific beliefs. For example, Dr. Dave Speijer, professor at the University of Amsterdam and an expert on the early evolution of organisms, wrote an article for *BioEssays*, a journal that calls for the use of clear markers of hostile content — "mandatory color coded banners warning of consistent factual errors or unscientific content, masquerading as science." He wishes to fight the "urgent problems with regard to confidence in vaccines," as well as "the example of climate science, which is well known."

When Speijer refers to "vaccines" and "climate science," he is *not* referring to the complexities and uncertainties related to immunology and the earth's climate. Instead, he is using terms that have become weaponized by opposing tribal journeys.

The paradigm of consilience can be thought of as a metalandscape that contains all journeys that people follow, including those that are scientific, political, sociological, artistic and religious. This metalandscape also contains a rapidly growing comprehension of the realities of human biology and social dependencies. As much as possible, and contrary to human instincts, we need to avoid making generalizations and facile judgments.

There is no harm in sympathizing with intellectuals who wish to fend off stupidity. At the same time, the dangers of censorship need to be pointed out. And we must ask, precisely whom would we trust to pronounce on what is correct? And what scientific evidence can Speijer point to that proves the censors can dissociate themselves from the pressures of their social circumstances?

— ▪ ○ 23 ○ ▪ —

Artifacts of Thinking

Quirks of our thought processes prevent us from seeing the limits of our understanding. The discipline of economics provides an example of overconfidence in people's ability to understand and control complex systems. It also shows how ideas are unavoidably personal and political.

CONSILIENCE IS FOUNDED ON THE FACT that reality is what it is. It can be known through direct observation, without the need to generalize and use labels. And, at least in theory, it could be possible to figure out the history of how reality came to be in the first few moments following the big bang. But the whole matter of human knowledge is challenging because of artifacts of the functioning of the human mind.

What do I mean by *artifacts* of how the mind works?

The first time I used a scanning electron microscope to look at brain tissue, I saw a fibrous smudge that could have been anything and was certainly nothing like the diagrams in the textbooks. This was during a second-year course at university, and Dr. Manning pointed out to his students some blurry shapes that looked like hairy plant roots. They were the neurons, the nerves of the brain. He had taught us how neurons transmitted impulses by firing *action potentials* across their cell walls, but at the time we didn't understand their complexity. He also pointed out the switch-like synapses. "Those are probably synapses," he said, pointing to some dots. "But," he cautioned, "you should know that there is some controversy about what the dots are. They could be artifacts."

It was startling to hear that we couldn't be absolutely sure of what we were looking at down a sophisticated microscope. When Dr. Manning talked of an "artifact," he meant that the very act of placing brain tissue in the microscope changed it, creating features that in the living animal might not have been there. For us to be able to see the brain tissue using a microscope, the tissue had to be altered — it had to be "fixed" to prevent decomposition, then set in resin to hold it firmly in place, and then sliced into very thin sheets by using a sharp glass blade. As well, chemicals were added to deflect the electron beam so an image of the brain tissue would register on a screen. Consequently, the tiny dots we saw might not have been synapses at all, but instead might have been the result of some kind of chemical reaction, possibly bubbles of gas or lumps of protein curdled by the chemicals.

We use our neural systems to perceive reality and, like the use of a scanning electron microscope that at the time was the only way for us to see the details of brain matter, it is challenging to recognize the difference between reality and artifacts of thinking.

Here is one of the many artifacts of our neural system: our use of words influences our actual experience. The brain creates melodies by putting together similar inputs and adding a label, that is, a word. When I saw smudges on the screen of the electron microscope, what I saw was affected by the fact that I already knew some of these smudges were called *neurons* and others were called *glial cells*. At that time neuroscientists described neurons as analogous to wires and glial cells as a supporting structure, like a plastic circuit board in an electronic device. It turns out there are more glial cells in the brain than neurons and, to date, four different types have been found: oligodendrocytes; astrocytes; ependymal cells; and microglia. Today, neuroscientists looking at a similar brain tissue image as I did years ago would likely see more types of these cells because of these new categorizations.

Glial cells are implicated in a number of brain diseases. Knowing how cells organize themselves — without regard to scientific categorizations —

my hunch is that glial cells are at least as important as neurons, and neuroscientists looking at images of brain tissue decades in the future will observe things differently. It may seem counterintuitive, but knowledge of new categories of cells and their functions will change what scientists see, as has been the case in the past.

A second artifact of neural systems is that we see the point of things, words and ideas, and arrange them accordingly. The brain arranges everything into a landscape that collectively has a point. Things that do not have a point are typically ignored. A person's neuronal landscape is formed during many interactions with other people — particularly close tribal members. When someone comes across ideas that do not serve a personal and collective purpose, these are placed in territories reserved for everything that is stupid, illogical, irrelevant or threatening.

A third artifact is that we take complex subjects and compress them into a single point that has significance for a particular tribe. This leads to no end of disagreement, particularly in matters of politics. When we hear words such as *democracy, capitalism* or *freedom,* we may think we know what they mean. But each of these words represents a massively complex subject, one that could take a lifetime to study, yet each word triggers a momentary feeling of "got it, I understand."

This challenge of understanding a complex subject applies to historical events. Think about the French Revolution, the American War of Independence or the First World War. You may know the causes and outcomes of these wars, but in each case the causes and effects involved many tiny incidents, which have been grouped together and labeled as a particular historical event with the perspective of a particular tribal group. The parts of history are not discrete events divorced from tribal motivations; instead, the goal-directed interactions of many people make up the ongoing unrolling of history.

To illustrate: the event that ended the First World War was the armistice signed on 11 November 1918. History books describe the signing of a document at the nondescript small village of Le Francport in Northern France by the French, British and Germans. This was a deeply meaningful moment in time. But the reality is that the people who walked out of the meeting were no different than when they had entered. That does not diminish the significance of the meeting. The world is still experiencing the results of the treaties that were signed afterward. When the current prime minister of Hungary, Viktor Orbán, makes speeches that irritate left-leaning politicians, undoubtedly, what he says reflects a continuation of the effects of events that occurred those many years ago. The signing of the armistice, marking the start of peace, is a discrete and objective event only in the mind.

A fourth artifact of the neural systems is that the landscape of human behavioral patterns is built from within the tribes we are associated with. For instance, a paragraph such as this, that defines the word *peace* in religious terms, will fractionate readers according to their tribal associations and loyalties. The word peace is derived from the Proto-Indo-European word **paḱ-*, which conveyed the idea of "to fasten or stick in place." At one time it meant "to shut up." In earlier centuries, the meaning of words was strongly influenced by their use in scripture. In the Old Testament, *peace* referred to a cosmic order, ordained by God through creation, and a realm where chaos — that is, sickness, war and social strife — could not enter. In the book of Isaiah, the point is made that peace is reached through a trust in God, rather than the dominance of armies. In the New Testament, Jesus spoke of "peace on earth," seemingly a sociological comment about the need to avoid interpersonal turmoil. The words above will strike practicing Jews and Christians differently than followers of Islamic practice, and those who are agnostic or atheist will react still differently. When we say that the treaty at the end of the First World War brought *peace* in the sense of personal tranquility, our understanding is necessarily and invisibly religious.

Let's consider how the four artifacts of neural systems play into each other in a social context. Earlier, using the example of psychology, I described how a single discipline made up of many ideas becomes pointified. Now I'll use the discipline of economics to illustrate how the artifacts of the mind have far-reaching consequences, not only on personal perceptions but also on public policy.

The discipline of economics got its start when the Scottish philosopher and overall genius, Adam Smith, spent his entire life writing two literary works: *The Theory of Moral Sentiments* and *An Inquiry into the Nature and Causes of the Wealth of Nations.* These two works consisted of eight and five books, respectively. Smith's aim in writing these books was to counter the prevailing view that trade was a means of acquiring wealth, much as a squirrel would collect nuts for winter from a limited supply. If the squirrel model of trade was correct, Scotland would be vulnerable to England taking its wealth and leaving many of its citizens as peasants. Smith's views laid the foundation for the market economy that encouraged trade and helped people of England, Scotland and all Western countries eliminate hunger and live relatively comfortably since that time. His books are feats of wisdom, candor and humor, with insights about human conduct and the dynamics of organizations that have not been matched since the books were published 240 years ago.

His many nuanced ideas have been condensed to simple ideas, such as "the invisible hand" and "division of labor," which have been used as ammunition in political arguments for both free market capitalism and socialism. Little by little, the discipline of economics ceased to take into account the complexity of individual behavior, instead treating people in the aggregate as "markets" that can be understood through the use of mathematical equations similar to the laws explaining the behavior of groups of particles, that is, the laws of thermodynamics. Economics has adopted the tenets of evolutionary science to visualize human beings as operating according to Darwinian principles in order to maximize their benefit or, to use the jargon, their "marginal utility."

It is affirming for both teachers of economics and their students to believe that the complexities of people can be understood by applying relatively simple theories. In this case, *Homo economicus* — or *Econs* for short — are imperfect, rational, self-interested agents who seek optimal, utility-maximizing outcomes and are motivated by money. Using science-like logic, aggregations of Econs make up an entity that is referred to as the "economy," which becomes something that can be measured using GDP and per capita incomes. Understanding and manipulating these measures has become the point of economics. Smith's wide-ranging observations on the complexities of human financial interactions have been turned into a quasi-science, with the objective to control an entity — the economy — that did not exist before.

This pointified view of human nature deviates from actual human conduct in many ways. Foremost is that human beings do not behave like Econs. Much of what people do is the result of factors other than money. People coalesce into social groupings to study books, enjoy music, drink expensive wine, listen to sermons, play sports, attempt to fish, build wonderful things for the fun of it, and act with extreme generosity and selflessness. They'll even climb over the lip of a trench toward enemy guns, facing certain death, without being paid a nickel. The idea that human beings are either entirely rational or entirely irrational does not accord with the reality that people sometimes buy things they don't need, fall in love with strangers, act cruelly to family members, have children and spend hours playing video games for no economic benefit.

The example of economics exposes a fifth artifact of thinking: we overestimate our ability to understand complex systems. Economic theories are a useful tool, but they are easy to overapply. Because an economist can manipulate the parameters in macroeconomic equations of supply and demand, it leads them to believe they can manipulate the economy in much the same way as an engineer controls the workings of an engine. Theories are inherently top-down, but economies are systems that operate from the bottom up. Markets conform to economic theories only under particular, restricted conditions.

Modern economics at an undergraduate level is explained by top-down generalizations and theories. Its practitioners follow well-trodden paths and in the process they overlook the interpersonal complexity of economic transactions. Money is not only a means of trading goods and services, but also a mode of communication – on many levels. Buying and selling things is subject to the quirks of relationships where people express themselves and imitate, leading to booms and bubbles in markets that repeatedly demonstrate the madness of crowds. Economies can only be understood as emergent systems that result from the conduct of individuals. Smith would not recognize modern economics. He understood that human *conduct* is complex and purposeful. He never used the generalizing word *behavior*.

Recently, economists have been taking the actual behavior of humans into account in the growing discipline of behavioral economics. Psychologist Daniel Kahneman and the late Amos Tversky have shown that people do not behave like Econs. For instance, people are possessive of the stuff they already own, which is neither rational nor irrational.

Nonetheless, the pointification of economics has effects that feed back onto itself. Those who learn about economic theory view people around them as acting like Econs, so they become more like that themselves. The habits and attitudes of economics professors and students have been well studied, and, compared to noneconomists, they give less to charities, are less ethical, are more accepting of greed and less concerned about fairness. They feel justified in this behavior because they are less trusting and believe that people are inherently selfish. Nobel Prize-winner Richard Thaler jokes that wherever the American Economic Association holds their annual conference, restaurant waiters should leave town because economists are notoriously stingy tippers.

A sixth artifact of thinking is that we use metaphors without realizing that in doing so we associate dissimilar things and treat them as equivalent. There is no better example than the subject of money.

A textbook definition of money says it's a medium of exchange that conveniently allows for trade of different items. Another way of thinking about money is that it is a shared belief in common value, so that pieces of paper printed with the same dollar bill motif are considered equivalent, even if some of them are crisp and others tattered.

Consider other meanings of money we intuitively know about, but rarely acknowledge. Money is a signal of appreciation. Giving a tip for a product or service transfers some economic value, as well as a money-where-your-mouth-is way of saying thank you. The nuances, however, vary with different cultures. In some parts of the world, leaving a tip is viewed in the same way as if you pulled out your wallet after visiting a friend's house and offered to pay for the cup of coffee they served you. It would be insulting.

Money can be used as a signal of social status. Someone who wants to demonstrate their wealth and show their station in life might give a large gratuity or donation. Money is also an expression of love, as when a parent gives their child a check when they go off to college. It is also sometimes an expression of commitment, as with a down payment on a house or a marriage dowry. Money is also used as a sexual signal. Males in particular exhibit their appeal by having money or showing what they have bought with it. A Ferrari is no better for navigating the streets of New York and London than a Honda Civic, but the Ferrari's main purpose is not transportation.

The various meanings of money are personal, but they are also controversial, because money is used to trade labor and, by implication, is a measure of one's personal worth and power relative to someone else's. For example, when two 30-year-old females who are physically similar stand side by side, what is their relative worth? If one is a well-educated lawyer, she can value an hour of her time at $500, whereas a caregiver's pay is valued at closer to $15 an hour. The lawyer has more freedom and power than the caregiver who is scraping by. The political and social implications are apparent; is such disparity fair? And what happens when the lawyer leaves the workforce to have a baby — what is her time worth then?

When someone uses money, its meaning depends on the context in which it is used and the motivations of the people involved. Money is a significant matter to nearly everyone, but discussing its many meanings is inevitably awkward because the very act of discussing it alters its meaning. Pointing out that money is valuable because it is metaphorical provokes a query about its apparent solidity. Acknowledging that it is a signal of hierarchy and power or a sexual signal immediately changes one's relationship to it and to the people who know what you are thinking.

We cannot avoid the artifacts of thinking. This means it is challenging to discuss the meanings of things that are significant to us, such as money — even if we aspire to objectivity — because each of us is personally, unavoidably, implicated in the matter.

24

Power and Social Justice

The social sciences have conceptualized society as a system of power hierarchies, thereby aggravating tribal divisions. Postmodernism was a move away from top-down categorizations.

IN FEBRUARY 2020 I WAS MOUNTAIN BIKING IN ECUADOR with a group of friends, whom we self-mockingly call the *Moab Ridazz*. The last thing on my mind as we traversed through lush forests, volcanic high terrain, around crater lakes and through Quicha villages was the possibility of writing a book. The year was shaping up to be busy, with my older daughter planning a wedding for May and my training trips with Aleks Gusev in preparation for a November rafting trip down the Karnali River in Nepal.

When I arrived back in Toronto everything changed. The world was locking down. In my newsfeed I saw accounts of dead bodies piling up in the streets of Quito, Ecuador's capital city, where we had strolled the previous week oblivious to news about the pandemic.

A few months earlier I had become interested in the issue of global warming after my company, as a side project, had helped a client run a seminar reporting on climate science. At the event I met Patrick Moore, one of the founders of Greenpeace. His perspectives on climate change contradicted accounts in the press. He cannot be classified as an armchair environmentalist as he has a doctorate in ecology and in his 20s helped sail an old fishing trawler into nuclear test zones that led ultimately to a comprehensive ban of nuclear weapons testing. After that he faced down harpoon guns to draw attention to the imminent extinction of large whales. I wanted to make up my own mind about anthropogenic global warming, so I began reading scientific papers and studying the history of the movement. I downloaded raw climate data for the United States, the United Kingdom and Canada from their meteorological service websites to analyze for myself. I was struck by the disparity between the clear-cut narrative in the press and the wild fluctuations evident in the actual data.

During the first few weeks of the lockdown I noticed that journalists, unable to get out to research topics firsthand, would parrot the talking points from public figures and echo the chatter on their social media feeds. The lack of insight about the political situation and social issues was so glaring that I stopped following the news. In its place I read articles published by *Quillette*, *Quanta* and other online journals, as well as following longform lectures and podcasts posted by all sorts of independent thinkers.

In the process, I witnessed how various groups were fracturing society with increasingly extreme viewpoints and mutual antagonism. Several people I was following online, who in my view were well informed and open to constructive dialogue, became subject to aggressive, coordinated campaigns to discredit them. Accused of being nazi, racist, sexist, homophobic — or attacked with other slurs and threatened with physical violence — they were often deplatformed.

An early example was Peterson. I came across one of his lectures on YouTube in 1999, posted by one of his students. He was articulate in explaining that our sense of reality is constructed in the brain. I hadn't seen a similar view expressed anywhere else, so I tried to find papers he'd written on the subject. I found nothing, so I forgot about him until 2016 when he appeared in headlines as the target of student demonstrations about gender pronouns. Most academics under similar circumstances would retreat quietly. He did the opposite and became the foremost critic of academia's embrace of "postmodern neo-Marxist" ideologies, as he labels them. His books and lectures were passionate, and his positions were well supported. At the time I did not understand why he was attacked so viciously, with *The Guardian* newspaper labeling him right-wing and saying "his arguments are riddled with 'pseudo-facts' and conspiracy theories," and *Jacobin,* a magazine that calls itself a leading voice of the American left, writing that "he's full of shit."

A growing movement — mainly of young people — is concerned about injustices in society and believes the way to fix them is by changing the system and muzzling dissenting voices. The various movements have been gaining momentum and, in the words of the economic historian, Niall Ferguson, the situation has become "a hideous mania, a cross between the early-modern witch craze and Mao's Cultural Revolution, in which implacable zealots conduct grotesque show trials, innocent individuals have their reputations, careers and sanity destroyed, and everyone else cowers, terrified that they will be next to be 'canceled.'" The so-called social justice movement is supported by a set of ideological and philosophical scholarship emanating from the social sciences.

In 2017, three people — magazine editor Helen Pluckrose, mathematician James Lindsay and philosopher Peter Boghossian — immersed themselves in social justice terminology and its "religious architecture" as they term it. They wrote 20 fake papers using its concepts and methods to document research findings that, as Pluckrose writes, "were identically methodologically shoddy, devoid of evidence or reason and ethically abhorrent." They submitted their papers to high-profile journals in fields including gender studies, queer studies and fat studies. One called *Our Struggle is My Struggle* was a translation into social justice terminology of Hitler's *Mein Kampf* multipoint requirements for Nazi party membership. Before they were unmasked, seven of their papers had been accepted for publication. Seven more were still going through various stages of the review process. Only six were rejected.

In the book, *Cynical Theories: How Activist Scholarship Made Everything about Race, Gender, and Identity — and Why This Harms Everybody,* Pluckrose and Lindsay sum up in this way:

> There is a problem that begins in our universities, and it comes down to Social Justice. The most immediate aspect of the problem is that Social Justice scholarship gets passed down to students, who then go out into the world. This effect is strongest within Social Justice fields, which teach students to be skeptical of science, reason, and evidence; to regard knowledge as tied to identity; to read oppressive power dynamics into every interaction; to politicize every facet of life; and to apply ethical principles unevenly, in accordance with identity.

My way of making sense of these movements and the divisions between political parties is different from the accounts commonly reported. I certainly don't see them as a battle between members of the left wing and the right wing that will be settled when one side or the other wins. Nor do I see them as an ideological battle between postmodernism and its approach of deconstructing the meaning of words versus the scientific certainty of modernism. Instead, I view everything through the lens of consilience that takes into account the dynamics of academia, the complexities of people, how they perceive the world and their individual life journeys.

Let's start by observing that the scientific insights recounted in this book, *How to Understand Everything* — about sensory perception, the role of words, social interaction and human feelings about hierarchies — are largely aligned with the writings of the pioneers of postmodernism: Foucault and Jacques Derrida.

The philosophies of postmodernism were in part created to displace the certainties of scientific, modernistic ways of thinking that contributed to the extreme racism of the two world wars and gave rise to Marxist regimes in the Soviet Union and in China that, far from creating a paradise for workers, resulted in the imprisoning of intellectuals and the starvation of tens of millions of their citizens.

Corroborating the theories of the postmodernists, the biological foundations of consilience enable us to see that the categorizations we use to make sense of our perceptions and the labels we attach to things are simplifications. Both postmodernism and consilience call into question the certainties of simplistic theories as they apply to people. Many "isms" — that is, Marxism, scientism, communism, socialism, capitalism and environmentalism — are banners used by the different tribal journeys, and they need to be deconstructed in order to figure out which parts are useful versus the parts that are shortsighted or self-serving.

The label *postmodernism* is itself an example of simplification. Foucault wrote 12 books, collaborated on several others, and gave many lectures and interviews. Derrida was prolific in the extreme, publishing more than 90 books and papers and eventually becoming a celebrity who was interviewed often on French TV. To bundle all their ideas together, treat them as a coherent body of knowledge and label them *postmodern* is a mental shorthand that ignores the authors' individual circumstances and the multiplicity of their ideas.

The academics in sociology departments simplify subjects to make them easy to teach and, over time, the subjects become pointified. Rather than just study how societies work, it is far more rewarding to aspire to improve societies. As with the development of marketing theory, the details of how people behave do not follow tidy rules and are difficult to make sense of, so sociologists take a top-down approach and treat society as a "system" of power structures. They use the politically charged and often complex writings of philosophers and theorists to create self-referencing bodies of knowledge that contribute to narratives of the Gather Together tribal journey toward a society of equality and peace.

That it is possible to reconfigure society and eliminate injustices through the application of simple sociological theories is a seductive idea. With the perspectives of consilience, however, we can see that the ideas of *power, systems* and *control* are metaphors, useful in the physical science for describing mechanical or engineered systems, have then been applied to groups of people.

Is the view that society is a system of power hierarchies a universal truth? People in the Middle Ages would not have been able to grasp that way of explaining their situation. The word *power* at that time meant having the ability and strength to do something — a meaning derived from the Latin word *posse,* which means "to be able." The word later took on the meaning of being able to exert influence over the behavior of other people. Three hundred years ago, *power* became a metaphor for energy, and 100 years ago it became used in conjunction with electricity. The power used in cars and homes is an unseen, but useful, physical force. In the 1960s, the word acquired its meaning as a societal force.

The use of the word *power* in its post-1960s meaning combines concepts from widely different domains. It associates an unseen physical force with top-down authority, feelings related to one's position in society and social obligations. These associations involve huge metaphorical leaps.

Most working people in the Middle Ages endured a never-ending struggle to stay warm, put food on the table and stay alive. Death was ever-present and imminent. Diseases of many kinds were common and often fatal, including the plague, dysentery, malaria, diphtheria, flu, typhoid, smallpox and leprosy. Death from hunger, accidents and fire was pervasive. Everyone lived with the fear that thieves, brigands or soldiers might appear, take their property and, for arbitrary reasons, cut them down. Pressures were local, such as payment of tithes and rent at often crippling rates. In every case people's concerns were tangible and immediate. Social hierarchies were well recognized, but the idea that societal "power" was playing a role in their lives would have baffled them.

Was it the power of the state that made my grandfather enlist to fight in World War I? No, it was not. I never had the chance to ask him about this, but he likely would have responded with words such as *duty* and *patriotism* — melodies associated with an array of feelings that can be traced back to human instincts that are part of our evolutionary makeup.

History shows that only minimal encouragement is needed to make people see tribal divisions and take sides. When people are told that a particular group is threatening their security, emotions galvanize abruptly. For example, my friends who lived in the former Yugoslavia used to mix with their neighbors and fellow students without much thought about each other's ethnicity. Then in 1991, within a span of weeks, talking to someone of a different ethnic group became an act of betrayal. People started losing their job because of their ethnic heritage — on occasion only noticeable because of their family name. Then a vicious civil war broke out that resulted in the deaths of 140,000 people.

The goal of understanding humanity and reconciling tribal differences so we can live together productively is surely worthwhile. Such a goal could spur the professors who teach students about society and human behavior to collaborate and organize multidisciplinary conferences of the life sciences, anthropology, history and computing. The collective knowledge from each discipline could help us address the facts of innate tribalism and teach practices that make tribal behavior productive or defuse it.

Politicians and communities need social wisdom, but unfortunately the social sciences create science-like categorizations and teach simplistic science-like theories, thereby igniting student anxieties and exacerbating tribal antagonisms in ways that last a lifetime and permeate society.

Rather than treating people as unique individuals and empowering them with the knowledge and capacity to live productively and harmoniously together, the social sciences do the opposite. Every student wants to be assured their chosen area of study is worthwhile and has utility beyond personal development. Additionally, to strengthen their feelings of self-worth, lecturers and professors ring-fence their area of specialization, with the result that subjects become increasingly pointified — each with the goal of changing society for the better.

Human nature makes it straightforward to draw distinctions between different departments, different philosophical perspectives, classes of citizens, amounts of wealth, differences in power, different races and skin colors, and an array of different genders to create distinct tribes that were not previously top-of-mind. Then it is easy to stir up anger, resentment and envy.

Social scientists fall prey to the human dynamics they should be teaching their students to be wary of. Certain of the correctness of their own ideological landscape, they employ metaphors and emotion-laden narratives delivered with opaque vocabularies, under the banner of Social Justice, to stir up animosities that are insoluble other than by overturning the system.

These ideologies angered Peterson, who said, "You cannot even call them pseudoscience because it is not science, it is just driven by a set of ideological presuppositions... Their goal can be found on their websites which is to bring down the oppressive patriarchal structures of the West by all means possible, including an assault on the basic categories that we used to orient ourselves in the world."

The artifacts of thinking, along with the anxieties of young people, as well as their need to settle on a purpose in life, end up accentuating the tribal rifts in society. The rifts were starkly illustrated in a 2018 interview of Peterson by Cathy Newman on BBC Four. Peterson is an outspoken advocate for the Hold Firm tribal journey and Newman represents Gather Together. From the first question, Newman made it clear the interview would also be about the tribal battle between men and women. She asked, "Does it bother you that your audience is predominantly male? Isn't that a bit divisive?... What's in it for the women?"

Peterson is a clinical psychologist whose videos have been particularly resonant with young males. Newman stated, "You say there are whole disciplines in universities forthrightly hostile toward men. These are the areas of study dominated by the postmodern/neo-Marxist claim that Western culture, in particular, is an oppressive structure, created by white men to dominate and exclude women," adding, "The gender pay-gap stands at just over 9%." In a lengthy exchange, Newman accused Peterson of wishing to hold women back in the workforce, which he denied repeatedly. The exchange became meme-worthy, because Newman prefaced every question with a statement such as "so what you are saying is..." and Peterson responded with "but that isn't what I'm saying." Subsequent media coverage exposed the ideological implications, including Newman's comment on the "appalling levels of misogynistic vilification" and that "social media companies should be taken to task for making so much of the online world a hostile environment for women."

From the standpoint of consilience, the human nervous system operates by making instant judgments about everything of significance. With only an eyeblink of information, we can sense if someone is a threat or sexually appealing. Peterson uses the example of lobsters to argue that animals have known their place in hierarchies since hundreds of millions of years ago. He says, "Lobsters exist in hierarchies and have a nervous system attuned to the hierarchy, and that nervous system runs on serotonin, just like our nervous systems do." He adds that hierarchies "are not a sociological construct of the Western patriarchy."

One questionable detail in Peterson's argument is the word *hierarchy*. Lobster brains do not have a neuronal category labeled hierarchy. Instead, hierarchies are an emergent result of the interaction of individual animals. It makes sense that when one animal squares off against another, before they fight to the death, they anticipate which one is likely to get the upper hand, then act accordingly, either engaging or retreating. The ability to anticipate outcomes in relation to others is deeply plumbed into every animal's nervous system because it reduces the chances of premature death. Lobsters, unlike humans, do not have a clue about where they stand in an overall hierarchy.

Humans have an innate ability to sense how we stack up against one another other along many dimensions. The dimensions are revealed by the words used to describe people, for example, strong–weak, fast–slow, intelligent–unintelligent, beautiful–ugly, hot–unappealing, funny–serious, hardworking–lazy, conscientious–careless, decisive–hesitant, confident–diffident, rich–poor.

Newman gives voice to concern about one's personal standing relative to the people around us. In Dale Carnegie's words, "the deepest principle in human nature is the craving to be appreciated." At the very least, nobody wants to be disrespected, discriminated against or treated unfairly.

Clear hierarchies exist throughout society. Corporate hierarchies include chief executive officers, managing directors, presidents, vice-presidents and on down to interns. Academic institutions have deans, professors, senior instructors, adjunct professors and on down to students. Governments have presidents and prime ministers, councillors and secretaries in a well-ordered hierarchy. The military hierarchy is clear cut, with generals at the top, then colonels, majors, captains, lieutenants, sergeants, corporals and privates. The hierarchical structure is part of what makes these social groupings effective, and they would likely not operate effectively without them — and that includes the BBC.

Although society benefits from the positive functionality of hierarchies, people are painfully aware that those considered to be high status and powerful are sometimes mean, self-serving and disrespectful. A corrupt organization or a bad boss can make life a living nightmare irrespective of the subordinates' capabilities.

In the social sciences, hierarchies are often portrayed as a result of the system. In terms of day in, day out experience, however, hierarchies constantly change according to circumstances. Presidents of organizations have higher rank than their employees, but they have lower rank than their largest customer's procurement manager. Customers, whatever their job title, have higher rank than waiters, service providers and salespeople. Doctors have higher status than their patients in a clinic or hospital. However, a doctor stopped for speeding by a law enforcement officer probably won't act like the top dog.

Here is another example of shifting hierarchies from my experiences backcountry skiing. This recreational activity involves eight to 12 skiers getting shuttled into a remote mountain location. We then plod up mountains and, after reaching the summit, we remove the furry skins from the bottom of the skis and ski down. A guide always comes with us because of numerous potential dangers — foremost being the danger of becoming buried in an avalanche and suffocating. There is never any question who is topmost in the hierarchy. It is the guide. Challenging the guide's authority on the mountain would be viewed by everyone in the party as reprehensible.

If a miscalculation occurs and an avalanche happens to bury one or more members of our party, including the guide, those remaining would need to sort themselves out quickly. The first order of business would be to appoint a leader to coordinate the search. The leader would check that everyone still standing had switched their transceivers from emit to SEARCH. Then we'd fan out across the path of the avalanche to locate and dig out the submerged skiers. The average survival time of someone buried in an avalanche is 18 minutes. Seconds count. There would be no question how the leader would be selected. It would be the person who had the most experience with backcountry skiing and who had exhibited confidence during the pre-trip training. No one would give a jot of consideration to the individual's strength, beauty, sex or their salary. It would be a matter of competence only.

If we relate this subject back to the environment of *Homo sapiens* and their need to operate as a high-performing team — when tracking down game, conducting offensive raids, or protecting settlements and offspring — the overall success of the party would count more than the status of each individual. When a leader was killed or injured, the roles of the individuals would adjust dynamically.

Our ability to make judgments is immediate and intuitive, and it determines how we feel from moment to moment. In situations where we sense that others judge us unfairly, feelings of irritation bubble up to our conscious mind and we conjure up an intellectually satisfying explanation.

The idea that hierarchies are fixed societal *systems,* with the people at the top exerting power over lower echelons does not square with the experience of leaders who have built organizations from the ground up. If a leader imagines they somehow have power over underlings, they will likely discover the most competent ones will leave and get a more fulfilling job. A more fruitful approach is for the leader to see themselves as a servant of the enterprise. A leader-as-servant dynamic will result in a more highly motivated and cohesive team.

News tabloids deliver endless chatter about the lives of royalty, celebrities and experts, not because of their intelligence and remarkable lives, but because deep in the human psyche there's a desire to look up to a guiding force. The pronouncements of political leaders dominate front page news, not because they are insightful, but because they represent the views of certain tribes and, if they are doing their jobs properly, their words provide reassurance. Even when we disagree with what a leader says, their leadership confirms our personal landscape of beliefs. The power of leaders does not arise because they exert control, but because members of a tribe willingly move together as a cohesive unit. Our feelings about societal relationships have deep-seated origins in our evolutionary past that are associated with the attachment instinct, parenting urges, and our physical and sexual status.

The Newman–Peterson debate is instructive because it exposes two presuppositions that would have been considered bizarre in earlier centuries: first, that males and females belong to separate and competing tribes; and second, that there is unquestioning social acceptance that a "pay gap" is a primary cause for concern — rather than say health, security, fulfillment, longevity, intellectual stimulation, creativity, raising a family and contributing to society. Ironically, Newman has adopted a landscape of meanings that is masculine in character; that is, to her, humans are *Homo economicus* and matters of finance are preeminent.

The use of words such as *power, system* and *pay gap* illustrate that we have grown accustomed to accepting that everything can be understood and organized from the top down. This mode of thinking is characteristic of all three tribal journeys. Consilience informs us of a new perspective: that human behavior is emergent from the details of human biology and the categorizations that result from our social interactions.

When I returned from Ecuador, I started writing this book as a form of self-therapy. In the news and on my social media I kept seeing unquestioning acceptance of different tribes and sub-tribes as embodiments of good or evil. I had trouble sympathizing with any of them.

Take the matter of racism. Before I went to university, I worked as a *commis de restaurant* (busboy) in the Hilton Hotel in the shadow of the Eiffel Tower in Paris. When I cleared the plates from tables in the hotel restaurant, I couldn't help noticing the contrasting behavior of people from different countries. I can still picture how groups of tourists from Japan would clear every speck of food from their plates, then each would hand them to me with two hands and bow their head in thanks.

As a 19-year-old, unskilled, British male, I was at the bottom of the totem pole — nearly. My position was made clear one night when I was walking home through the empty streets to my tiny apartment in Place École Militaire. Three work colleagues, who were French and the same age, appeared suddenly and surrounded me. Their purpose was to make sure I knew my place. Somehow I managed to avoid physical injury, but I certainly remember that lower than young-British-busboys in the hotel's hierarchy were employees from North Africa. Their jobs were to wash dishes and clean floors.

When I learn about the postmodern pioneer Derrida, I try to visualize his situation. Growing up in North Africa with parents who were heartbroken by the death of two of his brothers, he was an outsider from the start. At age 12, he was kicked out of school because of anti-Semitic laws. When he won a scholarship to attend the École Normale Supérieure in Paris, the odds were stacked against him. His combination of studiousness, athleticism, good looks plus some luck enabled him to eventually rise to intellectual stardom. Most important of all was the lyrical way he expressed himself that would leave his audience somewhat unsure of his point. I observed how this mode of discourse was appreciated by educated Parisians. On the weekends at dinner parties, through a forest of empty wine bottles and half-smoked Gauloises, I was mesmerized by the meandering conversations of my French host Madam Khan and her guests. They always started the evening by discussing food, then politics and, inevitably by the early morning, they would deconstruct sexuality.

— ▪ ○ ● ○ ▪ —

Our academic institutions have an invaluable role to play in helping us to collectively make our communities welcoming and stable. We should be alert to the dangers of simplistic categorization such as *black* versus *white*. Treating such categories as worthy of sociological scholarship is proving counterproductive.

These categories are certainly divorced from the way I have experienced the world. When I was 15 years old, I lived in a small home in Kakamega in western Kenya where I played golf every day with Nekesa and his friends who were members of the Luhya tribe. Nekesa played in his bare feet with only three clubs and a self-taught swing. He birdied most holes. I recall asking him, "Why do Luhyas hate Kikuyus so much?" He looked at me with a frown and said, "Because they are bad." When I asked what he would do if he met one, he flashed a broad smile and said, "I'd kill them." He did not appear to be joking.

My father visited dozens of the many hundreds of tribes in East Africa, taking photos of the intricate beadwork, piercings and scarification, and how it varied between villages. He had albums full of photos he took in the 1940s, and he was fascinated by how the people's appearance had changed over the decades. My mother was an expert on West African art and for many years catalogued the collection at Birmingham University. I grew up in a household surrounded by photographs, musical instruments, spears and carvings from around Africa. Whenever I meet anyone from Africa, or anywhere else in the world, I am acutely aware of the differences between countries and cultures, and I am not ashamed of my curiosity.

Nationalism is a term sometimes used disparagingly by those who view nations as the cause of conflict, particularly members of the Gather Together tribe. By contrast, I argue that we need to acknowledge that societies do not have a good record of being able to control tribal tendencies, and there seems little reason to believe this will change for the better any time soon. Borders between nations enable those living within them to work out their differences, help restrain the growth of authoritarian regimes and contain the inevitable tribal flare-ups.

While riding through Ecuador's young volcanic mountains, I noted the different Indigenous languages and wondered how the ancient bloodlines became mixed with those of the conquering Incans, and then the Spanish conquistadors. At the time I Googled the matter, but did not find much had been documented.

I noted the hardships of poverty and how peasant farmers in Ecuador and elsewhere have no time to worry about looking after the environment. I asked the guide, "Why are these people who are living on lush, fertile farmland with ample freshwater so impoverished?" He answered that all levels of government are corrupt, and public works projects are ill-disguised cronyism.

The picture I see in the Western world is not one of socialism versus capitalism or left versus right. I do not believe it is worth dwelling on the wounds of slavery and colonialism. Nor do I see systems of power and the validity of top-down categorizations. When I think about societies I look at them from the individual upward. If everyone has the capacity to lead a fulfilling, productive life, it could be possible for all of us to live sustainably and peacefully. However, if citizens believe that we can rewrite history and that someone in authority can arrange society according to some theory that will solve our individual and collective problems, I cannot see how this could work.

— ▪ ○ 25 ○ ▪ —

Consilience as Anti-Theory

Consilience aspires to be anti-theory and nontribal. It does not depend on categorizations and theories — unlike science. Consilience allows us to explore the idea of creationism historically.

IF ONE WERE LOOKING FOR A SIMPLE THEORY to sum up consilience, it might read something like this: *To truly understand something, one needs to dig into its details from every perspective.* However, with any attempt to distill complex matters down to basic principles, one is necessarily subject to the artifacts of thinking. Chief among these is that the words and ideas we create shape what we observe. Ironically, many notable examples can be found in the brain sciences.

For thousands of years the ability to reason calmly was viewed as a strength, and reason was upset by emotions. In books about the brain you will find statements such as "the amygdala is part of the limbic system, which is involved with different emotional responses." This perpetuates the idea that emotions are a distinct and separate system. Now that scientists are probing details of the brain's chemistry, it is clear that emotions are not separate from other aspects of brain function. They are part of a single integrated system.

We have the capacity to respond quickly to some stimuli, such as happens with the startle response, and also the ability to spend time considering matters. Kahneman describes these two capabilities as follows: "System 1, that operates automatically and quickly, with little or no effort and no sense of voluntary control"; and "System 2, that allocates attention to the effortful mental activities that demand it, including complex computations." While this is a useful concept in some instances, this distinction obscures the fact that the brain is a single, emergent, integrated system. It operates with a continuum of response times, from the startle response through to the development of skills, which can take years.

The idea persists that the brain is a modular system, not unlike a computer with separate chipsets involved with different functionalities. Consider some of the many parts of the brain: the visual cortex; Broca's area, associated with speech; Wernicke's area, necessary for language comprehension; sensory areas; and motor areas. Brain scientists continue their research, now by using increasingly sophisticated, high-resolution scanning technologies and watching the different parts of the brain light up. What is easy to overlook is that the scanning devices are calibrated to show small deviations from baseline activity. There is a growing acknowledgment that all parts of the brain are humming along *all* the time, with *all* the neurons operating on the knife-edge of criticality, ready to fire.

The words we use to understand and communicate about the natural world project culturally derived preconceptions — melodies of meaning — onto the messiness of reality. Obviously, the natural world did not arise to conform with how humans are able to understand it. To understand reality, we have to discount what we think we know — and that is a challenge.

The history of psychology and neurophysiology shows that scientists apply ideas that are familiar in everyday discourse and reflect these in the subject of their investigations.

Consider the subject of empathy and mirror neurons. In 1992, when a group of researchers in Parma, Italy, was studying the behavior of motor neurons in the brain of a monkey, they realized the neurons under investigation not only directed the muscles, but also were sensory. Luciano Fadiga, one of the researchers, stated, "They [the neurons] also had tactile receptive fields and, more interestingly, they responded to tactile stimulation *before* the stimulus even touched the skin!" Their findings contradicted the orthodox view that neurons are either motor *or* sensory, not both, and they called these neurons "strange neurons."

While their research continued, one day they noticed something completely unexpected. They were eating lunch and suddenly, "while someone was biting into a sandwich we clearly heard the discharge of a neuron through the loudspeaker connected to the amplifier." Fadiga said, "We had the immediate perception that something strange but important was happening. We put our food away, we took a video camera, and after testing the neuron to make sure that its response was not simply an artifact, we recorded the first mirror neuron. It was a *grasping-with-mouth-and-with-hand* mirror neuron." Sure enough, they had found a neuron that was activated not only when the monkey was eating, but also when it saw someone else use the same motion. News of the discovery of *mirror neurons* quickly spread through the scientific community and into popular culture. The news spread because it affirmed that feelings of empathy — the ability to feel things from the standpoint of others — are a basis of primate social behavior.

Empathy is a pleasing, human-created concept, and the word describes a particular feeling people may have toward one another. It is not a material thing, however, and it is not how neurons operate. Another way to interpret the Italian team's findings is that neuronal players sense and anticipate other people's movements as well as our own movement. There is no strict division of function between motor and sensory neurons, nor between what they detect in other people's movement and our own. Each neuron has a huge repertoire, and together they play along with sensations from different sources and arrange these according to their similarities. We can name the melody of a collection of neurons as empathy, but the neurons don't feel anything.

— ▪ ○ ● ○ ▪ —

In earlier chapters I've told a story of how worms evolved into fish, then pelycosaurs, then apes and early hominids, and ultimately *Homo sapiens*. Evolutionary psychology explains brain structures and behavioral traits as evolutionary adaptations that have provided survival and breeding advantages. Evolutionary psychology can, however, too easily confirm preconceptions about what happened in the past and use them to explain various traits.

Every conjecture has an unavoidable circular logic that goes something like this: it exists, it must have evolved for a reason and so that is why it exists. For example, most birds sing, and they sing because singing plays a part in mate selection, so their singing confers an evolutionary advantage over birds that do not sing. If most birds did not sing, however, the existence of non-singing birds could be used to argue that quietness confers an evolutionary advantage. The theory works both ways.

What kind of association can be made between bird singing and book writing? Dawkins writes, "We are survival machines — robot vehicles blindly programmed to preserve the selfish molecules known as genes." Perhaps writing books is a form of social signaling, somewhat similar to birds in the spring fanning out their tail feathers, chirping away and occasionally going at each other. In evolutionary terms birds are showing off and competing for the best mate. Are human communications, including the scientific endeavor, any different? Undoubtedly they have the same evolutionary roots, but in both cases we need to be careful about how we express the linkage.

Any explanation of behavior in terms of genes presumes a direct causal linkage between genes and behavior. Genes, along with the often-overlooked cellular machinery of microtubules, briefly described in chapter 6, encode biological structures. But saying that genes encode "memes" that are "a unit of cultural transmission, or a unit of imitation," as Dawkins terms them, is a problematic leap in logic. In many cases, the leap appears to be justified, particularly when dealing with relatively simple organisms such as C. *elegans* and social insects. In every case however, behaviors are emergent from the organism's structures and environment. To put it succinctly, genes encode structures, not behavior.

Another way to understand this is that the words used to describe the reasons for behaviors are human projections. For instance, it is said that peacocks have beautiful tails because they signal to the peahen a healthy mate and a better chance for healthy offspring. But in saying the words *beautiful, signal* and *healthy*, we map preconceptions onto a particular situation through small, seemingly reasonable leaps in logic. Beauty, health and signaling are human ideas. Perhaps the peahens' neuronal orchestra reacts positively to the repeated patterns in the peacock's tail and that is all.

Consider the subject of people's conception of physical beauty. Evolutionary psychologists sometimes presume that people are attracted to beautiful faces because they signal strong genes and the brain has evolved mechanisms to encourage breeding between partners with superior genes, to fulfill a goal of producing fitter offspring. It happens that if you take a large number of faces and digitally average them, you end up with a face that looks beautiful. Therefore, a simpler explanation is that the neuronal orchestra responds more positively to faces that are absolutely average and perfectly symmetrical — not because there is a goal. Signals of sexual fitness and physical health play a secondary role in mate selection and are harder to explain.

Rather than presume that evolution has programmed organisms to accomplish an objective, it is more logical to acknowledge that our conceptions of beauty in both the peacock's tail and the human form do not have a purpose in the ways we might have previously thought. To aim for objectivity, we need to remember the human propensity to project meaning onto things and resist it, unsatisfying as it happens to be.

Generally speaking, there are two ways to understand how something came into existence. First is by way of the scientific method, explaining observations according to theories that can be broadly applied.

In the case of the peacock's tail, the theory of evolution explains how it evolved. The details of evolutionary theory are complex, and researchers have progressively refined them ever since Darwin conceived the basic mechanisms. The second is by way of an historical approach, explaining what happened without resorting to broadly applied ideas, which means dispensing with theories and simply looking at how one thing causes another and leads to a result. In the case of the peacock, this would entail exploring how each cell is formed, and how each peacock survives and reproduces.

I have a purpose in writing this book, which is to promote civilized discourse about complex subjects that are important for humanity's ongoing survival, but consilience itself is an idea that does not have a goal. It is an approach that is agnostic with respect to the validity of various approaches to understanding. For instance, the Climb Higher and Hold Firm tribes often clash about whether or not evolution is factual. I would hope that from the standpoint of consilience we can accept that the theory of evolution is a powerful explanatory tool while at the same time acknowledging the dangers of using evolution as a model for human conduct.

For many people, creationism is a trigger word. It may appear to be a case of faith versus science: either you believe in Biblical accounts of Earth's creation or you believe in evolution. Contrary to most historical accounts, when Darwin and Alfred Wallace published their account of natural selection, there was no widespread religious backlash in either Europe or America. The idea that life undergoes metamorphosis had already been accepted for a long time and was a popular perspective in pre-Christian times. Metamorphosis is a recurring theme in the writings of the Roman poet Ovid. The gods Venus, Castor and Pollux were hatched out of shells. This inspired Erasmus Darwin, Charles Darwin's grandfather, in 1770 to paint a crest on his carriage door with the Latin words *E conchis omnia*: "Everything from shells." He felt that all species had descended from one microscopic ancestor, a single filament. It was not until nearly a century later that his grandson, Charles, figured out key elements of the evolutionary process.

Following Darwin's publications, evolution quickly became an accepted scientific fact. But in North America in the 1920s, there was outcry against it. The reasons for this outcry were potent. The world had just emerged from the Great War's tragedy, which had been fuelled by Darwinian theories. At the turn of the century, an intellectual movement in Germany, known as *monism*, had brought science and religion together into one coherent philosophy. The ideas of Darwin, through the writings of then-respected German scientist Ernst Haeckel, had been combined with the ideas of the German Romantic movement, which idolized an ideal of German purity and beauty — an ideology known as *volkism*. The monists pandered to feelings of the superiority of German culture and contributed directly to the rise of National Socialism and the slide toward all-out war. This same philosophy was echoed by Hitler in *Mein Kampf* and was the intellectual starting point for fascism, another world war and genocide.

An idea such as the theory of evolution might be scientifically correct, but its effect on people's behavior was catastrophic. Fear about the consequences of ideas is justified. From a scientific standpoint evolution is a fact, but from a historical standpoint it is also a fact that two world wars provide justification for people to be wary of the effects that ideas have on the behavior of people.

Creationism is part of the belief system for many followers of the Hold Firm tribe, particularly in the United States, and the reasons for their beliefs are, from a historical standpoint, understandable. The lingering fear after the Great War turned out to be justified. In a book written in 1923, *Hell and The High Schools*, the emotions and fervor jump off the page: "The Germans who poisoned the wells and springs of northern France and Belgium, and fed little children poisoned candy were angels compared to the text-book writers and publishers who are poisoning the books used in our schools... Next to the fall of Adam and Eve, Evolution and the teaching of Evolution in tax-supported schools is the greatest curse that ever fell upon this earth." This was by T.T. Martin, a religious firebrand from Mississippi. In view of what happened in the world during the following 25 years, his fears about the self-anointing ideologies related to the theory of evolution cannot be denied, although it needs to be emphasized that views about the nature of evolution were then, and continue to be, widely misunderstood.

To take the perspective of consilience, imagine how a Gliesian might see humanity, that is by ignoring human categorizations and not seeing ideas as tribal weapons. Perhaps we can aspire to see reality at its most basic levels of particulate matter, without the need for theories or the divisions between disciplines. With this undertaking, there would be no room for disagreement – scientific, sociological, psychological, political, religious or otherwise.

Human neuronal mechanisms attribute a point to things at every level, which is important for interactions with one another because it lets us make sense of motivations. That picture is, however, illusory because ascribing a point to things is an artifact of the neural system. When I observe a raindrop falling, I should not ascribe a motivation to it. It falls because that is the way gravity operates; it just happens. Human beings are considerably more complicated, but we are also the sum of physical processes. Just because we place ourselves in a category we reserve for things that are living and conscious does not mean that our physical selves are subject to processes that are different.

Throughout history there has been much discussion about the nature of free will, determinism and consciousness. Consilience allows us to acknowledge the significance of these concepts, but also how they get in the way of us being able to understand the underlying mechanisms of human thought and behavior.

The perspective of consilience does not diminish the value of ideas or the richness of human experience, but forces us to forgo the idea that the universe and everything in it has a purpose. Raindrops do not fall because plants need water. Gravity does not exist to anchor humans to the earth.

If the universe did not exist we would not be here, but it does not exist in order for us to be here. It is not science's role to provide a grounding for each person's search for meaning.

Where do these new insights lead? Imagine a student watching the sun rising over some distant hills, bathing the waking city below in a warm glow. He feels a deep sense of awe and for a few moments is overwhelmed. Then, from the heavens, an angel descends and quietly sits down beside him. He is startled and tries to conceal his confusion by commenting on the scene. "That is a stunning creation."

She dismisses his comment with a wave of her hand. "Everything is just fermions and bosons."

Indignant, he says, "What about the beauty of nature, stunning buildings, human culture? They are amazing creations!"

"Those things are all made up of leptons and baryons, just classes of fermions," she says, referring to the elementary particles that cosmologists have discovered. "Actually, the particles don't exist. You are merely sensing perturbations in quantum fields."

His voice drops, and he frowns. "Look at everything! Those aren't just perturbations! God must have had a purpose."

She responds, "Nothing has a purpose. God kicked the whole thing off, and it was an emergent system from that point on. If you want a purpose, you'll need to figure one out.

26

Guides for Living

Religious practice is described from a biological and historical perspective that acknowledges its point.

FAITH IN THE BIBLE IS CONSIDERED A MATTER OF BELIEF — rather than logic. But for the moment consider the genesis of the Bible from a secular standpoint, without adherence to the strictures of academics and theologians, but with embellishment from current thinking of historians and archeologists. Instead of using the historical names of places, I'll approximate to modern-day locations.

A tribe of *Homo sapiens* lived on the shores of East Africa, having retreated from the Rift Valley due to drought and predators. Then 70,000 years ago, some bands left Africa and ventured into Central Asia. By that time *Homo sapiens* wore clothes, had fire, twine, and the ability to plan ahead and work cooperatively as a group to fulfill their needs. They also made sharp weapons, and would have used them when they encountered Neanderthals and hominids from earlier waves of migration, as evidenced from fragments of bone.

Wherever they went, early humans built shelters within encampments to keep out enemies and predators. Like Darwin's finches spreading throughout a new island, their numbers increased, tribes grew and fractured, and they built encampments at new sites. As they dispersed, the tribes developed new skills, words and dialects.

During and after the last ice age, the climate changed quickly, not uniformly, but in a spatial and temporal patchwork. Localized climate catastrophes propelled tribes to move into new foraging territories.

Sea levels around 130 meters lower than current levels allowed early humans to spread to islands of Southeast Asia. By 60,000 years ago, tribes had spread to Japan and Australia, and by 24,000 years ago they had spread to the Americas.

In North Africa and the Middle East, particularly along the Nile, Tigris and Euphrates rivers, human settlements grew. Annual flooding of fields with silt-rich waters enabled the expansion of settlements protected from the summer droughts. Cities formed with thick battlements to protect their citizens from tribes who had fallen on hard times or were looking to plunder.

Archeological remains of every city in the region reveal layer upon layer of turmoil. Existence was precarious and always under threat from invaders, hunger, disease and interpersonal conflicts. Throughout the region slavery was common. Those living in the hills outside settlements were constantly at risk of being killed or taken into a city and put to work constructing buildings, digging irrigation ditches or performing menial duties.

A class of traders developed, traveling between settlements by boat and land. They traded food, pottery, animals, salt, perfume, ornaments, stories, music and new technologies. One transformative technology, bronze, spread through the region 5,500 years ago. Bronze is made by smelting copper and tin ores, both of which are uncommon and need to be transported from far-distant mines. Bronze was fashioned into blades and armor, giving its owners an advantage over others who used tools made of stone, wood and bone.

During the Bronze Age 5,500 years ago, large cities developed, with civic buildings, communal granaries and water supplies; outside the high city walls and gates there were fields of wheat, barley, rye, lentils, peas, fruit trees and date palms. Widespread trading of goods over long distances included amber from the Baltic, tin from southwest England, copper from Cyprus, gold from Egypt and silk from as far away as China. The names of civilizations at that time are familiar from the classics and Biblical stories: Babylonian, Mycenaean, Minoan, Hittite, Assyrian, Cypriot, Egyptian and Canaanite.

It is tempting to project modern ideas and institutions onto the ruins of cities from this epoch. For example, we see evidence of art, agriculture, kings, writing, trade, law and temples with gods and goddesses. We might speculate about the perspectives of people at the time, but politics, religion, commerce and the law were probably tightly interwoven. Citizens gathered in a central building — possibly every seven days, following the cycles of the moon — to discuss matters of public interest, plan projects, settle disputes, exchange goods, and commemorate births and marriages.

At a crucial point in history, the Bronze Age collapsed. Within a few years, cities turned to rubble, and once-prosperous peoples were expunged from regions as far apart as the Atlantic, North Africa, Southern Europe, the Caspian Sea and Northwest China. Massive and far-reaching, Armageddon — the name of one of the cities destroyed — cascaded into a series of mounting catastrophes. The cause was the eruption of Mt. Hekla, a volcano located on the southern side of Iceland. Later called the "gateway to hell," the mountain spewed seven cubic kilometers of rock and ash as high as the stratosphere. The sulphurous cloud blotted out the sun. As crops failed to germinate and hailstorms ripped fruit from the trees, hunger set in. Communities from Spain, Sardinia, Sicily, Crete, Italy, Libya and the Balkans bundled their families and weapons into boats to search for food and another life. As they moved east, they encountered people from former cities who were in the grip of starvation, and also feuding, raiding homes of the wealthy and rebelling against the ruling classes. A series of earthquakes toppled each city's fortifications, allowing refugees from other places to ransack them. City by city was picked over, burned, then abandoned, throughout Greece, Turkey, Syria, Lebanon, Israel, Jordan, Iraq and Iran.

The Egyptians managed to hold off the devastation. Ramesses III pulled his forces back from the Sinai, Israel and Jordan, then lay in wait for the arrival of the refugees from across the sea. When they arrived in the Nile Delta, the Egyptians overpowered them and stacked their dead bodies on the beaches.

Back in the Egyptian cities, scribes and slaves that generations earlier had been rounded up from Babylon and lands between migrated back to Israel and Jordan. One can imagine the scribes and working people returning from Egypt with their families, seeing the lands vacated by the Egyptians, the desecration of the cities, then sinking their faces in the pebbly sand and asking themselves what forces had excused them from death. When people speaking the same language descended from places of refuge in the hills, they gathered together and planned how to ward off similar subjugation and hardship in the future.

What did they decide? The first requirement was that rulers in each of the repopulating cities would be answerable to a higher authority; in fact, an unseen ruler of all the people of the region. Workers, scribes, prophets and kings would be prohibited from conjuring up their own deities and icons. Unity would be exalted, and anyone who forgot this would be in trouble. The second requirement was that, on the seventh day of the week, families would sit together, reflect on their common heritage and eat according to their custom.

Over time, scribes documented the customs and what they knew of their history. They stated that although bad things happen, by sticking together as a tribe they could overcome adversity. Their texts also incorporated practical commandments about moral and social behavior, food and health, and the requirement to mark days of the year to remember their shared heritage.

A third requirement was a prohibition against eating pork, since the people had seen whole cities weakened by parasites spread by pig meat. Today, public health authorities ensure that meat doesn't contain the eggs and larvae of nematodes (roundworms), cestodes (tapeworms) and protozoans.

The stories of the Hebrew Bible are based on recalled history. The garden of Eden recollects the fertile floodplains of the Tigris and Euphrates, before centuries of agriculture and hot summer sun pulled salt to the soil surface, killing the crops. Or perhaps Eden echoes even earlier times, when lakes and thick forests covered the Sahara for 3,000 years. The story of Noah's Ark is reminiscent of similar stories from around the world, describing how rising sea levels stranded populations on islands or valleys were inundated when moraine lakes burst in the Himalayas.

Eleven centuries after the Bronze Age collapse, the Romans invaded the Middle East with chariots and weapons made of steel, threatening the survival of the people. A charismatic preacher provided reassurance that the citizens craved. The Roman authorities executed him publicly, but his followers continued to teach his message and document his words. The symbol of his semi-naked body on the cross became a unifying symbol that to some was more meaningful than the symbology of the Holy Covenant described in the Hebrew Bible. Different visions of the meaning of the Bible developed, and a new sect took form.

Three centuries after the execution of Jesus, leaders of the new religion, under the direction of the Roman Emperor Constantine, wanted to reconcile inconsistencies between the laws of the Hebrew Bible that prohibited other gods and graven images, and the icon of Christ on the cross, which had become an image representing a deity. At a meeting just south of Istanbul in the city of Nicea, 300 religious leaders defined God as a holy trinity: Father, Son and Holy Spirit, being "coeternal, coequal and indivisibly united" in one being. This rationalization wasn't perfectly logical, but it reduced dissonance and brought members of the sect together with a shared belief. The Holy Trinity was the foundation of the Roman Catholic Church.

Over the past two millennia, the power of symbology and the supporting scriptures for Jews and Christians have provided a motivating and unifying force for many, many people. And in their time, the scriptures contained practical guidance to help people live together cooperatively, survive and raise families.

These days the word *God* has become pointified with a meaning that depends on one's personal allegiances. Consilience encourages us to consider the word in a more open-ended and inclusive way. The word *God* is a symbol of tribal loyalties as well as a metaphor for how believers should model their behavior. When males pattern their behavior according to the scriptures and take responsibility for themselves, their partners and children, it benefits the whole community. The role model of an omniscient, compassionate being makes the tribe more stable. On the other hand, if people follow instincts patterned in their genes and spread their seed like Genghis Khan, they will do well in a selfish-Darwinian sense, but only until they encounter a tribe whose doctrine allows them to pull together and get the upper hand.

Consilience allows us to view scripture and religious practices in a new light. For example, our neuronal mechanisms respond to human stories that have a point. Recall from chapter 3 the techniques used in marketing to make brand messages stick, and consider that scribes and storytellers have refined their skills over thousands of years of practice. We can see that the techniques used in the arts, business, religion and politics are, at the level of our biology, similar.

Christian belief has a single point: believe in Jesus Christ and the love of God. This point is supported by narratives intended to help believers make sense of, and handle, the vagaries of life. The act of believing in scripture is not a matter of understanding facts, in the way many scientists think about scientific theories, but is instead belief in an encoded account of acceptable behaviors that are symbolic of tribal loyalty. Those who share common beliefs and behave accordingly are part of the tribe. Non-believers are outsiders.

Tribal loyalties with their associated beliefs have powerful effects on human behavior. Beliefs affect how we perceive the world, and they become self-fulfilling. If we believe that humans are an innately violent, tribal species, we become more tribal and violent. Members of a religion that preaches the virtue of peace will act in ways that are more peaceful.

Every tribe on earth has a distinctive vocabulary, patterns of behavior and shared beliefs. Tribal forms include national identities, political parties, companies, institutions, and on down to sports teams and family units. These groupings are a productive and positive force in people's lives. It helps when everyone believes in their community and in what they do. Teachers, farmers, artists, journalists, other professionals and parents become more fulfilled, and likely more successful, when they are fully committed to the virtue of their practice.

I have argued that there is no such thing as complete objectivity in any field of human endeavour, including science. Nonetheless, it is productive that scientists believe in the merit of scientific objectivity. In the words of the physicist David Deutsch of Oxford University, "Science is about tolerance, respect for the truth, rationality and optimism... and it is not possible to have too much."

A countervailing view, however, is advanced by the English political philosopher John Nicholas Gray. "I think reason has its limits and I want people to be as reasonable as possible in politics and elsewhere," he states. "But the single most dangerous human belief at the moment is the belief in human rationality because it tells us that when you have a looming disaster people will avoid it. Well, human history would not be what it was if that were true."

We need to understand the realities of the human condition and the limits of reason. At the same time, it is productive for every professional group to appreciate and venerate the skills and contributions of others. There is little to be gained when any expert imagines they have a lock on truth and they belittle the skills of others, including those of historians, poets, writers, religious leaders and the wisdom of the scribes of earlier epochs.

We cannot escape our biology and the predisposition to form groups and become protective of our own, but our beliefs are under our control. If we so choose, we can work toward making them more cooperative and constructive.

—▪○ 27 ○▪—

Seeing the Light

Religious doctrines take shape in times of stress, and the related behaviors are often stabilizing and constructive.

GROWING UP IN ENGLAND I HARDLY NOTICED the lovingly built churches in every city, town and most villages. My study room at Durham University looked onto the intricate stained glass windows of the cathedral that has towered above the city for 1,000 years, dwarfing the castle and everything for miles around. It is the same throughout Europe. There are churches and cathedrals everywhere. Across North America even the smallest communities have several churches. In Australia and New Zealand, it is no different. In South America, the dominant buildings in almost every town are religious. These places of gathering are impressive in their artistic and structural details, and I am constantly in awe that people in small communities over the past 1,000 years had the resources, skills and commitment to create such magnificent buildings that are still standing.

Compared to many years ago, in recent decades fewer people, particularly in the cities, have been attending churches, temples and mosques. The sense of community that religious organizations once provided has been replaced by other gathering places, including people's workplaces, gyms and yoga studios, and by social media.

The followers of new atheism characterize people who belong to places of worship as slaves of their doctrines, but that doesn't match the data. Surveys in the United States show that Americans change religious affiliation early and often. In total, about half of American adults have changed religious affiliation at least once during their lives. Most people who change their religion leave their childhood faith before the age of 24.

Often people leave a religious group because of the religious doctrine. Two-thirds of former Catholics and half of former Protestants say they left their childhood faith because they stopped believing in its teachings or they think of religious people as hypocritical or judgmental. Other reasons include a dislike of the rules or a perception that religious leaders focus too much on power and money. They do not leave their religion because scientific rationalism satisfies their needs.

Religious ideas have appeared and taken hold at different periods of history. Why do some stick and others fade away? In this chapter I'll use the story of several Judeo-Christian groups to explore the intersection of human biology and religious ideas and practices, and also how they stick.

Recall that following the collapse of the Bronze Age scribes wrote the Hebrew Bible, and then the stress of Roman occupation in the eastern Mediterranean sparked the rise of Christianity. In both cases, the religious movements took hold during periods of intense social instability. The Romans by every measure were brutal rulers. When an adolescent Jew accompanying his parents to Jerusalem on a pilgrimage to commemorate Passover had a spiritual awakening, the Romans executed him on a cross, parading him as a warning to others.

The story of another young man, the tentmaker Saul of Tarsus, is a well-known Christian story. Saul had been given the job of rounding up Jesus's followers and persecuting them. While walking to Damascus, Saul experienced a personal transformation that led him to change allegiances; in a moment, the symbol the Romans used to project their power and humiliate deviants — a body slowly dying on a cross — became a symbol of love and sacrifice. Paul the Apostle, as Saul became known, must have realized the psychological power of this flip-flop in meaning and been proud of its insolence. That creative insight marked the start of Christianity.

Another example is Martin Luther. His awakening gave rise to the Protestant movement. Many Christian sects were hatched in similar circumstances. During a period of social stress, a young person feels anxious and hypersensitive. Then suddenly they experience a spiritual illumination, with a "jumping together" of insights or, in Whewell's terminology, a "consilience of inductions." In a flash, worrisome questions become answered. Then they make it their life's work to provide spiritual illumination to others.

I am familiar with some details about one nonconformist sect, Quakerism, because my forebears were attracted to it. George Fox, the son of a weaver and churchwarden, provided the seed. He left home in 1643 at the age of 19 and started a hike through northern England. He felt troubled which, given the circumstances, was understandable. At that time, anxieties were running high across Great Britain. King Charles had dissolved parliament and was trying to raise taxes. A long-running war in central Europe between Catholic and Protestant factions had killed one in five Germans. Anglican clergymen and their congregations worried that the king would reintroduce Catholicism. Independent-minded preachers became creative, which resulted in 2,000 of them being kicked out of the Anglican church. Scotland and Ireland were restless. The little ice age was at its worst, causing crop failure and hunger. A civil war had broken out between supporters of the king and those supporting the parliament, and troops were stationed in each of the towns George Fox passed through.

Young George was confused and angry about his situation. He looked for guidance in the words of the Bible; as a mass-produced book, it represented a transformative technology at the time, like the internet of today. He had lost faith in the priests who, depending on the church, advocated for either one side or the other in the civil war. He had a vision and realized his life could be illuminated directly by a light from within: "My heart did leap for joy. The Lord let me see why there was none upon the earth that could speak to my condition..."

George Fox's spiritual awakening happened on Pendle Hill in Lancashire, not far from his ancestral home. He began preaching outside churches and, as he traveled, he built up a band of supporters, who called themselves Children of the Light or Friends of the Truth; later, simply Friends or Quakers.

In 1661, two brothers, Thomas and John Beakbane, strolled over to the young man who was addressing a small crowd from the steps of a church and found his message appealing. Along with other followers they started meeting each Sunday at Swarthmore in Lancashire. Whenever the Friends were asked to swear an oath of allegiance to either the king or Parliament they refused and were put in jail. From that time on, their families and future generations were shut out of mainstream society. My forebears started enterprises along with other Quaker families, such as Dalton, Darby, Cadbury, Rowntree, Fry, Barclay and Clark. The businesses were relatively successful and enduring.

One of Fox's followers, William Penn, was jailed several times and later emigrated to the North American colonies. King Charles II, to repay a debt owed to Penn's father, granted him a vast tract of land stretching from the Delaware River in the east to Lake Erie and the Ohio River in the west. Called Pennsylvania, Penn helped create a haven for other Quakers and nonconforming religious people who were not welcome in Puritan-run Massachusetts. Penn negotiated treaties with the Indigenous communities, which have been peacefully upheld.

The number of Quakers did not multiply and Quakerism is on the verge of disappearing. How can this be explained?

For one thing, it is not clear what they believe in. Although brought up going to Quaker meetings most Sundays, I didn't know what to say when asked what Quakers believe, mostly because Quakerism is better defined by what Quakers don't believe. They don't believe in hierarchies and there are no priests. They don't believe in violence and war. Some believe in Jesus Christ and the Bible, but this is not essential. Quakers don't build ornate churches or have distinctive icons. At Quaker meetings, everyone meditates in silence, and, within the bounds of decency, they can get up and say whatever they wish. Nothing they believe is a conceptual stretch, such as wine turning into the blood of Christ. They believe "everyone is equal in the eyes of the Lord" and that God can be accessed through quiet introspection. They don't believe they are going to heaven, nor do they believe they are a chosen race or superior to followers of other religions. To sum it up, Quakerism is a nonbrand and is founded on the principle of being as nontribal as possible.

One could say that Quakerism is based on the rational premise that waging war is destructive, and if human beings quieten down and listen to our conscience, we can avoid stirring up animosities and live peacefully together. This premise, however, does not leave one with much to grasp that is visually or metaphorically memorable. It is not a concrete or sticky brand proposition, and (at least in my case) has not provided strong feelings of belonging to a community.

With perverse logic, a weakness in the Quaker doctrine can be explained by game theory, which is the mathematics of competing players. If you profess nonviolence you are easy prey for those who are violent. Over the long run, the threat of retaliation is a worthwhile tactic that helps preserve peace.

There is a marked contrast between Quakerism and other Judeo-Christian denominations, particularly Catholicism, with its many symbols and rituals, explicit hierarchies, entrenched doctrines.

Religious buildings provide a focus that strengthens communities. Churches, prior to telecommunications and particularly in the New World, provided a place for social gathering. The weekly congregation, with its singalong and the preacher's gentle reassurance or motivating pep talk, encouraged social behaviors that were constructive. The ritual of dressing in one's "Sunday best" and traveling to church from outlying areas, and having occasion for young ladies and men to eye each other, was a prelude to the church function of sanctifying marriages.

The doctrines of Catholicism have spread around the world, and the rules prohibiting abortion and contraception served the purpose of strengthening the institution of marriage and increasing the size of the congregation. For men and women who did not wish to be married, the priesthood and monastic orders provided a refuge and productive roles — notwithstanding ongoing controversies.

The functional aspect of scriptural practice is illustrated by the social and cultural elements of Judaism. Surveys of Jews in America show that the religious aspects are less significant than the cultural. Around 70% say they participate in a Seder at Passover. And more than 50%, including the 20% who state they are nonreligious, say they fast for all or part of Yom Kippur. The culture of getting together as a family at the end of the week, sometimes reciting a blessing, remembering one's shared heritage and eating together, builds a sense of community. Only one-quarter of Jews say religion is very important in their lives, compared with more than half of Americans. Among Orthodox Jews, the proportion is higher than 90%.

Of note, a high proportion of the scientific, literary and intellectual ideas I've referred to in this book were conceived by Jews. Although comprising less than 0.2% of the world's population, Jews have been awarded more than 20% of Nobel Prizes. To some extent, this abundance might be the result of genetic differences, but it is certainly cultural. Jewish culture does not shy away from complex narratives, encourages creative discourse, and values intellectual and artistic achievement. As well, Jewish communities in every country where they live, aside from a tiny parcel of land at the east end of the Mediterranean, represent a small minority within the surrounding population. To become accepted and secure in society requires extra effort and mutual support.

For Jewish people, two World Wars, political turmoil in Europe and genocide have been unusually traumatic. Living in situations of heightened vulnerability, being forced to emigrate and tearing families apart has provoked extraordinary creativity. Much of the output has been in the cause of understanding how apparently civilized people can collapse into abhorrent behavior. Philosophers including Hannah Arendt, Isaiah Berlin, David Bohm, Imre Lakatos, Karl Popper, and Émile Durkheim, as well as Derrida and Foucault, whom I mentioned in chapter 24, all tried to resolve personal feelings of disquiet and, through their writings, they hoped to head off further conflagrations.

Many aspects of religious practice and belief are functional and productive. To understand the purposes of religious behavior, we need to set aside our immediate point of view, and look beyond the labels and their emotional associations. The realities of human biology mean that our tribal instincts will never go away. The catastrophes of history have proven this time and time again.

Over the centuries much passion and wisdom have been brought to bear in the formulation of religious doctrines. It is conceivable that with intelligence, humility and respect, sensemakers, educators and politicians can use the parts that have proven to be helpful in the past to help orient individuals and communities to live together harmoniously and productively.

— ▪ ○ 28 ○ ▪ —

No Return to Eden

Looking beyond tribal loyalties related to concern about the environment and climate change, and presenting the argument that pointifying complex scientific matters obstructs our ability to find practical solutions.

HUNDREDS OF MILLIONS OF STUDENTS OF ALL AGES are worried sick about the climate. For those following the Gather Together tribal journey, the words *climate change* represent the desire to move toward a peaceful and egalitarian society, recapturing a time when humans lived harmoniously with nature. Many, perhaps most, journalists and educators believe climate change is the defining issue of this era and, unless we convert to green energy, a climate catastrophe is inevitable. Both left- and right-wing politicians are using the matter as political ammunition.

My perspective is that many aspects of the environment and human health need urgent attention and intelligent debate. Experts of all sorts have revealed details about health and climate, and it is increasingly clear that the science is exceedingly complex.

In this chapter, I'll discuss the birth of the worldwide climate change movement to illustrate the emergence of a new belief system and how complex scientific research becomes pointified.

The philosophy underpinning the Gather Together tribal journey was formulated by Jean-Jacques Rousseau, who wrote *Discourse on Inequality* and *The Social Contract* about 250 years ago. He imagined that the societies of classical Egypt, Greece, Rome and Constantinople were more virtuous than contemporary society. He wrote, "Our souls have been corrupted in proportion to the advancement of our science and arts toward perfection." Rousseau's ideas appealed to the poets of the Romantic movement and influenced generations of writers. The poet William Wordsworth, who loved the peace and solitude he found in the English countryside, wrote, "Nature never did betray the heart that loved her." The theme was also expounded in Henry David Thoreau's landmark book, *Walden*, published in 1854, that documented his life in a Massachusetts cabin: "We need the tonic of wildness."

The notion that we can return to an age of harmony with nature does not square with historical and archeological evidence. In societies that Rousseau venerated, the death rate for children under 15 was between 50 and 60%. In earlier ages, such as the time of the Garden of Eden documented in the Bible, archeologists estimate that child mortality rates were between 30 and 60%. Of the 286 people buried at a Bronze Age tomb at Tell Abraq in the Near East, 118 of them, 41%, died before reaching the age of 15 years. Twenty-eight, or 10%, of women died in the third trimester of pregnancy. Evidence from northern European sites indicates that young people were treated as expendable. Babies and youths appear to have been discarded rather than buried, and infanticide was common.

The BBC produced two documentaries that attempt to reenact life in an Iron Age village. One made in 1978, called *Living in the Past*, shows how the 12 adults and three children who started out in the series were ground down by the constant work, poor hygiene and stress of living in close quarters. The children with their parents did not make it through the planned 14 months. A remake filmed in 2001, *Surviving the Iron Age*, with 17 volunteers, including three children, filmed over seven weeks at a Celtic hill fort in Wales, was described by one of them as "hell on earth."

Each time I venture into the backcountry with all the benefits of modern technology, including lightweight waterproof fabrics, maps, stoves and hi-tech gadgets, it is often challenging, and I marvel how Indigenous communities survived in areas such as northern Canada and Alaska before the introduction of metal tools, fish hooks, nylon line and firearms. Day-to-day life would have required impressive skills, and often during winter months the people would have existed on the very edge of survival.

Studies of organisms in habitats untouched by humanity show that changes in populations are abrupt and impossible to predict. The idea of a "balance of nature" is a modern-day myth, so far from reality that it begs the question of how it persists. Perhaps a reason is a predominantly urban lifestyle or Disney's fantastical cartoons, where the natural world is portrayed as a stable backdrop; for example, *Snow White and the Seven Dwarves* (1937), *The Little Mermaid* (1989), and *A Bug's Life* (1999). The star in *Bambi* (1942), a cute fawn, is not felled by parasites or bitten to death by blackflies. Her only enemy is a man with a gun.

Documentaries, notably those produced by the BBC and narrated by David Attenborough, reinforce the popular conception of balance in nature. The scenes look natural enough, but they're engineered by dedicated teams of camera people and sound technicians, and the repeated message that humanity is on the verge of obliterating everything is poignant. I love watching them and hope they encourage the preservation of wildlife habitats, but they don't show the reality that natural ecosystems are rarely, if ever, stable.

There is widespread concern about rising sea levels and the state of coral reefs around the world. The premise, however, that coral reefs are stable habitats, like the ones in *Finding Nemo* (2003), is nothing short of a fairy tale. It is imperative that we address overfishing and ocean pollution, but humans cannot stop sea levels from changing or prevent coastal erosion. Tropical atolls exist on thick layers of dead coral formed around volcanoes whose ash and pumice has been washed away by waves. Coral reefs are regularly obliterated by typhoons and hurricanes, which have occurred for billions of years — long before corals first appeared on the planet. Periodically, the oceans have been wiped clear of corals, such as the time 252 million years ago when they did not reappear for several million years. In that case the cause was volcanic activity.

— ▪ ○ ● ○ ▪ —

Anxiety about human vulnerability to the forces of nature is justified. Evidence of environmental cataclysms on every scale throughout geological and human history is abundant. We need to acknowledge the possibility of meteor strikes, the eruption of supervolcanoes, pandemics far worse than COVID-19 and severe climate events — whatever their cause.

One aspect of human vulnerability is an increase in global temperatures. The climate change movement has chosen to focus on a single cause: atmospheric carbon dioxide produced by the burning of fossil fuels.

One individual above all others is responsible for the narrative linking carbon dioxide to climate change. Al Gore, in common with many people growing up in the 1960s, was anxious about a number of issues, including the threat of a nuclear war, soil erosion due to poor farming practices and harmful chemicals. He remembered his mother's troubled response to Rachel Carson's book about DDT and pesticide use, *Silent Spring*, published in 1962. While serving in the Vietnam War, he saw the effects of the herbicide Agent Orange, and subsequently learned that it caused chromosomal damage and birth defects. Agent Orange, he wrote, "is just one of the better-known examples of a whole new generation of powerful compounds created in the chemical revolution." The production of these chemicals rapidly increased after World War II. "Over the past fifty years, herbicides, pesticides, fungicides, chlorofluorocarbons (CFCs) and thousands of other compounds... have left a legacy of poison that we will be coming to terms with for many generations."

While studying at Harvard University, Gore became worried about the global environmental threat of higher levels of CO2. He recounts in his book, *Earth in the Balance*, "A great teacher of mine at Harvard, Dr. Roger Revelle, opened my eyes to the problem of global warming." Later he recalled, "The implications of his words were startling... Like all great teachers, he influenced the rest of my life." From that time, Gore has been on a mission to save the world from the effects of CO2 and global warming.

Gore's book describes his challenges in the political arena and how in the 1970s "most people thought of the environment in local or regional terms, so it was impossible to get adequate funding for research on global warming." Along with practiced public relations operatives, he set about galvanizing public opinion around the world.

In 2006, Gore released the documentary, *An Inconvenient Truth*, where he showed an abrupt upward curve in the concentrations of CO2, which he pointed to from the top of a scissor lift. The matter was framed as cut-and-dried science. His message: stop burning fossil fuels, otherwise there will be a global catastrophe. Those who disagreed were then likened to the cigarette companies that had used devious public relations practices to weaken the connection between smoking and cancer.

Gore secured Senate approval for funding for the United Nations Intergovernmental Panel on Climate Change (IPCC). The organization was tasked with reporting on "the scientific basis of risk of human-induced climate change." This was to become the vehicle to mobilize citizens and governments around the world to take action.

When the most powerful and respected government in the world embarks on a mission to protect everyone from environmental devastation, nearly everyone falls in line, particularly if their funding depends on it. IPCC, like every high-functioning organization, started work to deliver on its mandate.

Beginning in 1995 a huge annual climate conference attracted leaders from an array of United Nations bodies concerned with environmental and social issues — desertification, migration, biodiversity, endangered species, tobacco, nuclear weapons and pollution. As with other well-organized conferences, they took on a life of their own. They are motivating, uplifting and, for some, have generated a sense of a messianic fervor. In such an atmosphere, the international media is swept along, often forgetting professional tenets of skepticism and impartiality.

IPCC has carried out its mandate with extreme success. The same techniques used in marketing and public relations have been put to work, and a new brand — climate science — has been created. Prior to the 1990s, the study of climate was the territory of specialists such as climatologists, meteorologists, astrophysicists and oceanographers. Now hundreds of organizations and hundreds of thousands of specialists have committed to the climate change agenda. It has become normal to link the brand of *science* with the brand of *climate change*. For instance, the American Meteorological Society states that "Science is Confirmed as the Foundation for Global Climate Action." The discipline of meteorology has become pointified, and their scientists have a motivating purpose that goes beyond impartially documenting the weather and providing weather forecasts.

Climate science exemplifies the gap between the ideology of science, where reason supposedly exists independently of human foibles, and the reality of scientific practice, which cannot be unlinked from human interactions. Think about how science is practiced from the bottom up. When scientists look at data, they must decide what is relevant or irrelevant, miscalibrated or an artifact. All the time they will have in the back of their mind how their work will be received by their boss. Unconsciously or by design they will select the data that is more likely to elicit a positive response. In terms of climate data, a torrent is being collected from sensors in climate stations, on satellites and on thousands of ocean buoys. All data need to be calibrated. Some are wrong and need to be thrown out. Influenced by the prevailing orthodoxy, scientists are more likely to use data that fit with what they understand to be a fact: that the climate is warming,

This same mechanism would play out at every level in an organization. When people interact with one another they intend to make a point. They constantly make decisions about what to say or not say. When Gore wrote that Revelle "was the first person in the world to monitor carbon dioxide (CO2) in the atmosphere," he overlooked the more than 380 technical papers that were published between 1800 and 1961 that documented atmospheric carbon dioxide concentrations that jumped around, not following a tidy upward curve. He probably chose not to mention those findings in order to make the point about caring for the environment and to not confuse his readers by presenting contradictory evidence.

Scientists and nonscientists use scientific papers and books to support their arguments — just as I do throughout this book. In the process, the complexities of the subject matter become pointified. The theory that greenhouse gases cause global warming originated in the writings of two scientists, Svante Arrhenius and Guy Stewart Callendar. Arrhenius wrote a short, engaging book in 1908, *Worlds In The Making; The Evolution Of The Universe*. And Callendar wrote a paper, "The artificial production of carbon dioxide and its influence on temperature," in 1938. In both cases they expressed concern about global cooling and the onset of an ice age, rather than global warming. The central points made in these seminal papers are not included in the current pointified narrative about climate change.

Global warming evolved into *climate change*, which has now become a *climate emergency*. Now whenever an undesirable natural event occurs, such as wildfires in California and Australia, or die-offs of coral, humanity and the use of fossil fuels is the culprit.

Gore formed The Climate Project in 2006, changing its name to The Climate Reality Leadership Corps in 2011. It has run 39 training conventions and trained over 27,000 Climate Reality Leaders. These people are upset, militant, and gathering more and more followers. They have the communication skills to turn the online environment against anyone not embracing the climate emergency doctrine. For example, by searching the topic of climate science on Google or Wikipedia, you can see that those who have spoken up to query the orthodoxy have been maligned and deplatformed.

I would argue that the most intriguing aspect of climate science is that discoveries of frontline researchers show the situation is more complex than anyone could have imagined.

One example of the complexity of climate science is the melting of glaciers in western Canada, which I've witnessed myself since the 1980s.

There appears to be clear evidence that the climate has been warming since the end of the last ice age. Beryllium isotope dating of moraines in the area, however, shows that the last ice age ended with a period of abrupt warming 14,500 years ago. The temperature has been going up and down ever since, and differently in each region.

A second example concerns the long-held view that the sun is a relatively stable orb. This presumption changed in 2019 when NASA's Parker Solar Probe provided scientists with a close-up view of our star. In NASA's words, "The spacecraft confirmed that our picture of the Sun from Earth is deceptively simple. Parker is the closest spacecraft to the Sun, meaning we now have never-before-seen details about the solar wind and solar energetic particles." The sun is an extremely powerful, dynamic and unpredictable system.

A third example of climate science complexity is the measurement of average sea levels. While previously these measurements were obtained using tide gauges, an Arizona State University research team now uses a millimeter-accurate satellite-based radar to track the California coast's vertical motion. Their findings show that the land is moving like the slag on a crucible of molten metal. Santa Cruz is sinking about 8 mm/year, and San Jose is lifting about 3 mm/year.

Few people will likely look into the 150,000 papers published annually on the subject of Earth's climate. In any case, most are tedious, require math literacy and do not offer clear conclusions. The words *climate change* provide a brand shortcut, one that quickly helps us handle a significant, complex matter and figure out where we align with others on the subject.

Unfortunately, science journalism in the corporate press has become extinct, so people do not read about the fascinating complexities of the science; instead we see headlines that support competing tribal loyalties. Climate change has now become pointified to such an extent that people are unable to discuss basic questions such as, "How can we individually do our part to minimize our environmental impact?" And, "How can we spur breakthrough innovations in energy technologies that are job creating?"

The climate change movement exposes a psychological vulnerability that is troubling. Unquestionably, it is useful for humanity to know that our actions make a difference. We have a duty to this and future generations to leave the planet in better shape than we found it. But to promote the idea that we can control the climate and prevent natural disasters of all sorts is dangerous.

The perspective of consilience enables us to recognize that "the main source of hatred in the world" is not religion, as Hitchens pronounced, but belief systems that incubate fears about the future into tribal hatreds. When the arch-skeptic Michael Shermer, writer and founder of The Skeptics Society, and other scientists puzzle about the birth of religious movements, they need look no further than their belief in modernism and their embrace of the climate change orthodoxy.

We need to muster all the ingenuity and collective action we can to safeguard the future, but to imagine that we are in control of planet Earth is to believe that we have become godlike. History tells us what inevitably happens next.

— ▪ ○ 29 ○ ▪ —

Good Morning and Mean It

Based on a faulty understanding of the human brain, educational systems have fallen short in equipping young people with the skills and confidence to handle the challenges of modern life.

MY JOURNEY TO WRITE THIS BOOK STARTED 22 YEARS AGO when I attempted to write a manual called *Total Quality Communications* for my marketing communications company. In hindsight this initiative was provoked because at the time the young people I was recruiting didn't have the skills, the confidence and the resilience to do the job. And I had noticed that, paradoxically, the more education they had about marketing, the more frustrating it was to work with them.

Having wrestled with the question of why marketing textbooks — in fact, all textbooks I've come across related to human behavior — are not helpful, I've arrived at the conclusion that this problem has to do with the structure and needs of academic systems. Academic institutions are hierarchical and teachers need to keep order in their classroom — these factors underlie how scientists attempt to understand the human mind. This situation has had two adverse consequences. First, our understanding of how the brain works and the realities of human nature have been held back. Second, if educators believe the mind is a device that takes in knowledge and processes information using logic, children will not end up with the skills they need to live productively.

To illustrate this dynamic, meet two hypothetical professors who teach business: one is Professor Facts and the other is Professor Skills. At the beginning of the academic year, they have to compete for students by making a brief pitch that goes as follows:

Professor Facts says with a commanding tone, "This is an introductory business course where you will learn the laws of supply and demand. You will learn economic theories and consumer behavior. You will learn business strategy, and how to identify and build markets. You will become equipped to manage large budgets and build successful brands."

Professor Skills, with a less-confident tone explains, "In this course you will develop skills that are invaluable in every aspect of your life, including how to listen, understand, analyze and communicate. You will learn that every person is unique and that sales abilities are essential for building and leading organizations. You will become more sensitive to people's feelings. You will become equipped to appreciate and manage a communications toolbox of writing skills, design, music, analytics and programming."

Which professor is going to attract the bigger audience?

Facts are quicker to learn than the development of skills. Learning skills takes time and is generally frustrating. Malcolm Gladwell in his 2008 book, *Outliers: The Story of Success*, states that "ten thousand hours is the magic number of greatness." Paul McCartney read Gladwell's book and said there was a lot of truth in it, but "I don't think it's a rule that if you do that amount of work, you're going to be as successful as the Beatles." To become accomplished, you also need some natural talent as well as passion for what you are doing. On the whole, the main objective of college students is to graduate with high marks in the minimum amount of time, and so Professor Facts is likely to attract more students. Most professors are inclined to compete for positions that teach facts.

Facts are easier to teach than skills. Professor Facts can deliver lectures, hand out reading lists and, aside from marking papers, he doesn't need to get to know the students. Professor Skills, on the other hand, must respond to the efforts of every student and coach them.

While it is easy to pass judgement on the product of skilled activities such as writing, music and design, to teach the skills requires sensitivity and dedication. On the other hand, only specialists can assess the correctness of the answers from theoretical questions relatively quickly, especially those with a mathematical component.

— ▪ ○ ● ○ ▪ —

Theories often exist in isolation from the lives of people and their sensitivities. Academics can publish papers about theories in peer-reviewed journals, and they are left alone to continue in this way, because outside of academia no one cares what they are doing.

From the standpoint of someone running a business or wanting to start one, knowledge of economic and marketing theories is not useful. In practice, what has been taught about theories provides students with a false sense of confidence, which can be detrimental in the long term. From his experience working on the floor as a trader, Nassim Nicholas Taleb states, "Those who became practitioners after knowing theory always blow up. In other words, practice doesn't help you if you come from theory."

The most valuable skill in business is the ability to work productively as part of a team. This requires the ability to listen without being judgmental and the skills to think creatively. Being able to contribute at least one skill is useful, and appreciating the talents of others is itself a valuable aptitude, best learned through effort, experience, practice and oftentimes failure. Even if one never becomes an accomplished public speaker, writer, artist, performer, musician, analyst, programmer or artisan of any sort, the time taken to develop the skills is time well spent.

Deutsch is critical of the traditional view of education, which is seen to "transmit valuable knowledge faithfully, where knowledge is conceived of as a kind of valuable fluid which you pour from one generation to the next." He is an advocate of letting children learn in their own way and at the speed they choose, rather than according to parents' and teachers' prejudgments.

The presumption that the brain is an information storage and processing device, along with the well-intentioned desire to improve the quality of education so that "no child is left behind" (to paraphrase the United States education law), has led to widespread implementation of standardized testing. Testing and examinations are well-established techniques for motivating children to study and also for teachers to select high-performing students for further education. This approach, however, assumes it is best to teach all children in a similar manner, rather than as unique individuals. Over time, student testing has changed how education is perceived; now the purpose appears to be for children to score highly on tests and thereby climb to the next rung on the ladder of academic achievement.

For the sake of efficiency, many of the tests have become multiple choice. This implicitly promotes the notion that knowledge is about facts that are either right or wrong. And it presumes that the information-processing power of the brain can be assessed by means of IQ tests, which is thought of as a proxy for a child's ability to become productive in society.

I am not sure how unusual my education was 45 years ago, but through school and university I rarely had to take a multiple choice test. Instead, students were expected to demonstrate skills of observation, deduction and communication. As an example, for one high school exam in my final year of studying zoology, students nervously filed into the laboratory, and we sat at our appointed places. In front of each of us were three sheets of blank paper, a single object and, in some cases, a microscope. Each object was different, ranging from bones, fossils and coral to microscope slides of various tissues. We waited expectantly for the teacher, Ricky Schardt, to hand out the exam questions. "You have one-and-a-half hours," he said in an even tone. After a few moments, we realized that we were not going to get any further direction. Each of us started to draw the object in front of us. I had never before encountered the bone lying on my desk. I could tell it was a pelvic girdle and I deduced it was from a mammal about the size of a rabbit. By the end of the exam, each of us had filled the three sheets of paper with annotated drawings and a creative description of everything we could or could not deduce based on what we had learned or otherwise knew. When Schardt graded our work, there was no question of being right or wrong. He was evaluating our powers of observation, knowledge, logic and ability to express ourselves. The examination itself affirmed each of us because it demonstrated that, when faced with an object we had never seen before, we had nonetheless developed new abilities to observe, deduce and communicate.

Schardt was an unorthodox and sometimes mischievous teacher. He taught an extracurricular course, which he called human relationships. At the start of each class, the students would sit in a circle and wait for him to start teaching. He never did. He would sit quietly with us until someone said something, then we would spend the next hour discussing various curiosities about human dynamics. It was a form of self-therapy that taught us that it was OK to admit to vulnerabilities.

At one point, Schardt quietly mentioned to me that he considered teaching to be a hoax. I did not understand what he meant because he was a dedicated and effective teacher. With hindsight, I believe that he meant that a teacher presenting information in front of a class is not the best way for students to develop the skills they need for purposeful lives. The role of the teacher is to provide feedback, guidance and encouragement.

With an understanding of how human neuronal systems work, it becomes clear that the act of observing something, understanding what it is and being able to communicate about it, is a remarkable act of cognition. As well, it is evident that observation, deduction, creativity and physical action are tightly linked. Educators should be encouraged to move away from the practice of teaching "the usual second-order lucubrations on why scholars of different disciplines think this or that" — to use Wilson's terminology — and, instead, encourage their students to understand "material cause and effect."

The current polarization occurring in daily debates on social media is in part the result of the prevailing view that knowledge of facts and theories equates with being intelligent. Attempting to teach children theories and facts does little to encourage them to develop the skills and the curiosity to ask questions. I would advocate that whenever a young person hears someone say something with which they disagree, they should be coached to understand that person's viewpoint and preemptively plan how to journey toward a shared understanding.

An adverse consequence of multiple choice exams is that children think that achieving perfect scores in their work is possible and desirable. Children who have grown used to scoring 100% at school become stressed when future employers are unimpressed with their ability. A more fruitful view is that we should continually work to improve our skills in diverse areas of human endeavor throughout our lives.

Consilience teaches us that the human brain is a dynamic and flexible system that operates in the moment and enables the development of skills, and also can lose skills. The notion that a scoring system, such as IQ or exam results, is reflective of an individual's capacity to be productive is shortsighted. Students who score poorly in academic tests believe it reflects on their overall abilities, and they become either demotivated or overconfident. Either way, scoring badly or scoring well does not prepare young people with a sense of realism and the grit that can work to their advantage in the long term.

These days technology is changing at such a rate that students need curiosity and the skills to search out pertinent information and the motivation to teach themselves. At the same time the extraordinary volume and quality of the resources available on the internet is increasing by the day. Anyone with access to the internet can pick any point of interest, no matter how fringe it might be, and with a few clicks find tutorials, lectures, books and discussions.

The COVID-19 crisis might be an opportunity to reconceptualize the purpose and methods of education. For example, suppose a class of 14-year-old students has learned the basics of reading, writing and mathematics.

Now, instead of teaching the usual curriculum in the usual way, there is a single goal: to start every day by saying *good morning* and meaning it.

This might appear simplistic, but to be able to do this, the students need the basic skill of connecting emotionally with other people when addressing them. This involves both confidence in themselves and appreciation of others as unique and ever-changing individuals. They would also need to know they are developing the necessary skills to lead productive lives, and thereby feel optimistic about their future.

Many students are not passionate about the traditional academic disciplines, so this group of 14-year-old students would each select one subject to which they feel drawn. This might be a literary figure; or an animal, maybe a dinosaur, for biology; or a subduction zone, for geography; or the large hadron collider, for physics; or perhaps a non-academic subject, such as beauty cosmetics, the video game *Crossfire* or rap music. Then they would be encouraged to spend a year or two pursuing every avenue on that subject until they become an expert; disregarding the traditional boundaries of academic disciplines, expanding their horizons and going as far as they can.

For instance, if Leila likes rap music, she would be encouraged to write rap music, then work to refine her creation to a very good quality. She would be urged to study the history of rap music, the lives of famous rap artists and how rap evolved into the culture of hip-hop. She might study the physiology of the human vocal apparatus and look into the physics of the equipment needed for performances. She could study the legal, social and economic aspects of the rap business, and also be encouraged to look into the connection between gospel, jazz, blues and rock, and how these have fertilized the rap genre. Perhaps she would be drawn to study the life, the passions and the skills of Lin-Manuel Miranda, the creative mastermind behind the Broadway hit about American founding father Alexander Hamilton. She could investigate the economics of the various performances, and the role of social and corporate media in promoting them. She could be prompted to start a school club or join others in the community who share her interest.

By the time she is done, the objective would be for Leila to say good morning knowing that she has the skills to engage in a dialogue, really listening and responding in the moment, as though engaged in rap improv. She would have the confidence to dialogue with every type of person, irrespective of their professed level of expertise, responding to them as individuals rather than through prejudged stereotypes. And perhaps she'd be able to perform in front of her school and get a standing ovation. If she wished, she would be on the path to earning a living in the rap business — or steering clear of it, having discovered other avenues that suit her better.

If I were hiring to fill a position and Leila strode in, said good morning and looked at me like she meant it, my eyes would widen, because she would stand apart from the many I have interviewed over the past few years who become confused when I ask questions that deviate from the politically correct set pieces they have been practicing. If she was not offered the job, she would have the resilience to continue on and perhaps start a business of her own.

Not for one second would it cross her mind that the system was conspiring against her. She would not look to organizations and politicians to provide feelings of security. She would expect them only to provide a stable environment in which she can thrive.

If thousands like Leila were finishing school every year, there would be no need to worry about tribal battles or the stability of society. These students would have the mental fortitude to work toward understanding everything and the humility to grasp what they don't know. We could look to the future knowing we are in good hands.

— ▪ ○ 30 ○ ▪ —

Finding Our Path

Everyone is unique and has to find their own path to fulfillment, building on what their ancestors bequeathed them. Freedom to discuss should be safeguarded.

WHEN I STEPPED OFF THE AIRPLANE IN TORONTO IN 1980 I had nothing more than a suitcase half-full of unstylish clothes and $300 in my pocket. The change in my life was abrupt, yet nearly everyone I encountered was welcoming and positive. I had secured a job at Pepsi-Cola with a young team of highly motivated executives whose self-confidence and optimism was exhilarating. Also, I appreciated that whenever I entered a store or place of business, it was normal to smile and exchange good-natured comments.

As a student one summer years earlier, I encountered the same spirit in Philadelphia, where I bought a Sears bicycle for $70 and cycled via Washington, D.C., to Toronto along the banks of the Potomac. On the way, not having much money, I slept in a plastic-bag tent and pulled catfish from the river, wrapped them in foil and cooked them on a small fire. One evening in the heart of the Appalachians, surrounded by wooded hills, I reached the hamlet of Paw Paw and asked a stranger if there was a place I could pitch my tent. He pointed to a large colonial home and suggested I ask there. The door was opened by a lady with silver hair and a gentle Southern accent. She led me to a room with a solid oak, four-poster bed. In the morning, breakfast was laid out for me in a high-ceilinged dining room. When I offered to pay for the hospitality, she waved me on my way. I encountered welcoming hospitality, big and small. On the road to Pittsburgh, when I stopped to buy peaches at a roadside stand, the two boys, probably the sons of the farm owners, laughed and handed me three peaches, and I cycled off. Everyone I encountered had a natural affability and generous spirit.

It was that spirit that gave me confidence to start a computer graphics company after a few years of living in Toronto. I was able to grow the company, make a good living and, a short while later, get married and have children.

As with many adults, I am consumed with the pressures of earning a living and daily concerns; nonetheless, my journey has been profoundly rewarding and rarely a day goes by when I don't feel thankful. As you can tell from the subjects discussed in this book, I have many interests and mix with people from diverse backgrounds. I am comfortable conversing with people of every sort and also with those who have views outside the mainstream. I code-switch without effort or anxiety. I have always been perplexed, however, that my experiences with different people in different domains have been separated by what appear to be unbridgeable gaps. For instance, I might hug a baby and a short time later chat with a physicist about their research into the superpositions of cusp kernels. Most people would be content to keep those two encounters in entirely different domains, but for me this makes no sense.

Writing this book has been a transformative experience because I can now see the two — babies and scientists — are connected in many ways. Figuring out those connections has been the culmination of much deliberation, and has been a cathartic experience: much like experiences described in chapter 10 when people experience a mental awakening and a shift in how they perceive their place in the world. So now I can not only link the melodies in my mind labeled *babies* and *scientists,* but also better organize every other tune. In Whewell's terminology I have experienced "a consilience of inductions" and a "jumping together" of different domains. Everything I think about can be placed in a mental landscape called consilience.

The rearranging of neuronal melodies is a dynamic process, and I know I'll continue to clarify my thoughts as I discuss consilience in the future.

Reassuringly, I have become more comfortable with complexity and people's idiosyncrasies because of a foundational axiom of consilience: the metaphysical fact that everything is unique. Every particle has to exist in its own space at any moment in time. For instance there is much we don't know about those three specks I introduced at the beginning of this book — and will never know. But one thing is certain, they don't exist in the same spot at the same time. Therefore, every object and person and moment is unique.

I believe each of us has to find a path to fulfillment in our own way. My situation is a consequence of the contributions of many wise thinkers who, through the ages, have bequeathed a political and social environment that has enabled me — and others — to live safely and constructively. I feel blessed because of them.

One remarkable confluence of individuals, ideas and technologies happened close to where I grew up — an area between Birmingham and Liverpool. There, Erasmus Darwin, Matthew Boulton, James Watt, Joseph Priestley and Josiah Wedgwood met each month at the full moon. They came to be known as the Lunar Men.

The Lunar Men discussed their diverse interests and helped each other with their concerns. Darwin was a doctor who also wrote poetry and, like his grandson, mused about the origins of life. Priestly was a preacher and multi-talented thinker who discovered different "airs," including "dephlogisticated gas," now called *oxygen*. He invented carbonated water and was curious about the strange forces that could be transmitted through metal wires that paved the way for Michael Faraday to transform water into life-sustaining oxygen: a discovery that Whewell termed *electrolysis*. Boulton was a self-taught scientist who pioneered the use of steam engines in his factory that stamped coins and made elegant metal jugs. He worked with James Watt to refine steam engines that could be used to dewater mines, allowing coal to be brought up from deep underground. These gentlemen had ways of thinking and approaches to life that gave birth to the technologies that fueled the Industrial Revolution. Its products and processes quickly spread around the world.

My forebears to some extent participated in the dawn of this revolution. They certainly benefited from it. John Beakbane, the grandson of the Beakbane who met George Fox and became a Quaker, ran a pottery on the banks of the River Mersey and was a colleague of Wedgwood, whose efforts built a network of canals that enabled them to safely transport their delicate china to faraway markets. A distant uncle of mine, Daniel Eccleston, owned a shipping company, and when he traveled from Montreal to Boston with the King of the Caughnawaga Nation in a birchbark canoe, he reported that he "had the pleasure, and I may add, the honour of meeting General Washington."

The Lunar Men were nonconformists and some were radical thinkers, well acquainted with Biblical stories that they would have thought of as historical rather than mythical. Riding in a carriage through the Shropshire countryside, they would have seen the remains of a Roman town, Viroconium, with its palatial baths toppled to the ground and mostly buried by the work of earthworms. This is just five miles southeast of Shrewsbury, where Darwin grew up observing his father breed pigeons. The Lunar Men moved in the same circles as Thomas Jefferson and the founding fathers of America, who, when drafting the American constitution, were mindful of the grand sweep of history and the fallibilities of humans.

These men were familiar with names such as Kant, Schelling, Humboldt, Goethe, Hobbes, Bentham, Locke, Smith, Montesquieu, Rousseau and many others who thought hard about human nature and came up with insights that formed the framework for building modern society. For them, family, farming, science, music, literature, history, religion, commerce, personal growth and civic responsibilities overlapped. To them, creating a stable society was a process requiring reason along with wisdom and decorum. Their mindset was similar to consilience, but without the benefits of recent scientific discoveries.

— ▪ ○ ● ○ ▪ —

Whewell, the inventor of consilience, was well acquainted with the scientific, political, religious, philosophical and revolutionary ideas that had been gathering momentum through the 1700s to early 1800s. He believed that science and theology were separate, and should live by different rules. He said science needs to operate using evidence, causal relationships and rational inference to yield explanatory laws, whereas theology grows from revelation, hope and faith in "things not seen." Theology unveils the spiritual forces that erected the framework and authored the laws of the World, he believed, while the natural sciences are based on observation and experience. Nonetheless, they require concepts such as space, time and causality, which along with mathematics are creations of the human mind. "We do not see (ideas), we see through them," he wrote.

Mill viewed the situation differently. He was a modernist in philosophy and politics whose fundamental axiom was that "the greatest happiness of the greatest number is the measure of right and wrong." Building on this simple axiom, Mill articulated a complete system of beliefs relating to all aspects of modern existence.

Whewell and Mill participated in exchanges, much like those between Harris and Peterson, that reveal a deep split in views about how we pattern our thoughts. Mill's philosophies had far-reaching political implications that were apparent to socially progressive thinkers. His ideas provided a rational foundation for moves toward equality and a fairer society but, at the same time, buried the competing philosophy of German Romantics, along with their appreciation of wit, humor and beauty. The Romantics' admiration of the music of Beethoven, Brahms and Schubert was irksome to the likes of Mill and his muse, Jeremy Bentham, who were legal positivists and did not attach much importance to the sensual aspects of existence.

At the dawn of the twentieth century, Mill's ideas won out over Whewell's, which has had deep and lasting repercussions in the ways we think. Rationality has replaced wisdom as the respected doctrine in politics and education. In Whewell's era and earlier, humanity was considered to be subject to the whims of uncontrollable forces. They were realists who believed in fate, humility and stoicism.

From the standpoint of consilience, Whewell's ideas were wiser. No fundamental axiom of human society is correct in all instances. When we say "greatest happiness" what do we mean? An injection of heroin makes a person indescribably happy. Junk food, porn and violent video games also make people feel good, at least in the short run. Anyone in a position of authority is subject to the same pressures and has similar feelings as other humans. There is no reason to believe they will act in the best interests of the greatest number.

The consensus of crowds offers little wisdom. Human groups are not much wiser than skittish herds of ungulates. Democracy is necessary, not because the majority are correct, but because voting promotes feelings of inclusiveness and periodically turfing out government leaders prevents them from consolidating power. The purpose of government is to provide rules of conduct so that citizens can live constructively. Stable societies are built from the bottom up and are the cumulative result of people leading lives that are fulfilling.

The lessons of history show that whenever an elite imagines they are so smart they can control society's destiny — like gods — destruction is inevitable. After every conflagration, scribes, philosophers and historians, with trembling hands, spell out how leaders succumb to the pressures and intoxication of leadership, resulting in hegemony or conflict, or both. Wise people from the past witnessed the dark side of human nature that we can never banish. They realized human beings do not conform to simple axioms.

Perhaps the greatest blessing the Lunar Men and their contemporaries bequeathed in the Western world are the skills and political systems that allow us to explore diverse ideas through creative dialogue. There is no merit in believing that everyone will live harmoniously if they hold similar views, or that any group of intellectuals has a lock on virtue. Freedom to discuss whatever we please in a creative and forthright manner needs to be safeguarded.

— ▪ ○ 31 ○ ▪ —

New Ways to See

Japanese methods for quality management show the power of combining perspectives from the West and East. The post-war growth of Japanese industry hints at ways to develop productive and stabilizing tribal journeys.

FOR 20 YEARS I WORKED AS A NON-EXECUTIVE DIRECTOR of the manufacturing company my father started. The company produced components for the machine tool industry and, from that vantage point, I watched the effects of major changes in the economy and wanted to figure out their underlying causes.

Machine tools include lathes – milling and cutting machines that transform blocks of metal into products. While the machine tool sector accounts for less than 1% of the total manufacturing industry, it is the basis of nearly all manufactured goods. As such, it is strategically critical.

Until about 1965 the American machine tool industry was the biggest and best in the world. American innovation and get-'er-done attitude dominated in many aspects of life, including entertainment, retail and mass-production manufacturing. American machine tools commanded about 30% of the world market. In 1981, the U.S. industry went into freefall, and by 1992 it accounted for around 7% of the market, far behind Germany and Japan. The U.K. industry had less far to fall, but it also slid.

The reasons why this freefall happened are more deep rooted than currency fluctuations and shortsighted trade deals.

Many factors contributed to the success of manufacturing in the United States, such as plentiful natural resources, a favorable geography with natural waterways, numerous immigrants with craft skills, a sense of optimism and the freedom to create. An emerging scientific mindset was also changing manufacturing from skilled crafts to unskilled operations with sequences of simple, repeated tasks. One pioneer stands out: Frederick Winslow Taylor published *The Principles of Scientific Management* in 1909, and applied those principles of measurement and statistics to turn the Bethlehem Iron Company into the world's most modern factory, and a prototype for manufacturers and engineers in other industries. His ideas were put to use by Henry Ford, who pioneered the modern production line, and then by Alfred Sloan of General Motors, who scaled them up.

In Taylor's way of thinking, management provided the brains, and people manning the production lines were the arms and legs. "In our scheme, we do not ask for the initiative of our men," he said. "We do not want any initiative. All we want of them is to obey the orders we give them." In classical engineering terms, workers were thought of not unlike the dogs Pavlov used in his famous experiments — salivating in response to food. They were motivated through rewards, promotion and pay, or punished with "fines, discharge, assignment to less remunerative or less desirable work." The power of mechanistic logic shines through in Taylor's writing: "Rewards and Punishments Result in Action." He states, "There can be no doubt that a reward is an incentive." He used a simple Newtonian logic to show that a punishment is also an incentive. "The whole thing rests on the meaning of the word *action*. To be active is certainly the opposite of being at rest. This being true, punishment is just as surely an incentive to action as is reward." The topmost metric for measuring success was financial.

This story is pertinent to *How to Understand Everything* because manufacturing companies in the West became fractured. Management aligned with the modernist philosophies of the Climb Higher and Hold Firm tribal journeys, and workers coalesced under the banner of the Gather Together tribal journey.

The principles of scientific management were put to work in Japan after the war, but the outcomes were completely different. After the Second World War, Japan was utterly devastated. Three million Japanese had lost their lives. Blitzkriegs and the detonation of two atom bombs had flattened major Japanese cities, plus the country had suffered a series of earthquakes. The generation that would have stepped into the management ranks of industry had been killed in the war. Yet within 30 years the country transformed itself into a manufacturing powerhouse second only to the United States. In the words of the late Jack Welch, CEO of General Electric for 20 years, the transformation was "awesome and frightening." He recounted in his autobiography, "What I saw in Japan was occurring in many of our markets. The Japanese were tearing apart the cost structures in industry after industry. Television sets, automobiles, and copying machines were being hammered."

The rebuilding of Japanese industry was based on the implementation of techniques for quality control that had been pioneered in the United States. In the 1950s, the engineer and statistician William Edwards Deming trained hundreds of Japanese engineers, managers and scholars on how to improve quality through statistical process control.

Although the same techniques were used in North America, the differences between manufacturing in the United States and Japan made Jack Welch look for businesses that would "give us a place to hide."

The difference was that the Japanese layered science-inspired statistical process control onto patterns of behavior rooted in thousands of years of cultural practices inspired by the ideas of Confucius, Mencius and Laozi. These philosophers recognized that great change happens only when you address the question, "How are you living your life?" Then you start by working on simple daily practices and following rituals that free the mind from its usual patterns and ruts. The results are evident in the Japanese attention to detail that's apparent everywhere in their nation, from tea ceremonies and the manufacture of Samurai swords to the arrangement of sushi on a platter.

By contrast, in the West, companies treated the physical aspects of manufacturing as subordinate to the cerebral aspects. The craft skills required to make something were not highly regarded, and pleasing aesthetics — that are unquantifiable — were considered an indulgence. In the business world, the attitude that design takes second place to functionality was widespread — until Steve Jobs and Jony Ive showed that good design is necessary for product functionality and can add extraordinary value.

Profit rather than pride in one's craft became the point of working. Realizing their skills were not appreciated, the blue-collar workers coalesced into a tribe and set their energies to getting a greater share of the profit. The history of counterproductive industrial relations and strikes is well known; however, the effects of the competing tribal journeys went deeper, stifling innovation and taking down the machine tool industry.

In the early days of the machine tool industry, new machines could be developed with top-down approaches. When digital technologies started transforming all aspects of manufacturing, however, the electronics, servos, lasers, pneumatics, sensing devices and engineered metals needed to be intertwined in complex ways. That meant teams of designers, electrical engineers, mechanical engineers, programmers and operators had to work closely together. Innovation is always challenging, particularly with projects that require large teams with diverse skills. Things rarely work out on the first few tries. For companies with cultures of competing tribes, it is challenging to transition to a single, unified team that works together with trust and mutual respect. A positive dynamic cannot develop when white-collar managers believe their contributions are more valuable than those of the shop-floor workers. The workers cross their arms and wait for the managers to meet their comeuppance.

The Japanese companies did not have the same heritage of two competing tribes. When they implemented Deming's statistical process-control techniques, they started to produce elegant and sophisticated machining centers — more efficiently. Every year they have released new models that are increasingly fast, more precise, more versatile and easy to use. Now there are factories that take in blocks of steel at one end and assembled machines come out the other end. The companies operate round-the-clock, with lights off and few people on site. The fusion of Western scientific approaches with Eastern philosophies produced the techniques of *kaizen, lean* and *six sigma* that are now widely employed in manufacturing industries around the world.

— ▪ ○ ● ○ ▪ —

The impetus for writing the guidebook *Total Quality Communications* was triggered when I observed the managers of a Japanese machine tool company, Yamazaki Mazak, working with the personnel in the company my father started. I noticed that they thought and acted differently than our management. With everyone they encountered, irrespective of hierarchy, they were polite. Nor did they treat us as merely a supplier competing for dollars, but rather an integral part of their supply chain.

I didn't grasp it at the time, but the differences are more profound than I could have guessed. Japanese managers are quietly respectful, knowing that in Buddhist culture, through reincarnation, one might say "what goes around comes around." While companies in the West saw manual labor as drudgery made worthwhile by pay, the Japanese managers saw each act as part of a lifetime quest for betterment. To them, repetition was not boring, but a path to mental liberation. Michael Puett, a Harvard University professor, explains in *The Path: What Chinese Philosophers Can Teach Us About the Good Life* that through rituals we can free ourselves from the "patterns and ruts" that "limit what we can see, access, sense, and know."

This Eastern way of thinking is a world apart from the scientific mindset that posits that though *free will* we are constantly thinking and deciding. Gazzaniga's insights about how humans think and Ehrenberg's statistical analysis of market metrics reveal that modernist ways of thinking about human behavior are incorrect. In fact, our thoughts and attitudes follow on from our habits and routines.

Understanding can occur at even deeper levels. I believe that when the Japanese managers looked at our factory, they saw it differently than I did. They did not see the tribal divisions between white-collar and blue-collar team members, nor did they see each stage of the manufacturing process as a distinct operation; instead it appeared to them as a flowing river. The Japanese use the metaphor of a flowing fluid in many different domains, including to describe sound, communication, and the nature of thoughts and feelings. They often conceptualize life as moving like a river that washes around objects and gathers strength as it goes.

It is almost impossible to fathom these different ways of seeing. Words and metaphors influence our thoughts and actions in invisible ways because, like fish, we are unaware of the social liquid we are submersed in. We are usually completely unaware of the microhabits that make up our lives. We think about only the things we can think about, unless we stretch ourselves and seek to learn.

The practices of monks following the writings of the ancient text, *Tao Te Ching*, reveal an underlying reality of human perception and behavior as illustrated by the opening line: "The Tao that can be told is not the eternal Tao." The monks are like the visitors from the imaginary planet Gliesen, who observe humans and everything on earth without the human neuronal apparatus and the effects of words. Followers of the Tao aspire to do the same.

Is it feasible for the West to regain self-sufficiency in manufacturing? Perhaps. But only if we change how we see. Consilience gives us the power to understand the water we are swimming in and reformulate tribal journeys so they can lead to a shared mental destination.

How long will it take? Recall the utter devastation of Japan at the end of the war, and that the Japanese are living on a subduction zone — constantly attuned to the potential for earthquakes and tsunamis — and have almost no mineral resources, including oil and natural gas. But the nation rose phoenix-like to become an industrial powerhouse, producing goods that are the envy of the world. Within 35 years, their machine tool industry grew to take a 20% share of the world market. They were on a clear, yet unspoken, tribal journey to regain their national pride after Emperor Hirohito's humiliating surrender in August 1945.

Perhaps, for the good of the world, with technology and wisdom we can re-energize ourselves in the West.

— ▪ ○ 32 ○ ▪ —

Understanding People

Textbook representations of humans are misleading. Consilience allows each of us to knot together metaphors of humanity that are dynamic and more realistic.

I HAVE FOLLOWED MANY THREADS IN THIS BOOK to tie together different domains of human experience. This quest to understand everything can feel overwhelming, but there is still a pile of wool lying on the floor, and I'll pull these threads together by examining the question, "What is the best way to understand people?"

The answer has far-reaching consequences because the ways we conceptualize ourselves and other people influence how we interact. If we view the brain and human behavior in a way that is simplistic or misleading, we may feel irritated, unfulfilled or angry in dealing with people with whom we do not agree. This is a serious matter; however, I'm going to look at this example of human interaction with a touch of humor by drawing a caricature of the humans described in some textbooks.

First, there are those we encounter in marketing textbooks, referred to as *consumers*. These people are categorized by their age, sex and socioeconomic group, and have values and attitudes that don't change much over time. They do not have a sense of humor nor are they quirky or interesting, as they spend most of their time earning money, looking after a household, consuming media and making purchase decisions. Much of their behavior is the result of emotions. They behave differently to the less-emotional people who buy things in a business context. A consumer's level of rationality is proportional to their level of schooling. Those who are less intelligent and educated are particularly susceptible to the influence of advertising.

Consumers, even the stupid ones, have a sound understanding of their patterns of behavior and can impart the knowledge by answering survey questions. They respond to questions in a balanced manner even at inconvenient times during their day. Surveys that take 30 minutes or more provide greater insight into consumer behavior. When thousands of survey results are aggregated and statisticians have worked their magic, the findings are solidly scientific.

Second, there are the *Econs,* described in economics textbooks who share many similarities with consumers. These people have been molded by evolutionary forces to increase their brain's clock speed — or IQ — to maximize their economic advantage. However, glitches occur in their ability to make decisions correctly, particularly when they employ System 1, which is fast and often illogical. System 2, on the other hand, enables them to make rational decisions.

The Econ's brain, when analyzed in fMRI machines, appears divided into specialized modules. The motor parts of the brain are separate to the sensory parts; the creative parts are on the right, and the parts that process and store information are somewhere else. The lower, troublesome parts of the brain are unconscious, and harbor repressed traumas and reptilian urges. Set apart from the brain is the *mind* that houses consciousness.

Consumers and Econs evolved by climbing up the ladder toward consciousness and free will, as conceived by Aristotle. The rate of progress from primitivism to enlightenment is building momentum as science and technology make these people smarter than humans have ever been.

Davos Man is the most advanced stage of evolution. They have doctorates in the social and digital sciences. Their PowerPoint presentations spell out economic and political solutions that will propel humanity toward good order, rationality and harmony.

— ▪ ○ ● ○ ▪ —

Having presented this textbook picture, I have to say I have never met one of these mythical beings. And if I did, I would turn and run. The people I encounter are more intriguing and, on the whole, more convivial.

I would argue that just about every aspect of Textbook Man is completely incorrect and, in many respects, so misleading that the conception is counterproductive. Rather than recount point by point how the evidence from diverse sources — including markets, science, history and everyday experience — contradicts this portrayal, I'll paint an alternative picture, one that's aligned with scientific and other insights described in this book.

A principal noteworthy point is that the nervous system reacts in the moment. A computer gaming analogy is that the brain is online and playing live all the time. It does not operate by downloading data, going offline and processing it, then going back online with a response. When we contemplate something quietly, the neuronal orchestra plays scenarios forward and weighs the consequences of each. Nonetheless, during that time and at every moment, even at night, our neuronal systems are tuned to respond in fractions of a second.

Another noteworthy point is that the brain works in sync with the muscles. The entire system operates at the edge of criticality, constantly primed for instant movement. Speech and writing are muscular activities, little different from playing a musical instrument, making things, sports and dancing.

A further noteworthy point is that our perception of the world entails a constant process of re-creation, drawing upon all our past experiences. This capability is the basis of memory and the reason we can shut our eyes and bring to mind people and places, along with their many associated sights, sounds and tactile sensations.

One implication of these facts is that perceptions of reality are subjective. Everyone's sense of reality is dynamic, unique and specific to them.

The neuronal orchestra combines and arranges an array of different stimuli, and we label each particular arrangement with words. This function influences what we notice and remember. From the vast influx of impressions, we build up patterns — melodies — that help us make sense of experiences and ideas, as well as communicate.

Human behavior is the outcome of in-the-moment responses to incoming stimuli from the sense organs and body, which become interpreted in relation to previously encountered stimuli of the same nature. For the most part, conscious thought processes don't cause actions; however, thinking affects how we pattern incoming stimuli and potential courses of action.

In a dipolar way tending toward either attraction or repulsion, human behavior is tuned to look for the point of things and prepare an immediate response.

We do not have conscious access to the urges related to maintaining homeostasis — eating, drinking, holding a comfortable body temperature, keeping clean and protecting ourselves — nor the urges that preserve genes from generation to generation — having sex, being parented and parenting. The same instincts have been driving animal behavior for hundreds of millions of years. The parenting and being parented instincts underpin the human propensity to live and work cooperatively together.

The urge for social cohesion can, at any moment, turn into aggression against perceived threats. Humans are instinctively and fluidly tribal and protective of our own.

A range of emotions can arise during interactions with one another — envy, anger, irritation, love, affection, power or subjugation — and they relate to age-old biological realities. Feelings bubble up into the neuronal orchestra, where we attach words to them and arrange them as melodies related to objects, physical space and movement. Those melodies can be arranged in sequences, the narratives we use to write, speak and explain our situation.

This new picture I've given about human functioning is completely different to the one depicted in textbooks. From this perspective, I would argue that academics and everyone else who hold positions of responsibility need to acknowledge the scientific realities being revealed by frontline researchers.

Scientific findings about human biology and behavior, however, are complex and hard to visualize. They also do not conform to intuitive modes of thinking, which tend toward categorizations and generalizations. The new picture is not sticky.

For two decades, I've sought to understand the gaps between what I knew before and what I have learned from frontline thinkers. With the perspective of consilience, it becomes possible to helicopter above the landscape of people's minds and see how the rivulets of ideas have carved competing visions of our collective future. The various ideas become reinforced every time members of a group employ words with a shared understanding. While writing this book, I recognized my biases about each of the three tribal journeys; now I can accept them. Seeing the flow of the different rivers, I no longer feel compelled to take sides, which frees me to think about humanity completely differently.

In conversation with others, I no longer see them as solid, unchanging entities filled with information. They are not like the atoms pictured as billiard balls in the books I browsed in my bedroom, next to my cat Tipsy. To me, people are more like clouds of quantum potential. Each time someone says something, I don't presume I know what they mean, because what they mean depends on their condition at that moment and their perceptions of me.

I find this new perspective opens up new ways of interacting with people that are often creative, exhilarating and a lot of fun. I liken my interactions with people to one of my favorite pastimes: canoeing down a river through cascading rapids, alert to upcoming rocks and waves. From second to second I have to adjust my paddle strokes, sometimes leaning out wide, digging the water aggressively toward the boat; at other times gently paddling backward, aligning the canoe so it is ready for the next drop. I'm constantly aware of the actions of my canoeing partner, reading their body movement and sensing what to do next. The power of the water changes from moment to moment and, if I'm not careful, it could crush the boat. With the roar of the water all around and the threat of life-ending danger, the dance between the rocks and waves is intoxicating. When I reach the bottom of each cascade, I'll look to see how much water has splashed into the boat and relax for a moment knowing that my purpose, at least for that encounter, has been fulfilled.

This metaphor of rocks and rushing water appeals to me, but you can conceive metaphors that suit you better.

As I've stated repeatedly, a characteristic of our neuronal makeup is that we look for the point of everything. When we get out of bed in the morning, our day will be more fulfilling if we know the point. When we discuss something, there is always a point. As a community member, we need to be going somewhere collectively that has a point. Our river has to be flowing somewhere we wish to go. We need a purpose in life.

When I paddle through whitewater, my purpose is clear: get through the rapids as safely and as stylishly as I can. Our collective goals in Western society are not as easy to figure out. But we need to, because we cannot be sure of what we might encounter around the next bend in the river. We can never be sure it will work out well.

Epilogue: What's Next?

THE COVID-19 CRISIS, THE 2020 U.S. ELECTION and its aftermath have been exposing the deep rifts among the three tribal ideologies with which we have been living.

We can make sense of the situation through consilience. We can see that our behavior results in the moment from the state of our body, prior experiences, what our senses are taking in, our tribal loyalties and our vision of where we are going.

How we react to people and things depends on the particular melodies we've created in the neuronal orchestra. When we see a neighbor, how do we feel? Secure or fearful? When we hear a national leader speak, do we hear beyond the words?

When we think of our respective nations, what do we see? Do we see a zero-sum game? Or do we witness societies that, relative to previous eras, are better off? Do we focus on the injustices or see unlimited potential?

Places of worship can be seen as power structures of depravity and captive to anti-science superstitions. They might also be sanctuaries for community and sensemaking, or as cumulations of wisdom from the past.

All can be true. Can we acknowledge complexity and have the curiosity to ask deeper questions? Exactly who is involved? What are their motivations? How are they actually behaving? It is up to each of us to figure out the point of things, how everything fits together and where this will lead us.

While the title of this book is cocky, my principal message is that we need to acknowledge the limitations of our individual and collective ability to understand. Consilience requires humility. I hope its dawning kicks off new modes of public discourse.

The ideas in this book are based on the work of many dedicated researchers and thinkers. Their cumulative effects promise to be exciting. I am willing to concede that my interpretation of their ideas may be partly or, in some cases, completely incorrect; however, the overarching conclusions, I would argue, are inescapable.

I'd like to finish with a request. Please seek out individuals who are making an effort to study human vulnerabilities as well as ways to help individuals and communities become stronger. Modern-day thinkers and spiritual sooths — sensemakers — offer hope for the future and, by engaging in thoughtful dialogue, we can fan the embers of constructive ideas to fire.

Also, please let me know your views about consilience. You can reach me through the contact page on https://howtounderstandeverything.beakbane.com/contact/

Made in the USA
Monee, IL
16 June 2021

71446005R00174